THE DVD

In this enlightening 2-hour presentation, Joshua Jay performs and teaches 35 tricks from the book. Use the DVD and book together to learn step-by-step techniques, then watch Jay's up-close performances so that you can master the essential elements of timing, rhythm, and misdirection.

(See the inside back cover for DVD contents)

DVD INCLUDED
Watch Joshua Jay Perform
and Explain 35 Tricks

MAGIC

THE COMPLETE COURSE

by Joshua Jay

WORKMAN PUBLISHING · NEW YORK

Library of Congress Cataloging-in-Publication Data is available.

ISBN 978-0-7611-4987-3

Design by Janet Parker and Kate Lin

Illustrations by Kagan McLeod

Permission to photocopy page 270.

Workman books are available at special discounts when purchased in bulk for premiums and sales promotions as well as for fund-raising or educational use. Special editions or book excerpts also can be created to specification. For details, contact the Special Sales Director at the address below.

Workman Publishing Company, Inc.
225 Varick Street
New York, NY 10014-4381
www.workman.com

Printed in the United States of America
First printing October 2008

10 9 8 7 6 5 4 3 2

Credits

Front Cover: Photography by Rafael Fuchs
Stylist: Tina Latonero
Hair and Makeup: Dina Kinion

Back Cover: Photography by David Arky

DVD Title Page: Photography by Felipe Abreu

Interior photography by David Arky Photography

Additional Photography:
p. vi (right) Richard Faverty/Beckett Studios, p. x H. Armstrong Roberts/Getty Images, p. 11 Anne White Photography, p. 21 Mike Caveney's Egyptian Hall Museum, p. 25 The Nielsen Magic Poster Collection, p. 28 Richard Faverty/Beckett Studios, p. 30 Gary O'Brien, p. 47 The Nielsen Magic Poster Collection, p. 68 Mike Caveney's Egyptian Hall Museum, p. 78 (lower left) Richard Faverty/Beckett Studios, p. 93 Courtesy of Simon Aronson, p. 99 Mike Caveney's Egyptian Hall Museum, p. 102 Jeff Davis, p. 114 Richard Faverty/Beckett Studios, p. 122 Mike Caveney's Egyptian Hall Museum, p. 127 Courtesy of Gregory Wilson, p. 141 Mark J. Terrill/AP Images, p. 149 Anne White Photography, p. 161 Mike Caveney's Egyptian Hall Museum, p. 183 Mike Caveney's Egyptian Hall Museum, p. 186 Shutterstock, p. 187 (left) The Nielsen Magic Poster Collection, (right) The Houdini Museum, p. 189 Courtesy of Peter Martin, p. 210 Courtesy of David Regal, p. 218 Courtesy of Barrie Richardson, p. 225 Courtesy of Gene Anderson, p. 237 Courtesy of Tom Frank, p. 251 (top left and right background) Shutterstock, p. 251 (bottom) Mike Caveney's Egyptian Hall Museum, p. 254 Courtesy of Andi Gladwin, p. 268 The Nielsen Magic Poster Collection. p. 271 Extended Credits: (left) Anne White Photography, (middle, top to bottom) Richard Faverty/Beckett Studios, Gary O'Brien, Courtesy of Banachek, (right, top to bottom) Courtesy of Simon Aronson, Mike Caveney's Egyptian Hall Museum, Mike Caveney's Egyptian Hall Museum, p. 272 (left, top to bottom) Jeff Davis, Richard Faverty/Beckett Studios, Courtesy of Gregory Wilson, Courtesy of Daniel Garcia (middle, top to bottom) Courtesy of Clive Grewcock, Courtesy of Curtis Hickman, Anne White Photography, Courtesy of Barry Richardson, (right) Courtesy of Andi Gladwin.

Contents

Match-ic Wand

Spoon Switch

Chapter Four | **THE TEN GREATEST CARD TRICKS OF ALL TIME** |
Becoming a Card Expert

Finding Four Aces

Chapter Five | **KID CONJURING** |
Magic for Kids, and Magic by Kids

Cutting a Child in Two

Chapter Six | **WORKING MIRACLES** | *Magic and Mischief in the Office*

Chapter Seven | **MONEY MAGIC** | *Conjuring with Currency*

The Miser's Dream

Chapter Eight | PARLOR PRESTIDIGITATION |
Conquer Your Fear of Large Audiences

Money Mischief

Chapter Nine | TELEPHONE TRICKERY | *Magic Without Boundaries*

Chapter Ten | GET YOUR ACT TOGETHER |
Five Complete Shows to Amaze Any Audience

IN CLOSING

Introduction

*The most beautiful experience we can have
is the mysterious.
It is the fundamental emotion which stands at the
cradle of true art and true science.*

—ALBERT EINSTEIN

*What's the point of a magician?
He comes on, he fools you, you feel stupid,
show's over.*

—JERRY SEINFELD

Magic needs a makeover. Toss the tuxedo. Lose that top hat and set the rabbit free. And that goatee has to go. No more impaling women in boxes, and enough with the corny insults. Just stop.

Magic is the most mysterious of the performing arts. Why has she become so trivial?

The tricks. Most of the material magicians use is outdated or out of context. Consider the rabbit-from-the-top-hat effect. No birthday party is complete without it, and for fifty bucks the Amazing Larry will do the honors. And every time a rabbit comes out of a hat, another dozen nine-year-olds think magic sucks.

But as Einstein pointed out, magic can be moving. The moment we experience a great trick, we are instantly children again. For a fleeting moment—after the magic happens and before logic sets in—the world is boundless and anything is possible. Only magic can do that.

Magic is filled with amazing effects. And they're even more amazing because they're simple. Good magic is easy to describe and easy to remember: "She made a hundred bucks appear" or "He cut through a lady."

But consider the classic "Cut and Restored String"—a version of which appears in every bad beginner's book. You thread a piece of string through a straw . . . then you put the straw in a tube . . . then, in some cases, you cover the tube with a handkerchief . . . then you cut the whole mess in two . . . poof . . . it's restored. Straws? Tubes? Handkerchiefs? Too complicated, thank you.

You're about to learn over a hundred *magical* effects. Make a coin appear. Make your pet disappear. *Simple.* Read the one-sentence tag accompanying every entry in this book and you'll know exactly what you're getting into.

Remember that simple doesn't mean easy. While most effects in this book can be performed immediately after reading them, some require real practice. The difficulty ratings, 1 through 5, are there to help you decide which tricks to tackle first.

What separates this collection from many others is that the magic is relevant. That is, there's an emotional hook for the viewer. Sometimes the connection is obvious. In fact, you will even find several ways to make money appear at your fingertips. This is a skill *everyone* wants.

Magicians have a name for adding meaning to magic: the Ham Sandwich Theory. This theory states that if I reach into the air and produce a Ham Sandwich, you won't care. But if you said to me, "Josh, I'm hungry," and *then* I plucked one from thin air, you would be amazed. The magic fulfilled your desire. It had relevance.

An example: Tearing and restoring a plain old piece of paper is a meaningless trick because the audience doesn't care about paper. But in "Trash to Treasure" you restore a torn dollar bill. People can't stand to see money ruined, so there's an emotional connection to the bill's restoration.

Every effect in this book matters. Use borrowed objects to perform effects that fulfill audience desires: Predict thoughts and phone numbers, make money appear, control a participant's decision, and demonstrate a superhuman memory. The scripts are topical, the props familiar, and the magic unbelievable. It's all here, performance-ready.

This is the book I wish had existed when I started magic. When I was eight, I checked out every magic book at the library, but the information in each one was incomplete. How can you teach magic—a visual art—without photos? The effects in older books are tersely described, and no emphasis is given to the most important part: the performance of magic. There's a difference between explaining how tricks are done and how to do tricks.

With *Magic,* you'll learn the mechanics *and* presentation skills necessary for an amazing performance. Only a mastery of both makes a real magician. Good material is useless without proper delivery. In these pages both what to do and how to do it are treated with care and precision. No prior knowledge is assumed and no prior skills are required. This is a complete course in magic.

In addition, after each effect I have included a Master Class section, where you'll learn the subtle, professional nuances that make these effects come alive in the minds of your participants.

RABBIT FROM THE HAT

Pulling a rabbit from a hat wasn't always a bad trick. It was first recorded in an early American conjuring book in 1836. Imagine the period: Every man you know wears a hat; the wealthier men wear top hats. You're extremely wealthy, of course. So you invite John Henry Anderson—the Great Wizard of the North—into your drawing room to entertain your guests. At one point, he removes your top hat and pulls out the unthinkable: a live rabbit!

Today, pulling a rabbit from a hat is an ancient relic from a different time. Fuzzy bunnies and top hats still adorn magicians' business cards and neon magic shop signs, but the trick itself went out of style about the same time as the venerable top hat.

CHAPTER ONE

MAGIC SCHOOL

IN THIS CHAPTER

The Observation Test

Using This Book

EXPOSURE, OR HOW TO VANISH AN ELEPHANT

You're holding a book of secrets. Powerful secrets. And true to my profession, I know what you're thinking: *Isn't this against the rules? Breaking the magician's code . . . or something like that?* Exposure is the elephant in the room. For my first trick, I shall make it disappear.

There is a difference between exposing and teaching, and magicians have long debated what that difference is. It boils down to this: effort. This book is not exposure because you had to open it. My expectation is that you opened this book because you want to learn the art of magic.

You are not seeing the tricks exposed on TV or looking up videos of "magic secrets revealed" on the Internet. You are expending *effort* to learn magic.

Poof. The elephant is gone.

THE OBSERVATION TEST

In sixty seconds, you'll perform your first magic effect. Don't be nervous. You'll do fine.

You will be both magician and audience, and if you follow my instructions exactly, you'll fool yourself. When you turn this page in a moment, you'll see a scene from the greatest city in the world, New York—but that's all I can tell you. Being a magician requires you to be acutely observant, so study the drawing carefully. You need a timer; give yourself thirty seconds. After that, turn the page again and answer the questions about what you observed.

Ready? Remember, just thirty seconds. Go.

Welcome back.

That was a lot to take in in only thirty seconds. Now, without turning back, answer the following questions aloud (remember, no peeking):

1. There is a message painted on the side of the truck. What does it say?

2. There are two flags in the drawing, one in front of the Statue of Liberty and the other in front of the Empire State Building. What is on each flag?

You're almost there.
You have to turn the page again for the last question.
And just like last time, no turning back.

ANSWERS

1. The sign on the truck says, "World Peace, Man." Those hippies. You have to admire their optimism.

2. One flag is the United States flag. The other says, "Hi, Mom."

3. The third question seems easiest, yet it's trickier than it seems. Did you say the Statue of Liberty? 98 percent of readers do.

If you did, then congratulations on your first magic performance! This is your first step into a bigger world.

You just performed the most famous illusion of the last three decades—the one that made David Copperfield an international star. You made the Statue of Liberty disappear!

The drawing you studied never depicted the Statue of Liberty. But I conditioned you to "see" it there, both by implication and explication. This statue is New York's most famous landmark. That's why Copperfield used it. You simply assumed it was there, alongside its sister skyscrapers.

I cheated, too. "There are two flags in the drawing," I said, which is true, "One in front of the Statue of Liberty and the other in front of the Empire State Building." I didn't *ask* you whether the Statue of Liberty was there. I implied it, camouflaged within a different question. I imbedded a false memory in your head.

The same techniques that you fooled yourself with will fool your friends.

By the time you turned the page, the false memory was implanted in your head. Not only did you believe the statue was in the picture, you would have *bet* on it.

USING THIS BOOK

Before you begin using this book, a few notes...

Welcome to orientation. By the end of this book, you'll have both the material and the knowledge to perform amazing magic on a professional level. But first things first.

MAGIC WORDS

There are three words to immediately remove from your magic vocabulary:

1. Trick

2. Misdirection

3. Spectator

Here's why:

1. Dogs do tricks. Magicians do magic.

Magic tricks belong in the oxymoron bin, with jumbo shrimp and honest politicians. For what is magic isn't a trick and what can be proven a trick isn't magic. An appearing tiger is magic. But if you see the trap door, you're watching an appearing-tiger magic *trick*.

And tricks have a negative connotation. I hate being tricked. Use the word "effect" instead. Magicians identify their material as effects, and this is a useful term. What effect are we conveying? A vanish? Telepathy? Synchronicity? Every piece of magic in this book can be broken down to its simplest form—its essence. Its *effect*.

2. Getting the "Mis" Out of Misdirection

Misdirection is another loaded term, misunderstood and misused. "Hey Ricky, where'd that coin go?"

"I don't know. I was misdirected." Ricky may not know where the coin went, but he knew he was misdirected. If you're aware you're being misdirected, then the misdirection has failed. At that moment, the effect is ruined. It's like Mom's secret ingredient. Its use is so subtle that you don't even realize its there until she points it out. And if she tells you what it is, it doesn't seem so special anymore.

Magician Tommy Wonder articulated a better name: *direction*. Though he undoubtedly wasn't the first, he observed that the philosophy of misdirection is flawed; the idea is to force someone to look away from a secret move or action. Instead, we should direct someone's attention *toward* an object of interest. He proposed using "direction" to describe every moment during an effect, not just when we wish to distract the audience's attention. Wonder's revolutionary rethinking changed the way magic effects are structured. *Magic* adheres to this new framework. You'll hear quite a bit about direction, and not much more about misdirection.

3. Spectators Don't Exist

In theater-speak, the fourth wall is the invisible barrier that separates the magician from the audience. Magic penetrates this fourth wall. Movies, live theater, juggling, and ballet play out the same way, regardless of who is watching. But every magic show is unique. In the best magic shows, we are treated to the feeling that we, the viewers, impact how the effects unfold.

Magic doesn't exist without an audience—an active audience. In this spirit, I have replaced "spectator" with "participant," in the hope that you'll consider your audience as vital as the magic you show them.

THE LESSONS

I begin each chapter with a warm-up section that introduces the concepts you will need to practice and master in order to perform the effects properly. Don't worry—we'll take it nice and slow.

And be patient; all magic requires practice. Every effect in this book has a difficulty rating of 1 through 5 (look for the dagger icons), that will tell you at a glance how much technical skill is involved.

> Self-working. These routines are essentially foolproof.

> Still within the range of children. You can focus your practice time on the *presentation* of these effects.

> Simple sleight of hand; some practice required.

> A combination of sleights and principles; substantial practice required.

> Extremely difficult; see you in 200 hours!

SPOTLIGHT ON TOMMY WONDER

Magic is an industry full of virtuosos you've never heard of, and Dutch magician Tommy Wonder (1953–2006) is arguably the greatest modern example. He combined his theater background and engineering skills with refined sleight of hand. The results were extraordinary.

But his performances weren't his only gift to magicians. He was one of magic's most critical thinkers. In an influential essay, he wrote: "It's truly unfortunate that in magic we have many terms and expressions that don't accurately reflect what they are intended to. This is a pity because the use of correct terminology helps to keep one's thinking straight, and greatly simplifies matters when magicians communicate with each other."

All effects are illustrated in full-color photos. A "Concealed View"—a step in which the action is hidden from the participant (and sometimes the magician)—is outlined in blue and noted accordingly. Practice your effects in front of a mirror so you can make sure all of the hidden actions stay hidden while you perform.

The effects in this book are described for righties. That said, any lefty can easily reverse or adapt the techniques explained here. It by no means puts you at a disadvantage as a magician. I just went with the odds here: Nine in ten people are right-handed. My sincerest apologies to southpaws worldwide.

Magic has traditionally been dominated by men and doesn't have a good history of being welcoming to women. However, trends are slowly changing. In 1948, British magician Paula Baird was the first woman to win a prize (tied for second place in the manipulation category) at the World Championship of Magic. In the years that followed, at least seventeen more women won awards through the International Federation of Magic Societies (FISM)—and that's not including teams. Female magicians are winning top awards in other contests, as well—in 1990, magician Jade won the coveted Gold Medal from the International Brotherhood of Magicians—and there are a growing number of female members of both major international magic organizations. Accordingly, I have purposely included a mix of "shes" along with the "hes" when referring to the archetypal magician in this book. And to reflect the reality that *everybody* appreciates magic, I've also used both "shes" and "hes" for the participants.

BREATHE NEW LIFE INTO OLD PROPS

On Saturdays when I was eight, I would go down to the local magic shop where other young magicians used to hang out and trade effects and swap ideas. We were like the comic book shop kids or Boy Scouts, but dorkier. And each Saturday I would spend my allowance on a new trick. My magician friends helped me learn each one.

The Internet has changed everything, including magic. Now magicians hang out in chat rooms and "buy" magic via video download. Brick and mortar magic shops are becoming fewer and farther between.

People are still buying magic, but there are very few teachers. Magic instructions are notoriously bad, so props

arrive in the mail but nobody can decipher how to perform with them. Inevitably, the props end up in the back of your closet, next to the carrot juicer you ordered on TV.

But I'd like to change all that. Throughout the book, under the heading "Old Dog, New Trick," I've included detailed instructions on how to use many classic props, including Linking Rings, False Thumbtips, and Gaffed Decks. I also explain something you can't buy online: the presentations that make these effects *entertaining*.

Old Dog, New Trick: Using a False Thumbtip

A Pinch of Salt

MATERIALS:
A magician's false thumb tip
(available in all magic novelty

THE EFFECT Make a fistful of salt disap
bill, form it into a cone, and fill it with salt. When y
gone!

THE DVD

Just when you thought it couldn't get any better, check the inside front cover of your book. In the envelope is a feature-length companion DVD jam-packed with some of my favorite effects in the book. I perform ("Watch Magic") and teach ("Learn Magic") 35 effects in great detail, with particular emphasis on the rhythms, actions, and script adaptations that are harder to describe in print. Timing and misdirection are especially apparent in performance, and the DVD will help you learn and practice the nuances and flourishes associated with each effect. Look for the DVD icon throughout the book to note which effects are included. Slide the disc into any DVD player and navigate through the menus to your heart's content.

GETTING HELP

Magic is a collaborative art, and every magician needs a safe environment to grow. For some, this might mean inviting the family into the basement after dinner for a show. But to really improve your *technique*, you must seek the audience of other knowledgeable magicians.

The best way, perhaps, is to join your local magic club. There are two fine magic organizations with clubs all over the world: The International Brotherhood of Magicians (I.B.M.) and the Society of American Magicians (S.A.M.). These groups are made up of professional magicians, magic hobbyists, collectors,

historians, and general magic lovers, and typically meet about once a month.

Every magician needs feedback, and there is no substitute for personal instruction. Your local magic club can fulfill that need—and you just might make some great friends, too.

IMPROMPTU MAGIC

IN THIS CHAPTER

MAKING THE ORDINARY EXTRAORDINARY

To become a magician, you must learn to think like a magician. Forget any notion of having to perform on a stage; you're already on it. The local restaurant, classroom, front yard, kitchen, at work—the magic is everywhere. It's your job to help others see it. *Think* magic.

This chapter will help you see the magic potential in everyday objects. Here are seven of the most powerful conjuring effects. Not only is each piece a reputation-maker, but you can do each one right now. There is no preparation necessary.

Think of this chapter as a magician's desert island survival kit. You'll make miracles from nothing, make objects disappear, and control the choices your participants make. These tools have limitless applications, but only if you're thinking magically.

You'll learn how to make an entire booklet of matches appear in a straw, cause pool chalk to appear in a participant's hand, and restore a torn napkin. I've also included "Four Elements," arguably the greatest bar bet of all time. Use this stunt at the pub or cafeteria and you'll never pay for drinks or donuts again.

The contents of this chapter involve only borrowed objects, so you're already prepared to turn the page. What follows is your crash course in how to take the ordinary and do the extraordinary.

THE WARM-UP

Finger Flexibility

This simple stretching exercise is the perfect way to warm up before a show or effect, and will keep your digits nimble and flexible.

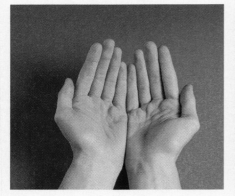

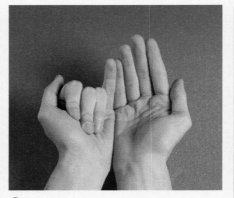

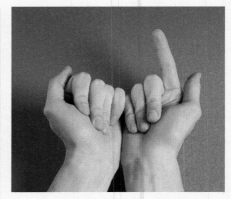

1 Hold your hands next to one another with the palms up. The little fingers should be touching.

2 Bend your left first finger inward. In quick, fluid succession, bend your left second, third, and fourth fingers inward.

3 Continue the "wave" action by bending your right fourth, third, second, and first finger inward.

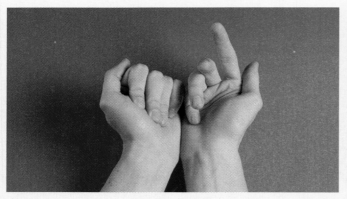

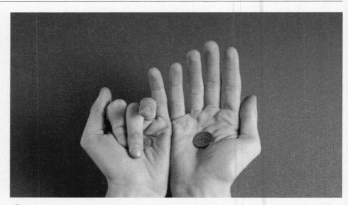

4 Now complete the actions in reverse. That is, extend your right first finger, followed by the right second, third, and fourth fingers. Continue this action across your left hand. Repeat this back-and-forth motion, striving for speed and grace. There should be no pause between hands.

5 Once you have mastered "the wave," try it again with a coin on each palm. Magic often involves moving the hands while concealing an object.

The Palm

Palming is a technique to practice with any small object at any time. Like any basic effect, it can be applied in many situations to a variety of effects.

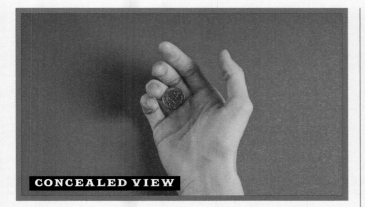

CONCEALED VIEW

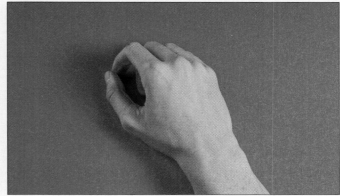

❶ Place any small object—like a coin—in your right hand. Position the coin at the base of your right fingers, between the second and third fingers. Gently curl the fingers inward to secure the coin in place. It's obvious to you that you're holding a coin.

❷ But if you turn your hand palm down, it looks completely natural.

The goal of palming is learning to live guilt-free (this has fringe benefits). Remember that you're the only one who knows you're holding a coin, and you can't let this secret knowledge intimidate the way you perform.

❸ Conquer this guilt by practicing often. Practice while you walk to your car or sit at your desk. Keep a coin palmed while you talk with friends or when you're reading in bed. Once you're comfortable with how inconspicuous your covert actions are, start carrying out tasks with your fingers while maintaining the coin in palm position. Unlock doors, open packages, and answer phones. You'll quickly find that your second and third fingers are still somewhat functional while they conceal the coin.

False Transfer

Whether you use coins, napkins, or gum balls, you'll need the following technique in your repertoire in order to vanish objects throughout Magic.

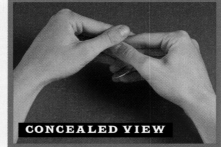

CONCEALED VIEW

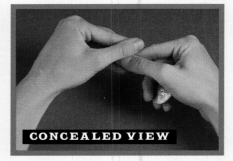

CONCEALED VIEW

❶ Display a coin in the palm of your right hand then maneuver the coin so you hold it between your right thumb and first finger. Notice that the right second, third, and fourth fingers rest beneath the displayed coin, extended.

❷ Move your left hand into view, with the left fingers pointed toward the ground and the left palm angled toward your body, concealing the coin from the audience's view.

❸ Under cover of the left hand, secretly pinch the coin between your right second and third fingertips. The right fingers are used as pincers, and their grip should support the coin independent of the first finger and thumb. Still concealing the coin, curl the right second and third fingers toward the right palm.

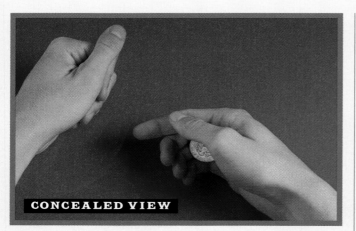

CONCEALED VIEW

❹ Close the left hand into a fist and move away, apparently with the right hand's coin. Stare intently at your left fist, as if it contains the coin. Drop your right hand casually to your side. When nobody is looking, allow the coin to fall onto the curled right fingertips, where it remains concealed in palm position (see "The Palm," page 17).

PRACTICING

The *false transfer*, like all magic, is an acquired skill. You have to practice the sleight until it's second nature. Keep these hints in mind:

1. Magic is an art of concealing art. Your false transfer must not look like sleight of hand. It must look exactly like the action you're simulating: transferring a coin from one hand to the other. When you practice, alternate between *actually* passing a coin between your hands and performing the false transfer. When the two look identical, you've mastered the move.

2. Practice doesn't make perfect; practice makes consistent. Rather than risk learning the move incorrectly, practice in front of a mirror so you can see what your audience sees.

3. Don't look at your hands. The false transfer, like most sleight-of-hand moves, simulates a simple action. In the course of a normal day, we perform actions like this dozens of times without looking. If you're looking at your hands, you draw unwanted audience attention.

Phoenix Matches

MATERIALS:
Matchbook (drawer-box matches won't work).

SETUP: Before you perform, angle a match upright from the booklet's front row. The match should stand perpendicular to the others and separate from them. Tear another match from the booklet, light it, and carefully use it to ignite the attached, angled match. Extinguish both matches and then discard the loose burnt match.

DIFFICULTY: †††††

THE EFFECT As you strike a match to light a candle at dinner, you gather everyone around and recount the tale of the Phoenix, a mythic bird that is burned alive so it can be reborn. To illustrate, **you cause the burnt match (your Phoenix-bird) to disappear, only to show it has been reborn (reattached itself) inside the matchbook**.

THE SECRET "Phoenix Matches" is accomplished with a simple vanish and your ability to conceal a burnt, attached match as you display a matchbook.

THE PERFORMANCE

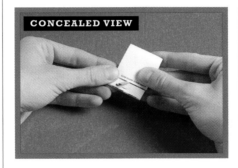
CONCEALED VIEW

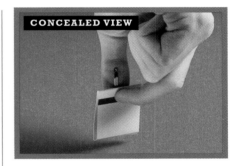
CONCEALED VIEW

❶ Close the matchbook cover, taking care that the burnt attached match that you prepared during the setup remains outside the closed matchbook.

❷ Hold the matchbook pinched in your right hand, concealing the burnt match with your right thumb.

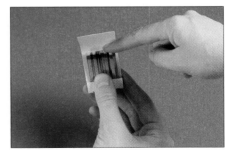

❸ Before lighting a candle or while chatting over glasses of wine, present the matchbook to your participants: *"The sacred Egyptian bird, the Phoenix,"* you say, *"is one of the most famous icons of all time, and it's one of my favorite stories."*

❹ Keep your right thumb over the burnt match as you peel open the booklet with your left thumb and fingers. *"Would you please choose a Phoenix?"* Point to the matches in the booklet and ask one of your participants to touch one.

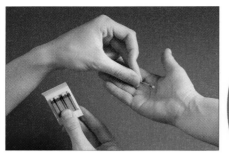

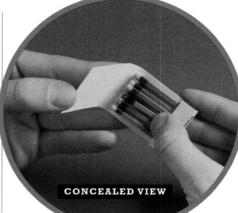

CONCEALED VIEW

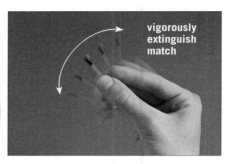

vigorously
extinguish
match

5 Keeping your right thumb anchored on top of the burnt match, tear the selected match from the booklet and hand it to your participant. It's an exciting feeling to call your participant's attention to the matches in the booklet, all the while concealing a burnt match. It is right under his nose . . . but he never notices it!

6 Angle the back of the matchbook toward your participant. As you close the matchbook with both hands, secretly fold back the hidden match so that it rests alongside the other matches.

"*The Phoenix,*" you say, reaching for the selected match, "*reaches the end of its life cycle and builds a nest. Suddenly, the nest and the bird ignite.*"

7 Pick up the match between your right thumb and fingers and light it against the booklet's striking pad. Set the matchbook on the participant's outstretched palm. Extinguish the match by shaking it back and forth. When you see smoke, continue shaking in a large left and right action as you prepare to secretly toss the extinguished match to the floor.

CONCEALED VIEW

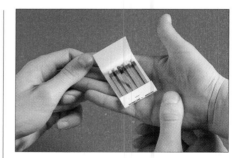

8 As you shake to the left (toward your body), lower your hand beneath the surface of the table.

The moment your fingers dip beneath the table's edge, drop the match to the floor. Keep your fingers clenched, as if you still hold a match, and continue to move your hand back and forth, as if shaking the match until it cools.

9 The smoke doesn't dissipate for a few seconds, and this hovering cloud gives the illusion that you're holding a match long after you have ditched it.

"*The bird burns until it is no more,*" you say, slowing your right hand to a stop. Open your fingers and show the match is gone. This vanish is more surprising than you might think, so don't underplay it. You just made a match disappear! Next comes the real shocker. . . .

10 "*But then the bird is reborn, in the Arizona desert city that bears its name—wait, that's not how it goes. The bird is reborn where it originated!*" Ask the participant to open the matchbook, and remind him that it has been in his possession throughout the effect.

"*I think you'll find the vanished match 'reborn,' still covered in ash!*" Allow the participant to discover the burned match in the booklet. When he tries to remove it, he'll find yet another layer to the mystery: The match has reattached itself!

MASTER CLASS

"Phoenix Matches" is one of the greatest impromptu effects of all time. Professional magicians have used it with great results for more than a century. But the version described here has two points worth exploring.

The first is the notion of using magic to illustrate a story. This is one of the most effective techniques to remove the sting from a magic "trick." I've already discussed how much I loathe the word "trick" because it implies a sneakiness and suggests that our audiences are getting bested. Alleviating that impression with a story, we recount a classic tale and punctuate it with devastating magic. For the audience, it's no longer a "trick," but a special "effect" of the story.

"Phoenix Matches" is also a great example of good choreography. For example, it's important to ask the participant to choose a match. It doesn't matter which match he chooses, but your request forces him to look at the booklet closely. He'll form a mental image of the matchbook—a vivid picture *without* a burnt match. Later, he will recall this image and conclude that the burnt match "appeared."

Also, notice that you place the matchbook in the participant's hand during the effect. Don't put it in your pocket or on the table—you want to involve your audience as much as possible. The match reappears in the booklet, but that's not how the participant will remember it. He will remember that the match *reappeared in his hand.*

This effect must be performed by or under supervision of an adult. As with all effects involving fire, use extreme caution and make sure you have a supply of water nearby.

CREDIT: **Milbourne Christopher invented this trick and published it as "Match Stickler" in** *The Phoenix* **in 1952.**

THE FIRST MAGIC BOOK

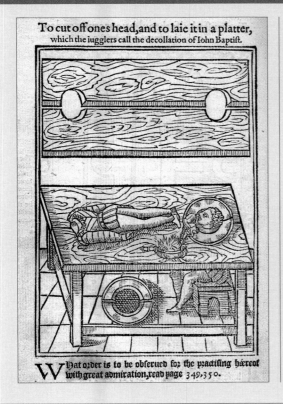

To cut off ones head, and to laie it in a platter, which the iugglers call the decollation of Iohn Baptist.

What order is to be obserued for the practising hereof with great admiration, read page 349, 350.

The year 1584 was a bad time to be a magician. Conjuring, at the time, was often classified as black magic, and magicians worked in fear of being tried for witchcraft. But with the publication of Reginald Scot's *Discoverie of Witchcraft* in England, everything changed.

This was, in part, the first magic book published in the English language. It sought to clarify the difference between witchcraft and magic as entertainment. Nevertheless, the book was considered sacrilegious, and King James I decreed that all copies should be burned. Fortunately, copies survived.

The section on magic effects illuminates what sort of material magicians were using in 1584. What follows are some of my favorite effects in the book:

- *To thrust a peece of lead into one eie, and to drive it about (with a sticke) betweene the skin and flesh of the forehead, until it be brought to the other eie, and there thrust out.*
- *To cut halfe your nose asunder, and to heale it againe presentlie without anie salve.*
- *To Cut off ones head, and to laie it in a platter . . . which the jugglers call the decollation of John Baptist.*

Thanks to Scot, you can perform the magic in this book—or his—without risk of being burned at the stake.

The re-creation of the beheading of John the Baptist became a popular illusion of the time. Remnants of this effect are present in modern-day illusions where assistants are beheaded, impaled, or sawed in two.

Match-ic Wand

THE EFFECT You display a book of matches and ask a participant to wave her wand (a wrapped straw) over the closed booklet. **Matches disappear in her hand! Where did they go? Inside a sealed straw!**

THE SECRET It's a little-known fact that you can pre-load small objects (matches, in this case) into one end of a wrapped straw. The hole in the wrapper is invisible. Thus, you can encourage the participant to examine the match-loaded straw, or "magic wand."

MATERIALS:

Two matchbooks (drawer-box matches won't work) and a straw with a paper wrapper.

DIFFICULTY: †††††

SETUP: This is a good restaurant effect as everything you need for "Match-ic Wand" is readily available and can be picked up on the way to your table. For best results, "plant" the following props on the table in advance; this way, it will appear you "borrow" all the objects.

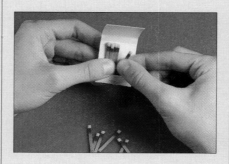

❶ Grab two booklets of matches. Tear out all the matches from one booklet.

❷ Stuff them, one by one, into a small hole at one end of a wrapped straw. Clear straws work best, but any straw will suffice.

❸ Once the matches are loaded, twirl the wrapper's end to further conceal the small hole you created in the paper.

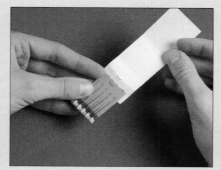

❹ Unfold the other matchbook completely and pull the bank of matches free from the staple that keeps them in place.

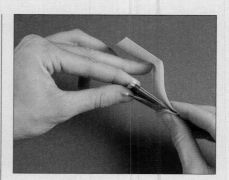

❺ Carefully remove the staple and then replace the match-insert *behind* the stumps in the other empty matchbook. At a glance, this prepared matchbook looks normal.

THE PERFORMANCE "Match-ic Wand" is perfect for a role-reversal presentation. There are a lot of directions to follow here, but with practice you will get it. The role-reversal itself is actually a rather simple concept and it's a lot of fun to perform.

You tell the participant that *she* will be the magician, and you'll cue her lines. From that point forward, you whisper to her what she is supposed to say back to you (and to the rest of the audience). The audience hears you cue her (it's all done tongue-in-cheek), and this allows for hilarious moments of ambiguity (where she will be unsure whether you're cuing her line or merely telling her something). Visualize the performance as a dialogue between two people and all will become clear.

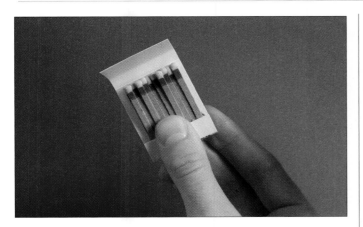

❶ *"Mary, you're going to be the magician for this next piece."* Pick up the prepared book of matches and open the cover. Use your fingers to keep the match insert in place. *"Don't worry. This will be a lot of fun, and I'll tell you what to say."*

Point toward the matches and give her the first cue: *"These matches will do fine."*

She will immediately repeat, *"These matches will do fine."* When cuing your participant, you want to stage-whisper. This is drama-speak for projecting with a raspy voice. You want everyone to hear you cuing the helper, but you also want to pretend that you're feeding her lines "secretly." Open the matchbook and display the matches.

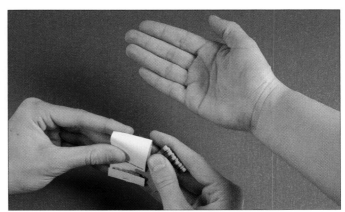

❷ Cue her again: *"And now,"* you say, allowing her to repeat, *"I need you to remove your magic wand from your pocket."* Allow her to repeat the second part of the sentence. As she does, you will secretly steal the match insert from the cover. To do this, simply hold the matchbook between your hands. Just before closing the booklet, use both thumbs to slide the insert into the curled fingers of your right hand.

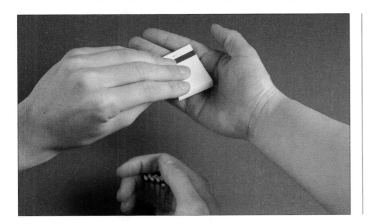

❸ Continue to close the matchbook cover. With your left hand, place the cover in the participant's hand. With your right hand, move to your pocket. Place the insert in your pocket and remove your right hand, pretending to hold an invisible wand. Cue your participant further: *"Here, you can use my invisible wand. Wave it over the matches."*

Continues on next page ☞

4 Cue her, *"Now I'll wave my magic wand over the matches."* She will repeat this. Do nothing. Just wait. She will stare at the audience with a blank expression. Eventually "remember" what to do, and say, *"Here, you can use my magic wand."*

She'll repeat, "Here, you can use . . ."

Cut her off, smiling. *"No, I'm telling you. You can use my magic wand. Use this."* Pick up the prepared straw, give it to the participant, and let her wave it over the matches.

"And the matches are gone," you say.

"And the matches are gone," she repeats after you.

5 *"Prove it,"* you say, encouraging her to unfold the matchbook. When she opens the cover, she'll discover that all the matches are gone. *"Thank you very much,"* you say, leading the applause. Allow her to repeat your thanks, and then get her deserved applause.

Say, *"Do you know how I did that?"* and allow her to repeat. Pause a moment and then say, *"No, how?"* This is funny on several levels. If she perceives this comment as a question, she'll be speechless (since she doesn't know she did it). If she repeats "No, how?" then make a joke: *"That's what I asked you!"*

Continue the banter and say, *"I did it with my magic wand. See?"*

6 She says, "I did it with my magic wand. See?" Allow her to unwrap the "wand" and pour out the matches. Shake her hand and congratulate her on her first magic effect. *"Now let's see you saw this guy in half."*

MASTER CLASS

In a magic show, the notion of a role reversal is daunting but ultimately empowering. It's hard for any magician to give up power, even if the power is only theatrical. Many people get into magic to inflate their own egos (but those people eventually ditch magic for politics). It's hard to share the spotlight with a participant.

From the audience's perspective, there is no doubt that you're in control. In fact, really great magicians do empower those around them. That, in itself, is an incredible effect. With this role reversal, you're creating a more memorable experience for your participant. She becomes the magician.

CREDIT: "Matches All Gone" was first published in my column in *MAGIC* magazine. This book's chief consultant, Joel Givens, created it. Givens is a professional magician from Clayton, North Carolina, who has performed for such corporations as IBM and CYSCO Systems and celebrities like Michael Jordan and Kevin Costner. Thanks to Chuck Fayne for guidance with Karrell Fox's role-reversal presentation.

HOW HOUDINI DIED

Aside from Merlin, Harry Houdini (Ehrich Weiss, 1874–1926) has become the most recognizable magician of all time. Yet his death remains shrouded in mystery, just as Houdini would have liked it.

In *Houdini*, the 1953 film starring Tony Curtis, the magician perishes after an underwater escape. This ending is romantic, but inaccurate.

In *The Secret Life of Houdini* (2006) authors Bill Kallush and Larry Sloman proposed murder by poison as a possible cause of death. They contend that Spiritualists may have carefully orchestrated Houdini's murder. Houdini spent the latter part of his life debunking and discrediting these supposed spirit mediums. He detested that these petty charlatans claimed authentic powers.

Houdini's death certificate offers yet another explanation. The official cause of death is peritonitis caused by "ruptured appendicitis." Precisely how Houdini's appendix was ruptured is a mystery. Some scientists contend he had an undiagnosed condition and that the rupture occurred naturally.

But there was a peculiar event that preceded his death. Houdini was backstage before a show in Montreal when J. Gordon Whitehead, a student at McGill University, approached the magician and asked if it was true that he could withstand punches to his gut. The second Houdini began to answer, Whitehead hit him with a volley of blows to the stomach. Whitehead caught Houdini completely off guard. These unexpected punches may have aggravated or instigated peritonitis.

Houdini insisted the injury wasn't serious and went untreated for days. Eventually he was hospitalized, but it was too late. Nearing death, Houdini pulled his surgeon close and told him that as a boy, he had wanted to become a doctor.

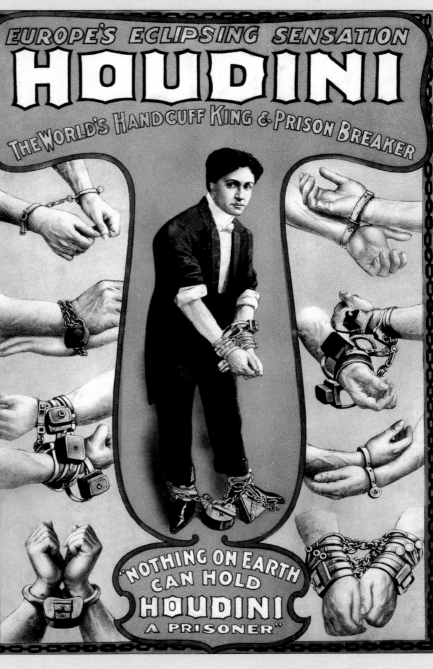

The surgeon tried to make Houdini understand the impact he had had on the world, saying, "Here you are, the greatest magician and the greatest entertainer of your age. You make countless thousands of people happy."

Houdini replied, "Perhaps those things are true, doctor, but the difference between me and you is that you actually *do* things for people. I, in almost every respect, am a fake."

Trick Shot ON DVD

MATERIALS:
Pool chalk.

SETUP: Just before the eight ball falls in and ends your game, stick your right first finger inside a cube of pool chalk. Allow the game to end and order the next round (it's on you because you sank the eight ball).

DIFFICULTY: ✝✝✝✝✝

THE EFFECT Between games of pool, you pull aside an opponent and ask him to make a fist with either hand, promising an unparalleled trick shot. You retrieve a cube of blue pool chalk from the pool table. Now the weird part: You chalk up your right first finger like it's a pool stick and then **make the chalk mark appear inside the participant's fist without touching him**.

THE SECRET Before the effect begins, you secretly transfer a blue chalk mark to the participant's palm (without his knowledge). He makes a fist without knowing the chalk mark is already there. The rest is presentation.

THE PERFORMANCE

❶ You're playing pool and you propose a trick shot better than any your friends have ever seen.

"Have you seen guys on television do amazing trick shots where all the balls fall in from one shot? Well, this is my claim to fame."

Approach your participant and instruct him, *"Hold out both hands, palms down."* Grip each of his hands with yours, fingers beneath and thumb on top. *"Lower your hands just a bit, like that."* You're grabbing his hands under the guise of lowering them a few inches so you can transfer the chalk mark on your right finger to his palm.

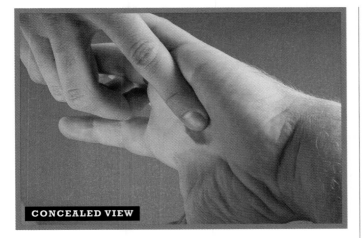

CONCEALED VIEW

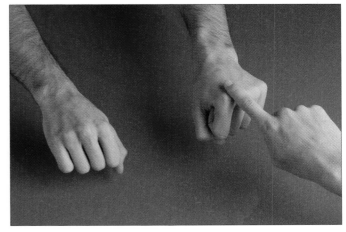

2 When your hands contact his, touch your chalk-covered right fingertip to the middle of his left palm. You don't need to transfer a lot of chalk—its appearance, no matter how small, is enough to freak out anyone.

Ask your participant to make a fist with each hand. As you talk, step back a little. Say, *"We're only going to use one target for this trick shot, so we need to eliminate a hand. I'll let you decide. Raise one of your fists."*

Here we're using a powerful principle known as *equivoque*. Although it appears the participant gets to choose which fist he will use, *you* make the real decision. Notice how the script is worded: You announce that you need to eliminate one fist, but you don't say whether the fist your participant chooses will be used or eliminated.

3 For example, suppose he raises his left fist, the one with the chalk. *"Perfect,"* you say, *"we'll use that fist as the target. You can relax your other hand."* If he raises his right fist, continue with the same confidence. *"Perfect. We'll eliminate that fist. You can relax that hand by your side. Keep your left fist tight."*

In both scenarios, your participant will be clenching his left fist. Unbeknownst to him, it already contains a dab of pool chalk.

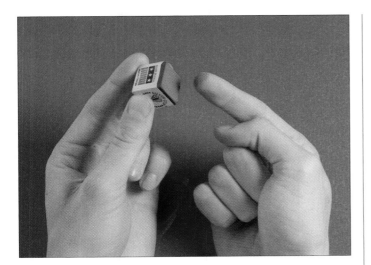

4 Your finger may still have some remnants of chalk, but you'll camouflage this evidence by openly adding more: Retrieve the chalk from the pool table and apply it to your right first finger. Only now, after you have loaded the chalk onto your target, should you begin to talk specifically about the effect.

Hold up your blue-tipped first finger. *"This is my pool cue. Oh, and I use an invisible cue ball. Your fist—which I haven't touched—is the corner pocket."* Now you mime the action of hitting an invisible ball with your finger. *"It bounces off the rail,"* you say, commentating like a sports announcer, *"then off that light, then around John's head, then off the floor, it's rolling . . . rolling . . . and into the pocket!"* With your eyes, intensely follow the imaginary cue ball all over the pool hall.

continued

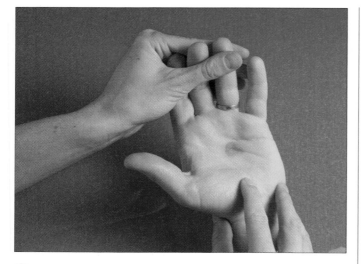

5 Eventually relax and announce that you've made your shot. The audience doesn't seem very impressed. *"I'll prove it,"* you say to your participant. Reiterate that you haven't touched him throughout the effect, then say to him *"Open your hand."* When your participant opens his fist, he discovers an unmistakable trace of chalk—a magical remnant of the best trick, and proof of the best trick shot he has ever seen.

MASTER CLASS

"Trick Shot" works because you do the sneaky part (loading the pool chalk onto the participant's palm) before he even realizes the trick has begun. In this effect, you use your audience's assumptions to your advantage.

Michael Close, one of magic's current great philosophers, articulated this concept:

"Assumption lies at the heart of deception; in fact, I'm not sure deception can exist without it. . . .When we perform, the spectators assume that we are beginning the show. But what if the show actually began earlier? After all, how can you begin to reconstruct a method if part of the show happened before you began to watch?"

CREDIT: "Trick Shot" is Jay Sankey's excellent adaptation of the classic "Ashes on Palm" effect which is derived from an old Indian feat called the "Potsherd Trick." The original effect was performed with cigarette ashes, but pool chalk provides the perfect presentation. Jay Sankey is one of magic's most prolific creators: He has published over 800 effects and put out nearly 50 instructional DVDs.

MODERN MASTER

MICHAEL CLOSE

Michael Close is a magician from Las Vegas. But unlike other Vegas magicians, he doesn't do illusions. Michael Close is a close-up magician; his stage is your table.

He has revitalized the industry of tableside entertainment. No more balloon twisting or bar tricks. When Close approaches your table, you get a polished, professional show. There's

interaction, drama, scripting and, of course, world-class sleight of hand. All this before the appetizers are served!

Blister Vanish

MATERIALS:
A house key that has a round hole, and salt.

SETUP: When nobody is looking, remove a key from your key chain and press the pad of your right middle finger firmly against the hole for thirty seconds. You can even do this in front of your audience, forming the "burn" under cover of your pants pocket. The longer you hold, the more discolored the "blister" will look. Once you've got a good "blister," you must perform quickly . . . it will fade within forty-five seconds.

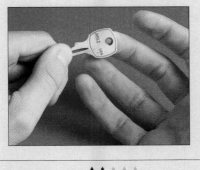

DIFFICULTY ✝✝ ✝✝✝

THE EFFECT "Ouch!" you say as you pull your finger away from a scalding hot pot. "I didn't know the burner was on." Your friend grabs your hand and notices a huge pink burn blister.

"It's okay," you say, "it only hurts a little. And I know a secret family remedy. Can you get me some salt?" You pour dry salt on the blister and its color starts to fade. "Now I just have to concentrate on what my finger looked like before I burned it," you say, rubbing the blister lightly. When you show your finger again, **the blister on your finger has melted away right before everybody's eyes.**

THE SECRET It's not as painful as it looks. You create a temporary "burn" by forming a circular impression on your finger, using a key hidden in your pocket as your template.

THE PERFORMANCE

❶ Pick a situation where there's a potentially hazardous, hot object nearby (lighters, stoves, hot plates, and cigarettes work well). If you can't find a real hot object, just fake it! Your blister is proof enough of the heat.

Pretend to touch the object with your right hand, then flinch in pain, using your best acting skills. Display the faux blister you created on the pad of your middle finger, but underplay it. Let your participants validate its severity: *"No, this is serious,"* or *"I'll get the first-aid kit,"* they might say. Let them sweat.

continued ☞

❷ *"I've got an idea—an old family remedy,"* you say. Ask for salt. You could ask for anything on hand, so long as it sounds homegrown (*"I need brown sugar, quick!"*). Pour salt over the blister. Although salt has nothing to do with it, your blister will begin to fade (because twenty seconds have gone by). What's beautiful about this illusion is that the color fades *before* the impression goes away. So it seems that the salt really takes out the blister's color.

Complete the illusion by rubbing your left thumb and fingers over the blister. Rubbing expedites the blister's fade; simply stretch the skin back and forth until the bubble is gone. Lift your hand as you exhale, exhausted and relieved.

MASTER CLASS

This impromptu stunt can be performed more formally if you have a small bandage. Simply form it into a ring that loosely fits your middle finger. Keep this in the same pocket as your "impression" key. Once you've formed your makeshift blister, slip on the bandage and show it to your audience for their sympathy, saying, *"I burned myself the other night."* As you gently remove the bandage, assure everyone that you'll demonstrate your "magic powers of healing." Display the burn. *"Careful,"* you say, *"it's sensitive."* Now make it disappear by the will of your mind.

CREDIT: **Jack Kent Tillar created "Blister" and published it in *The Tarbell Course in Magic: Volume Seven.***

MODERN MASTER
MARTIN GARDNER

Ninety-four-year-old Martin Gardner is one of the world's most respected intellectuals. He's an internationally renowned logician, mathematician, and skeptic, and has written more than seventy books on an impressive array of subjects (from string theory to an annotated *Alice in Wonderland*). And all of these areas help inform his other passion: impromptu magic. Gardner is considered the authority on off-the-cuff effects, done with borrowed or unprepared objects—like many of the ones found in this chapter. The effects he designs are based on simple scientific principles or mathematical puzzles, and he has a particular knack for presentations that obscure how the effects work. He says of his work and passion, "Science reminds us of the reason behind things. Magic . . . reminds us of the unreason behind things."

Hand-Eye Coordination ON DVD

MATERIALS:
Two plain paper cocktail napkins and a permanent marker.

SETUP: This quick preparation can be done in a matter of seconds, away from your audience. Unfold a cocktail napkin once and draw a hand on one half and an eye at the facing half. This is your duplicate napkin. The drawings don't have to be masterpieces, but you must be able to recreate them during the effect. Crumple this napkin into a tight ball and place it in your left pocket. Keep a matching napkin and a pen nearby, and you're ready for performance.

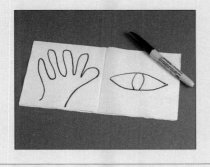

DIFFICULTY ✝✝✝✝

THE EFFECT "You've heard the expression, 'the hand is quicker than the eye,'" you say, "but I'm going to prove it." You tear a cocktail napkin in two pieces and draw a hand on one piece and an eye on the other. You separate the pieces, placing one in your participant's hand and one in yours. But when the participant opens his hand, he has both pieces. **You've proved that the hand really is quicker than the eye.**

THE SECRET You use two napkins and some sleight of hand.

THE PERFORMANCE

Most folks have heard the adage, "The hand is quicker than the eye," and many will assign this vague untruth to all your magic. "I know how he did that; the hand is quicker than the eye," they'll say. Whenever someone brings this up, this is the perfect effect to perform. And if nobody raises this point, bring it up yourself: *"I'll prove the hand is quicker than the eye."*

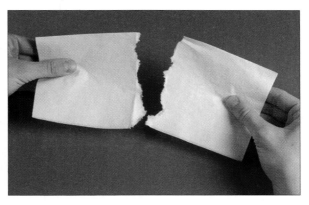

❶ Display a cocktail napkin and clearly tear it into two pieces.

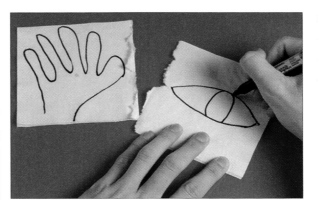

❷ Present the pen and draw a hand on one piece and an eye on the other. As mentioned in the setup, try to approximate the drawings you've already made on the duplicate napkin. They don't have to be exact, but they need to be close.

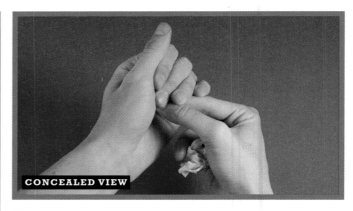

3 *"I'll put the hand in my hand,"* you say, as you crumple up the "hand" piece. Here you begin the false transfer. Hold the napkin between your right thumb and right first and second fingers. Position your other right fingers next to your thumb and even with your second finger.

4 Pretend to put the napkin piece into your left hand while retaining it in your right fingers: The right hand moves toward the left hand and touches the napkin to the base of the left fingers.

Start to close your left fingers. As you do, pinch the napkin piece between your second and third fingers and curl them inward, shifting the napkin into your right palm. Notice that your right thumb and first finger remain straight throughout the false transfer, as if they hold the napkin right up until you form your left hand into a fist, apparently holding the napkin piece.

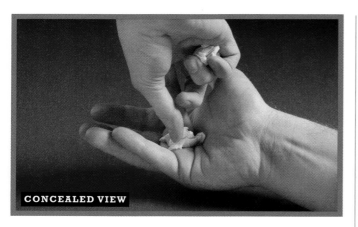

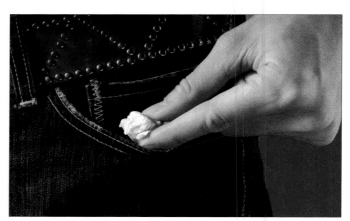

5 To provide added cover for your concealed move, ask the participant to crumple the "eye" piece as you execute the false transfer. With your right first finger and thumb still extended, retrieve that piece. Openly take it into your right fist, secretly adding it to the palmed "hand" piece. *"I'll give you the 'eye,'"* you say, handing *both* pieces as one to your participant. Ask him to close his hand in a fist around the "eye." Since the pieces are from the same napkin, they camouflage each other. And since napkins have a spongy quality, the participant won't be able to feel a difference between one or two halves.

6 Your participant thinks you have one napkin half and he has the other. Actually, your left fist is empty and he's holding both halves. Place your empty left fist into your pocket, saying, *"I'll put the hand in my hand in my pocket."* Retrieve your duplicate napkin from your left pocket, pulling it out for just a moment—just enough so your participant sees what appears to be you stuffing the "hand" piece into your pocket. It's a decoy, of course, but now he has a visual of you pocketing your "hand."

Pretend to put the duplicate back in your pocket but keep it concealed in your left fist. *"Now keep one eye on my hand and one eye on your eye."*

CONCEALED VIEW

7 Ask the participant to open his hand. He discovers both pieces, the "hand" and "eye." He can even unfold the pieces to verify the doodles. While he is reacting to the magic, pull your left hand from your pocket, concealing the balled-up duplicate napkin in your left second, third, and fourth fingers. Your first finger and thumb should extend from your fist, ready to grasp a napkin piece.

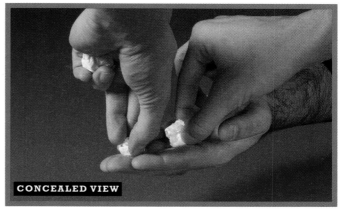

CONCEALED VIEW

8 Reach into the participant's palm and take one piece in each hand. Your hands should mirror each other, which looks disarming and helps conceal the palmed duplicate napkin in your left fingers.

9 Momentarily place both pieces into your right hand. Pretend to take one back into your left hand, taking care not to flash the concealed duplicate. To do this, put your hands together and release the palmed duplicate napkin from your left fingers into your right fingers.

10 In a continuing action, pick up the duplicate as if it were one of the pieces and place it into the participant's hand. Ask him to make a fist around it. This is a *palm switch* (see page 180).

As you move your left hand toward your participant, close your right hand and say, *"This time I'll put an eye in my pocket and a hand in your hand. Keep one eye on my pocket, one eye on your fist, and one eye on me."* Put your right hand into your pocket and ditch both pieces. Once you have dumped the pieces, retract your hand and show it empty.

Ask the participant to open his hand. At first, he will think you have failed (because he sees only one piece). Ask him to open the piece. He'll discover that it is both pieces, and that they have somehow fused back together. *"I told you,"* you say, *"the hand is quicker than the eye."* *continued* 👉

MASTER CLASS

"Hand-Eye Coordination" is a thin disguise for the classic "Sponge Balls" trick introduced by Jesse L. Lybarger in the 1920s and used and abused by magicians worldwide ever since. You know sponge balls—the red pieces of sponge, usually manipulated by magicians in ill-fitting tuxedos.

But contemporary magic theory challenges sponge balls, and the "costumes" magicians perform them in. The problem is *context*. Why does this strange man have red sponge balls in his hands? Are they candy?

Bloody cotton balls? Clown noses? And why is he dressed like that? Did he just come from a wedding?

The truth is, Sponge Balls—for all the laughter they garner—are just silly magic props. And tuxedos only work if you're James Bond.

It's time for an update. Instead of abstract pieces of sponge, "Hand-Eye Coordination" employs cocktail napkins. These are props found everywhere drinks are sold and so our audiences have a *context* for what they're seeing. Now we add the classic presentational hook, *"The hand is quicker than the eye,"* and we've taken an antiquated magic trick and turned it into modern magic simply by replacing an obvious magic prop with an everyday item.

Now, what to wear?

DRESSING THE PART

In 1810, magicians dressed in robes and hats—a Harry Potter party gone wrong. Cue magician Jean-Eugène Robert-Houdin who, in characteristically French style, burst onto the scene in dapper evening wear, much like the clothing his Victorian audiences wore to his theater.

More than a century later, many magicians still wear tuxedos and top hats even though virtually nobody else does. Robert-Houdin said, "A magician is an actor playing the part of a magician." Dead for more than 130 years, Jean-Eugène Robert-Houdin continues to influence how we play that part—and in ways he didn't intend.

So what should you wear when you perform? The general guideline is that a magician should dress like the most formal person in his audience. So if you're going to perform strolling magic at a cocktail party and some people will be wearing jeans and others will be wearing dress slacks, you wear dress slacks. If half the men are wearing ties, you wear a tie, too. But if you're going to do a kids' show outdoors in July, a suit and tie is overdoing it; wear a collared shirt and slacks.

The same goes for women. If most women at the cocktail party will be wearing a long dress, wear a long dress. (Note: You may have to get creative when performing effects that require you to have pockets.) But if it's a barbecue, wear comfortable attire and footwear.

Your costume should always be practical. Choose clothing with as many pockets as possible, and always dress for comfort.

The Game

ON DVD

MATERIALS:
A matchbook, a pen and paper, and a small group of borrowed objects.

SETUP: You can perform this effect without any preparation, but there is room for cleverness here, too. If you're sure a woman has lipstick in her purse, you can prepare a matchbook in advance by asking someone to kiss it, leaving an unmistakable prediction.

DIFFICULTY ⚔️⚔️⚔️⚔️⚔️

THE EFFECT You write a secret prediction on a matchbook and ask someone to hold it without peeking. Then you assemble a small grouping of borrowed objects: keys, an olive, a cell phone, a tube of lipstick, a shoe—any collection of objects. **You and the participant play a game of elimination until only one object remains: the lipstick. Your prediction? You will be left with a lipstick imprint . . . of a kiss.**

THE SECRET The PATEO force. PATEO, an acronym for Pick Any Two, Eliminate One, is a classic counterintuitive swindle in which you and your participant take turns eliminating objects. Despite your participant's total freedom of choices, you can "force" him to select any desired object.

THE PERFORMANCE

"**I**'ve got a prediction written on the flap of this matchbook," you say. Entrust a participant to hold the matchbook, and insist that she not peek at it until the end.

"*Now we need some borrowed objects. Everyone help me by putting something in the middle of the table.*" Invite each participant to lend you a possession. Bizarre objects are a great opportunity for humor and interaction: shoes, heart medication—it's all good. "*Wow, John's lending us a five-dollar bill. But where was John when the bar tab came last night?*"

If nobody volunteers a tube of lipstick, volunteer it yourself. "Janie," you might say, "*let's get a few more objects. Do you have, say, lipstick, in your purse?*" Then camouflage your request with a few more: "*John, why don't you put your cell phone on the table. At least that way I know you won't talk on it for the rest of the performance! And Mary, would you mind lending me your bracelet?*"

Line up the objects in one or two rows. Your objective is to have an odd number of objects. If the number is even, simply add an object from your own pockets.

Select a participant, like Mary. "*Mary, this is how the game is played. I will point to any two objects, and you will eliminate one of them. Then you will point to any two objects, and I'll eliminate one.*" This is the PATEO force.

continued

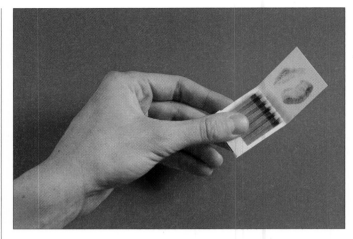

1 *"I'll go first,"* you say. You must always go first. And as long as you obey one simple rule, you can force any object: never point to the force object. Since you go first, you can point to any two objects—just don't point to the lipstick. Ask your participant to eliminate one of the two objects. Encourage her to remove it from the table.

Now it's her turn. Your participant can point to any two objects and you choose one to eliminate. If one of her chosen "two" happens to be the lipstick, simply eliminate the other object. Remember: You *never* point to the lipstick.

Continue in this manner, alternating between choosing two and eliminating one. During the last round, the participant will be left with only two objects to point to: the lipstick and an inconsequential object. Not coincidentally, it's your turn to decide which one is finally eliminated. I think you know what to do. . . .

2 *"You made a series of choices I couldn't control . . . or could I?"* Invite the participant to unfold the matchbook and reveal the prediction. *"Now that,"* you say, *"definitely deserves a kiss."*

MASTER CLASS

The PATEO force is a powerful tool to have in your arsenal. Its flexibility is matched only by its impact. You can do this anytime, anywhere, and for any number of people—no preparation necessary. And people have been obsessed with predicting the future since before Nostradamus.

Obviously, you shouldn't use more than one presentation in the same show, or else the "game" becomes laborious and transparent, but here are some other applications for the PATEO force that you may try:

Card Force: Spread a batch of playing cards on the table and predict which one a participant will select.

Last Man Standing: Line up your colleagues at the office, and predict who will be the "Last Man Standing."

The Chosen One: Predict the birthday girl by lining up a classroom full of students.

The Gift: Display five envelopes to your audience and explain that you'll keep only one. Four contain only a penny and one has fifty bucks inside. Mix the envelopes around (keeping track of where the money is), and line them up. Now do the PATEO force so all the others are eliminated. You're left with fifty bucks.

CREDIT: Roy Baker's PATEO force first appeared in *Baker's Bonanza* in 1968. "The Gift" is a version of Tom Sellers' plot, known as "Just Chance" or "Bank Night," devised in 1935.

Four Elements

MATERIALS:
A saucer, an empty glass, a lemon peel, and a book of matches.

DIFFICULTY

THE EFFECT **Never pay for drinks again; this bar bet looks like magic!** You pour water onto a saucer and invert a glass on top. You bet a friend that you can cause all the water on the plate to go inside the glass without touching the saucer or the water. And you do it.

THE SECRET Science! This is magic without the element (sorry) of deception. To make this stunt work, just follow the steps outlined below.

THE PERFORMANCE

Bar bets require suckers, and while there is one born every minute, they are not always easy to find. In those cases, you can use this as a display of out-of-the-box thinking—not exactly magic, but a fascinating stunt.

1 *"The Ancient Greeks believed that all problems could be solved by using the four elements: earth, wind, and fire."* Pause here. Then continue, *"Oh, and water.*

"Anyway, I think there's something to that philosophy. The other day, a guy walked into this bar and poured water on a saucer, like this." Suiting actions to words, you pour some water from your glass onto a saucer so that it almost overflows. Put the clear glass upside down in the middle of the saucer. *"He bet me a drink that I couldn't get all the water into the glass without touching the plate or the water. Would you bet a drink on that?"*

continued 👉

2 Some won't. Then again, some will. Continue, *"I was about to give up on the bet when I remembered the Greek philosophy—the one about the four elements."* Now you go on a scavenger hunt around the bar. Retrieve a lemon peel (an olive or cherry will also work). Find a book of matches, too.

"We already have water," you say, pointing to the saucer. *"And this lemon came from a tree that was grown in the earth."* Remove the inverted glass for a moment and drop the lemon in the middle of the plate. *"And this will represent fire."* Stick an unlit match into the lemon wedge.

3 *"It looks like a drunk's birthday cake,"* you might observe wryly. *"The last element is wind, and that's what makes this work. Together, like this."* Light another match and use it to ignite the one protruding from the lemon wedge.

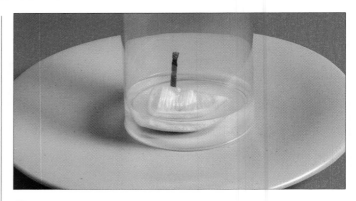

4 Replace the inverted glass over the flame.

Now enjoy the show. The moment you put the glass down, a small cloud of smoke will form at the top of the glass. Meanwhile, the water at the opening of the glass will begin to bubble and hum as it is sucked into the glass!

5 *"What you're seeing is a vacuum,"* you say with authority. *"The fire inside the glass burns away the oxygen, which creates a vacuum at the glass's edge."* This pulls the water inside the glass and eventually extinguishes the match. *"Now, about that drink. . . ."*

MASTER CLASS

Even though this isn't a magic effect, it works like magic. Using items found in any bar or kitchen, you can create a truly bizarre and memorable experience.

We do magic to give people that inexplicable feeling of wonder, particularly when we perform impromptu magic. And while "Four Elements" has no real secret, it certainly invokes wonder.

CREDIT: This stunt has been paying for drinks for a long time, and its origins are unknown.

DINNER
DECEPTIONS

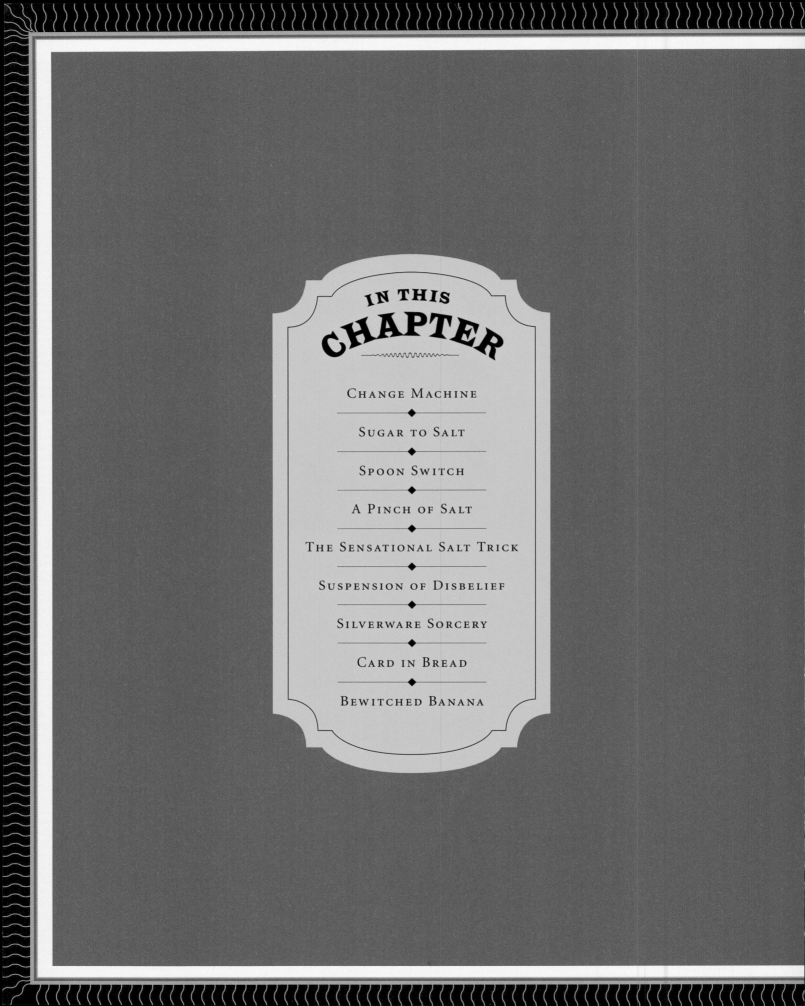

IN THIS CHAPTER

MAKING MEALTIME MAGIC

Finally, an excuse to play with your food! The dinner table is the perfect spot for a magic show. Your participants are close—so close they can touch the magic. Everyone is seated, captive. You're seated, too, which opens up a host of secret possibilities (you're about to learn how to vanish and produce items from your lap). And at this close range, your audience is very important. The people in your audience aren't strangers. They're your friends, your family . . . and they are in for an unforgettable magic show.

Bend Dad's spoon or change it into a knife. Push a saltshaker through the table. Make your sister's chosen card appear in her own dinner roll! Each one of these mealtime mysteries features all the components of memorable magic: audience interaction, an engaging presentation, and an amazing experience.

THE WARM-UP

Lapping

CONCEALING: *Lapping is a magician's jargon for concealing an object in your lap. Before you learn the sleight, you must become comfortable sitting in front of people with spoons or saltshakers hidden in your lap, beneath the table. Remember, you're the only one who knows the object is there . . . so don't worry about it.*

1 Seat yourself at a table and place an object—say, a banana—in your lap. Now turn your torso left and right, as you might move to talk to people on either end of the table. All the while keep your hands in sight and, above all, don't look at or touch the banana.

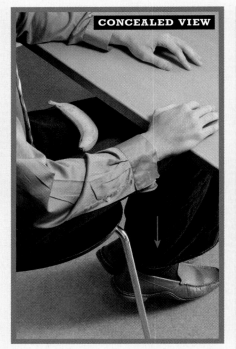

2 The exact position is important. Make sure your thighs aren't sloped. This may involve pressing your toes against the floor and raising your heels to give your legs a few extra inches.

3 Keep your knees pressed firmly together so your concealed item doesn't inadvertently fall to the floor.

continued ☞

THE TECHNIQUE: *Throughout this chapter, you will be using this, the lapping principle, to effect vanishes, productions, and changes. Here's how to secretly move an object into your lap.*

CONCEALED VIEW

4 Now let's try a simple lapping technique. Place the banana on the table's edge so both ends curve toward you.

5 Cup both hands around the fruit so that it is entirely concealed from audience view. Slide the banana toward yourself until it falls from the table's edge into your lap. The key here is not to blink (or wince) when it lands.

6 Eye contact is critical at this point. Keep focused on your hands, *not* the banana. In a continuing action, pretend to raise the banana to chest height. Since you've already dropped the banana, you actually move your cupped hands upward with nothing in them.

7 In a continuing action, move both hands upward as a unit, as if you still hold the banana between your fingers. Once both hands, as a single unit, are at chest height, blow on your fingers and reveal that the banana is gone.

Change Machine

MATERIALS:
You will need a cloth napkin. The other materials vary depending on how you use the effect. The explanation below uses a bottle of water and glass of juice or wine.

SETUP: Let's assume you're feeling Biblical and you want to change water into wine. Conspire to have a glass of wine in your lap, filled less than halfway. (If you fill the glass with too much liquid, you run the risk of spilling it.) Grape juice works fine, and real wine works even better.

Situate a bottle of water on the table, in front of you. Make sure the cap is screwed on tightly. If you're at a restaurant the waiter may remove the cap from the bottle, so you may need to change this a bit. You must be seated to perform the effect, and you must have a cloth napkin nearby.

DIFFICULTY: ✝✝✝✝✝

THE EFFECT **This devious sleight allows you to secretly exchange two small objects**. This will work with any object you wish as long as it fits in your lap such as:

- change water into wine
- make a glass of soda appear, replacing an empty duplicate glass
- change sugar into salt (see "Sugar to Salt," page 48)
- bend an ordinary spoon (See "Spoon Switch," page 50)

Practice the effect to mastery and then introduce new objects.

THE SECRET The objects are secretly exchanged in your lap.

THE PERFORMANCE

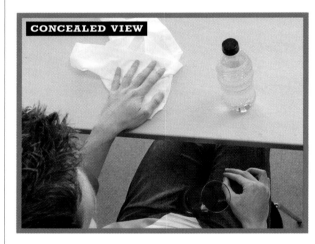

CONCEALED VIEW

❶ With the glass of wine in your lap and water bottle on the table in front of you, move your left hand toward the napkin on the table. Drop your right hand into the lap one second after you move your left.

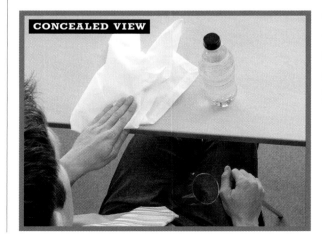

CONCEALED VIEW

❷ With the fingers of your left hand, casually slide the napkin to the edge of the table, toward your left side.

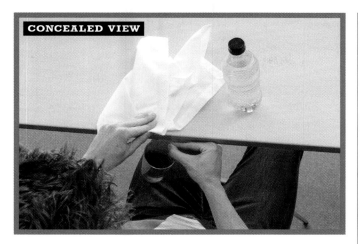

CONCEALED VIEW

3 Situate your left hand at the table's edge and keep hold of the napkin under your left first and second fingers.

Simultaneously, pinch the lip of the glass between your right thumb and first and second fingers.

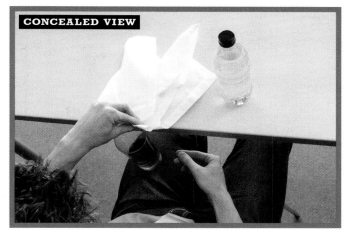

CONCEALED VIEW

4 Move the glass to your left. Secretly transfer the glass of wine to your left fingers. Pinch the lip of the glass between your left first finger and thumb, just beneath the table's edge. Hold the glass in position while still grasping the napkin between the other fingers.

5 From the front, it should look as though you're simply holding a napkin on the table.

CONCEALED VIEW

6 Move your empty right hand back onto the surface of the table and pick up the water bottle. You will apparently cover the water bottle with the napkin. Actually, you'll drop the bottle into your lap under cover of the napkin, and take hold of the concealed glass of wine. To do this, hold the water bottle near the edge of the table. Lift your left hand up and to the right. The napkin conceals the glass of wine.

continued ☞

CONCEALED VIEW

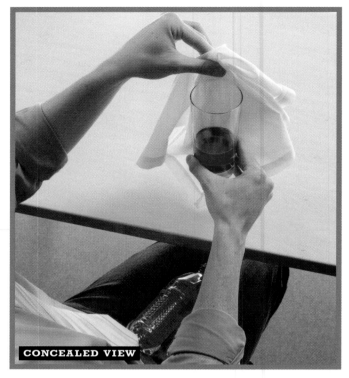

CONCEALED VIEW

7 Cover the water bottle with the napkin. As soon as the bottle is out of view, drop it onto your lap. Look out at the people around the table as you do.

Don't worry about the sound the falling water bottle makes on your lap. The bottle only falls a few inches, and this noise is muffled by the sound of the napkin rubbing against the hidden glass.

8 Continuing the action, grip the base of the wine glass with your right fingers. Maintain eye contact with your participants.

9 Move both hands upward and apart as you whisk away the napkin, revealing the change.

For best results, move your hands forward as you reveal the change. This way, the magic happens several inches away from your body, and far enough from the table's edge.

MASTER CLASS

John Ramsay, one of magic's greatest thinkers, sums up misdirection, or, more aptly termed "direction," in two principles: *"If you want someone to look at your hands, look at your hands yourself. If you want someone to look at you, look at them."*

Both principles are used in the sequence described in "Change Machine." You look at your audience while you are making the switch. In turn, the participants are directed toward you, and misdirected from what's happening under the napkin. After you've made the switch (but before you have revealed it), you look at your hands. This directs the participants to look at your hands, where they will be amazed by the wine's appearance.

CREDIT: Lapping is an ancient technique. My guess is that it has been around as long as people have been sitting at tables. Ross Bertram used to perform a similar type of effect, as did the world-reknown Slydini (the undisputed master of lapping).

SPOTLIGHT ON MALINI

"So, how long do I wait?" you're asking, anxious to get rid of the water bottle resting in your lap.

"You vait a veek," Max Malini, who spoke with a thick Polish accent, would have said. Born Max Katz in 1873, Malini remains one of magic's cleverest performers, and one who understood that a magician must be *guiltless*. Sure, you've got a water bottle in your lap. But only you know that! In the audience's mind, the water bottle is still on the table—because the water has *become* a glass of wine.

"You vait a veek," he used to say—his message encouraged other magicians, inspired by Malini, *not* to fuss with concealed objects. Malini was one of the first close-up experts, and he specialized in baffling illusions. For example, he would borrow a gentleman's hat and from it produce a real block of ice! This required Malini to wait, hiding a block of melting ice. But you can't rush miracles, and Malini knew this. He would "vait a veek," until his audience begged for a particular performance. Only then would he ask for a hat, and produce the block of ice.

Malini's theory on "waiting" paid off. Rumors spread of a short, stocky Polish magician who could do *anything* upon request. Partly due to his mastery of timing, Malini played engagements for audiences as diverse as presidents, royalty, and Al Capone.

Sugar to Salt

MATERIALS:
A packet of sugar, a shaker of salt, and a cloth napkin.

SETUP: Begin with a saltshaker in your lap. It's best to sneak the shaker from the table into your lap, hiding it between your legs. Wait for someone to ask for the salt, and begin your performance in response.

You must be seated to perform this effect.

DIFFICULTY: ††† ††

THE EFFECT Change a packet of sugar into a shaker of salt.

THE SECRET The same principle as "Change Machine"—the objects are concealed and secretly exchanged in the lap.

THE PERFORMANCE

CONCEALED VIEW

1 *"Could someone pass the salt?"* a friend might ask.

Drop your right hand into your lap and retrieve the saltshaker. As you do so, slide the napkin with the fingers of your left hand to the table's edge, toward your left side.

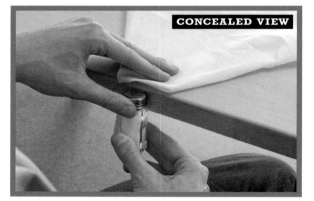

CONCEALED VIEW

2 Situate your left hand at the table's edge and keep hold of the napkin under your left first and second fingers. Move the shaker with your right hand so you can grasp it between your left fingers.

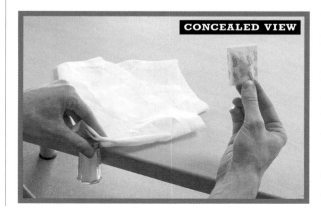

CONCEALED VIEW

3 Openly retrieve a packet of sugar and display it in your right hand. (Keep holding the saltshaker hidden behind the napkin and below the table.) *"Do you want sugar for your fries?"* you ask. In most cases, the answer is no.

CONCEALED VIEW

❹ Now perform "Change Machine" step 6 (page 45), with the saltshaker playing the part of the wine and the sugar packet playing the water bottle. Lift the napkin (with the saltshaker concealed behind it) to cover the sugar packet in your right hand.

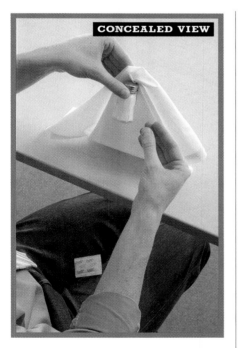

CONCEALED VIEW

❺ Once the sugar is out of view behind the napkin, allow it to fall into your lap. At the same time, take hold of the saltshaker between your right thumb and fingers and release the saltshaker from your left fingers. Look out at the people around the table as you perform these actions.

❻ Move both hands upward and apart as you whisk away the napkin with your left hand to reveal the change. For best results, move your hands foward as you reveal the change. This way, the magic happens several inches away from the table's edge. Oh, and don't forget to pass the salt.

MASTER CLASS

In the introduction, we explored the Ham Sandwich Theory, and this is a prime example. Changing sugar into salt only demonstrates an ability, which doesn't necessarily make for a powerful trick.

When someone asks for the salt and you produce it for them, however, you have fulfilled a participant's desire (albeit a small desire). More importantly, you have made your magic meaningful.

Spoon Switch

MATERIALS:

Two spoons and a napkin.

SETUP: Bend one of the spoons in advance of the performance. Get into the standard "Change Machine" (page 44) position, with the pre-bent spoon hidden in your lap and the napkin and straight spoon on the table. You must be seated to perform this effect.

DIFFICULTY: ††††

THE EFFECT This third application of "Change Machine" (page 44) works perfectly in a restaurant setting: **You bend a spoon with the power of your mind.**

THE SECRET You begin with one spoon on the table and an identical, but pre-bent, spoon in your lap. It appears that you transform the spoon in your right hand, but you actually "lap it" as you place the bent spoon between your right thumb and fingers.

THE PERFORMANCE

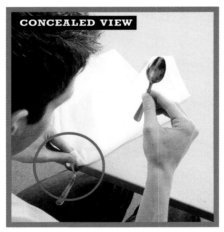

CONCEALED VIEW

1 With the fingers of your left hand, slide the napkin to the edge of the table toward your left side. Simultaneously grasp the bent spoon in your right fingers and move it toward the napkin, keeping it hidden beneath the table's edge. Pinch the bent spoon behind the napkin, between your left thumb and first and second fingers. Move your empty right hand back to the surface of the table and pick up the regular spoon.

2 From the front, it should look as though you're simply holding a napkin on the table while you present the straight spoon. Make sure you maintain eye contact with your participants throughout the following actions.

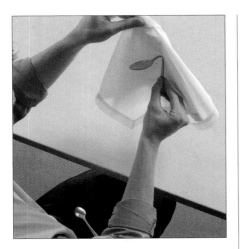

3 Move the napkin and concealed bent spoon in your left hand toward the spoon in your right hand. As soon as the straight spoon is out of view, drop it into your lap and take hold of the concealed bent spoon, gripping it by the end of the handle.

4 Without revealing anything, rearrange the napkin so it covers the spoon and your right hand; withdraw your left hand (photos 4 through 6 show a transparent napkin for clarity). Pause for a moment while the spoon is still covered.

5 Move your left hand away from the napkin and toward your head. Concentrate, touching your left fingers to your temple.

6 As you concentrate, allow the bent spoon to rotate counterclockwise by easing the grip of your right fingers and thumb.

7 Now use your left hand to whisk away the napkin, pivoting the bent spoon upright as you pull the napkin clear of the fingers of your right hand.

CREDIT: **Uri Geller popularized the "magical bending" of solid (metal and other) objects in the 1970s. This is a simple but effective way to re-create that illusion. "The Filling Glass" is attributed to Lennert Green.**

MASTER CLASS

Each application for "Change Machine" shows how different EFFECT and SECRET can be. For us, changing water into wine requires the *exact same actions* as sugar to salt. But how different the effects are to your audience! Of course, you wouldn't perform these three effects in the same show, but with the mechanics of "Change Machine," there are even more possibilities:

The Filling Glass: Cover an empty glass with a napkin. Whisk the napkin away and show that the glass is now full.

Appearing Flower: Cause a flower to appear in an empty vase.

Bill to Cash: What better way to pay a bar bill than to change it into cash?

Choose an effect to suit the occasion or try to come up with your own.

Old Dog, New Trick: Using a False Thumbtip

A Pinch of Salt

MATERIALS:
A magician's false thumbtip (available in all magic novelty shops), saltshaker, and a dollar bill.

SETUP: Begin with the thumbtip on your right thumb.

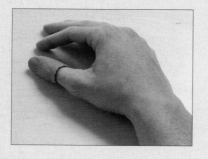

DIFFICULTY: ✝✝✝✝✝

THE EFFECT **Make a fistful of salt disappear.** You borrow a dollar bill, form it into a cone, and fill it with salt. When you unroll the bill and display it, the salt is miraculously gone!

THE SECRET The salt goes into a hollow, traditionally plastic, thumb that fits over your own thumb. The thumbtip is a sneaky device; the members of your audience see it without realizing what they're looking at.

THE PERFORMANCE

1 Borrow a dollar bill from a participant, saying, *"I'd like to show you a trick that requires three things. Your bill, you, and a pinch of salt."* Form the bill into a cone around your right thumb.

2 Pinch the thumbtip through the cone and then move your right hand away, leaving the thumbtip concealed inside the bill-cone.

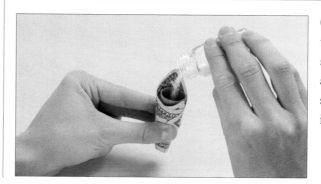

3 Ask your participant to unscrew the lid of a saltshaker. Take the shaker and begin pouring the salt into the cone (and into the thumbtip).

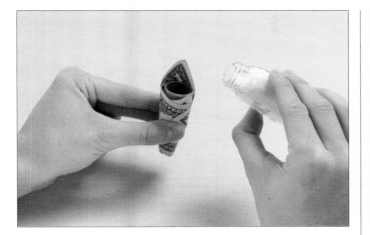

❹ Fill the thumbtip about half an inch. This doesn't sound like much salt, but if you pour slowly, you can give your participant the illusion that the cone is almost full.

❺ Move your hands together and openly slip your thumb back into the tip inside the bill-cone to make the salt vanish. Slide your thumb into the tip until it's securely wedged, and then unroll the bill with both hands. Show both sides of the bill.

❻ You can flash your hands to the audience as long as you aim your thumb at the participants. From the front, everything appears normal.

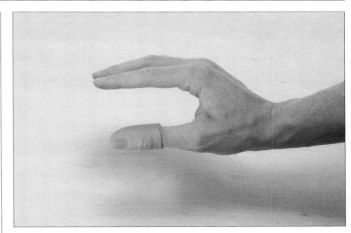

❼ From the side, the thumbtip is quite obvious. So, don't hold the position too long, and watch your angles!

Ditching the thumbtip is as simple as placing your hands in your pocket. Don't rush this part; nobody suspects a thumbtip. The best time to ditch this gimmick is long after the effect has ended, when participants aren't watching you closely.

MASTER CLASS

Despite the ubiquity of false thumbtips in traditional magic kits, beginners are often self-conscious about using them, afraid everyone will notice. But I've seen magicians use red thumbtips just to illustrate how little our thumbs show when we're handling objects like salt or pepper shakers or currency.

CREDIT: The original false thumbtip was built using a modeling material akin to papier-mâché by Professor Herwin circa 1885. By the 20th century, most commercially manufactured thumbtips were made out of metal, and plastic and rubber dominate the field today.

The Sensational Salt Trick

MATERIALS:
A saltshaker, a pepper shaker, and a cloth or paper napkin.

SETUP: None, except that you must be seated, with the napkin in your lap.

DIFFICULTY:

THE EFFECT   "Which do you like better, salt or pepper?" you ask the person sitting across from you. "Salt," he says. Without a moment's hesitation, **you push the saltshaker through the tabletop!**

THE SECRET   You secretly drop the saltshaker in your lap. A napkin formed into the shape of a saltshaker is used as a decoy.

THE PERFORMANCE

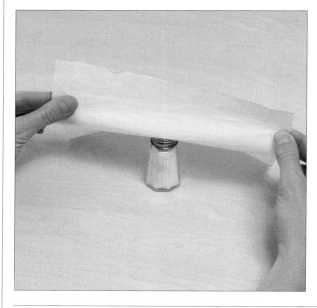

1 Hold a napkin between your hands and openly cover the saltshaker with a flourish as you ask your participant if he prefers salt or pepper.

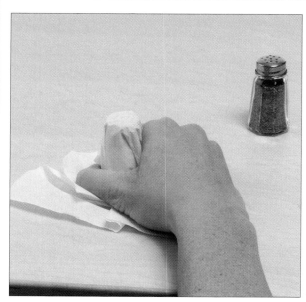

2 Grip the covered shaker from the sides with your right hand. Give it a good squeeze so the napkin forms around the saltshaker.

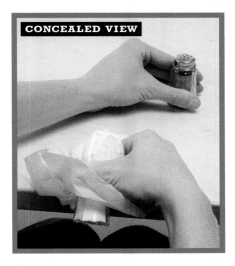

CONCEALED VIEW

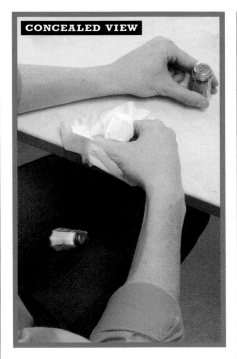

CONCEALED VIEW

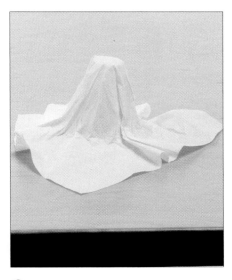

3 As you reach for the pepper shaker with your left hand, retract your right hand to the table's edge. Follow your left hand's actions with your eyes, as you retrieve the pepper shaker.

As you do, secretly drop the saltshaker into your lap by loosening your right hand's grip so the saltshaker "squirts" from the napkin into your lap.

4 Pinch your knees together so the saltshaker lands quietly in your lap. Your right fingers remain motionless, gripping the napkin as if the saltshaker was still inside it.

5 The napkin retains the mold of the saltshaker.

When your dinner guest answers your question (from Step 1), the response doesn't really matter; the saltshaker always goes through the table. If he requests salt, say, *"Then I'll push the salt through the table."*

6 If he requests pepper, say, *"Me, too. I hate salt!"* Either way, the salt goes through. Here's how. You raise both hands off the table to display both "choices."

continued ☞

7 With your left hand, place the pepper shaker on the table, off to the side. At the same time, lower your right hand so that the napkin rests on the tabletop, close to the table's center. The sound of the pepper shaker against the table masks the silence of the supposed saltshaker. Move your left hand above the "saltshaker" (the napkin).

8 Pretend to push the shaker through the table as you crush the napkin.

If you're dining at a restaurant with hard-surface floors, here's a nice touch: spread your knees as you pretend to push the shaker through. The saltshaker on your lap will fall to the floor audibly, allowing your participants to not only see but also *hear* the magic as it happens.

MASTER CLASS

The restaurant you're in dictates the quality of your napkin. Both paper and cloth napkins have advantages. The advantage of a paper napkin is that it holds its shape well—so well that you can even rest the napkin on the table without holding it.

The advantage of a cloth napkin is that it's thicker and thus less apparent when you ditch the saltshaker.

CREDIT: "Saltshaker through Table" is a staple of the beginner's repertoire, but it's always taught in the context of an illogical presentation. Historically, the magician offers to push a coin through the table. She covers the coin with the saltshaker and the saltshaker with a napkin. A moment later, the saltshaker—not the coin—goes through the table.

But what about the coin? The magician promised to push a coin through the table . . . and didn't fulfill that promise. The explanation above details a more logical, impressive way to perform this tattered classic.

Suspension of Disbelief

MATERIALS:
A spoon, a table knife, and a cloth napkin.

SETUP: Begin with a table knife strapped against the inside of your wrist using your watchband. The blade should extend just short of where your fingers begin. Obviously, don't use a sharp knife (otherwise you run the risk of accidentally performing a different feat, called "Stigmata").

You must be seated for this routine.

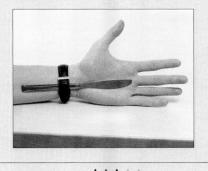

DIFFICULTY: ✝✝✝✝✝

THE EFFECT While seated, you demonstrate an obvious way to suspend a spoon against your palm (some participants might even know this one); then, **you really suspend the spoon in midair and change it into a knife!**

THE SECRET To suspend a spoon on your hand, you'll employ the aid of a "third hand," namely, a table knife stowed under your watch. To change the spoon into a knife, you will secretly ditch the spoon into your lap as you reveal the knife under your watch.

THE PERFORMANCE

Throughout this sequence, be mindful of your angles. Make sure your right-most participants can't see the knife on the underside of your left wrist. If you're concerned, sit with your knees and shoulders squared to the right-most participant. This way, you ensure your angles are perfect from every perspective.

❶ Pick up a spoon from the table and perform the classic "Spoon Suspension" we all did for each other in the school cafeteria back in the day. Hold the spoon in your left fist, taking care to keep the back of your hand toward your audience. Be careful that the knife and spoon don't clink against each other.

CONCEALED VIEW

❷ Grip your left wrist with your right hand and secretly extend your first finger forward so that it contacts the spoon.

3 Slowly open your hand and show that the spoon is suspended. Needless to say, this is underwhelming from your particpants' perspective.

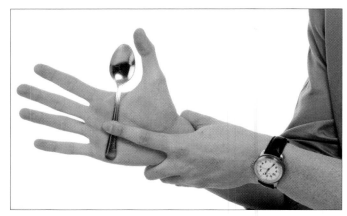

4 Offer to teach the stunt to anyone not already familiar with it. Transfer the spoon to your right hand and repeat the effect, this time with your right palm facing the audience and your left first finger extended to hold the spoon. The secret is immediately clear, and you can invite your participants to try it.

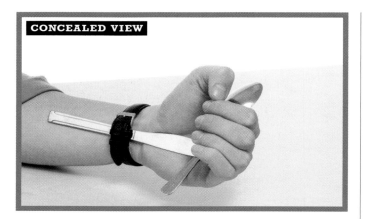

CONCEALED VIEW

5 With the audience's attention slightly diverted, transfer the spoon back to your left hand and quietly maneuver it between your hand and the knife. In a continuing action, maneuver your right hand around your left wrist, as before. You want the audience to think you're repeating the stunt. But wait until they see what comes next. . . .

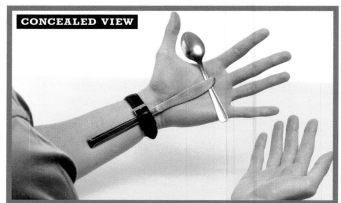

CONCEALED VIEW

6 Slowly remove your right hand as you uncurl your left fingers and push your left palm gently toward your body. This pins the spoon in position, lodged between your palm and the secreted knife.

7 It's obvious from your angle, but from the audience's viewpoint, this looks way cool.

Now for the transformation. Offer the following riddle as you retrieve a cloth napkin from the table: *"How do you cut a steak with a spoon?"*

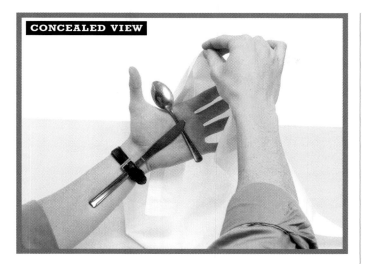

8 Cover your hand and the suspended spoon with the napkin as you slowly move them toward your body. Allow the ends of the napkin to extend just beneath the table's edge, and only for a moment.

9 During that moment, bend your left wrist back slightly, allowing the spoon to fall silently from your hand to your lap. Don't watch as the spoon falls. Instead, when you feel it hit your lap, raise your hands a bit and move forward, focused intently on the utensil under the napkin. By moving forward, you disguise any extraneous movement from the covert switch that takes place at the table's edge.

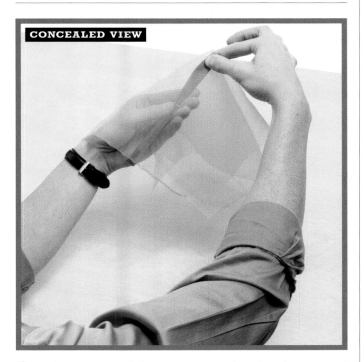

10 Dislodge the knife from your watchband under cover of the napkin (photo shows a transparent cloth for clarity).

11 Reach around to the outside of the napkin and pinch the tip of the knife.

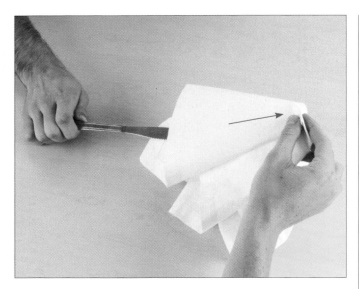

⑫ While you pinch the tip of the knife through the napkin, ask your participant to pinch the end of the "spoon" (actually the knife).

Explain the solution to the riddle: *"You change the spoon into a knife, and then you cut your steak!"* You (or you can invite your participant to) uncover the spoon. He will discover only a knife; the spoon has changed in his hand!

MASTER CLASS

This classic effect has been taught in several books on magic but here it's completely overhauled. The effect has historically been performed as a stunt or a "gotcha" moment. I've turned up the audience interaction and added a fresh, impossible ending.

In doing so, I have *routined* the effect into three phases. The first one is an exposé: You *teach* someone a cute stunt. Once you have taught her the perceived secret, you *shatter her perceptions* by using a different method (you suspend the spoon with one hand). For the third phase, you *perform an even better effect*—and the magic happens in your participant's hands.

The technical problem with the original effect has always been what to do after the spoon is suspended in your hand. You've got a knife under your watch and—let's face it—that's not cool. With the third phase, the problem becomes a solution. Rather than eat your entire meal with one hand, you produce the secret knife!

Silverware Sorcery

MATERIALS:
A fork.

SETUP: Just before performing, bend one fork tine backward (away from the utensil's curve). With most forks, this requires only a modicum of pressure. (Your best bet is to perform this at inexpensive restaurants. The ritzier places use sturdier flatware.)

Place the pre-bent fork back on the table next to your other flatware, and steer the conversation toward metal bending.

DIFFICULTY: ⚔⚔⚔⚔⚔

THE EFFECT Wriggling a fork by the bottom of its handle, **you cause a tine of the fork to visibly bend forward.**

THE SECRET The tine is bent before you begin the effect, but the wriggling action conceals this fact until just the right moment. Your words and an optical illusion paint the picture of the fork bending while you shake it.

THE PERFORMANCE

❶ Pick up your fork from the table, as if you're inventing this experiment on the spot. Once you touch the fork, keep it in motion; you don't want dinner companions to notice the bent tine. That said, nobody is expressly looking for a bent tine in your fork, so act natural.

❷ Transfer the fork to your left fingers, gripping it near the bottom. (Keep your fingers well away from the tines of the fork throughout the trick.) Aim the fork at one of your participants (choose wisely— this person gets the best view). Notice that, from the front, a person with ordinary depth perception can't distinguish that the tine is bent. *"I wonder . . . "* you start. *"Sometimes I can force a reaction to occur at the ends of the tines . . . don't take your eyes off the ends as I shake a bend into them."*

❸ Immediately shake the fork gently, forward and backward. Don't shake violently. Rather, use a gentle rocking action—just enough to blur the end of the fork. As you shake, turn your hand to the side very slowly so the fork's profile comes into view. The more you turn, the more you accentuate the bend. This turning action gives the perfect illusion of a bending tine; your participants actually *see* the metal bend.

❹ Stop shaking and allow the participants to see the permanent bend in the tine.

Emphasize that you only touched the handle while you pass around the fork for verification.

MASTER CLASS

As I noted under "The Secret," your words paint the picture of the fork bending while you shake it.

This simply means that what you say will influence how your participants interpret what they see.

As you bend the fork in step 2 or 3, you might also say, *"I'll heat the metal with my mind so that it becomes softer, softer . . . now it's soft like cookie dough."* This paints a vivid picture of liquid-soft metal bending.

If you use the script as written in step 2, you paint a different picture. In this case, the action of your left wrist causes the bend (as opposed to your mind).

This concept is easier to think about if we change our view of magic. Don't think about magic in terms of what happens in your hands; think about what's happening in the audience's mind.

CREDIT: **Uri Geller popularized the bending spoon. This method of bending a fork tine was invented by Banachek, one of the world's greatest mentalists.**

THAT'S TIGHT

If an experienced magician approaches you after a show and says your performance is "tight," say thank you! Don't worry, he's not calling your props cheap. Quite simply, this magician has noticed that you figured out what parts of an effect are important . . . and that you edited out everything else. A mark of an accomplished magician and a very high compliment, indeed.

Card in Bread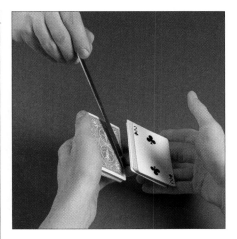
ON DVD

ON DVD

MATERIALS:

A pack of cards, a duplicate Three of Clubs, and a dinner roll.

SETUP: Position the Three of Clubs on top of your deck. Take a duplicate Three of Clubs and fold it into fourths. Make a narrow slit in a dinner roll and load the folded card inside without anyone noticing. Here are a few ways:

• Excuse yourself to go the restroom; as soon as you are out of sight of your table, ask a busboy for an extra roll. Load the card before you retake your seat, and then place the prepared roll in the basket when the participant isn't looking.

• Arrive early, prepare a roll, and explain what's happening to your server. Ask him to include the "loaded" roll in the basket when he brings out the bread.

• Prepare the roll beneath the tabletop, provided you practice loading the card without looking. Sneak the roll back into the basket.

DIFFICULTY: ♱♱♱♱♱

THE EFFECT You ask the participant to insert a butter knife anywhere into your deck of cards and to remember the card next to the knife: the Three of Clubs. You throw the cards toward the center of the table and they fall onto and around a basket of bread. **The participant tears open a dinner roll. Folded inside is the chosen card—the Three of Clubs.**

THE SECRET You force the participant to select the Three of Clubs. The card discovered inside the roll is a duplicate Three of Clubs, which you preloaded before your dinner companion arrived.

THE PERFORMANCE

"*T his,*" you say, holding up the table knife from your place setting, "*is usually used to butter bread. But it's also an excellent way to stab someone.*" Pause. "*Or something.*" Present your deck of cards.

❶ Hand the knife to the participant and ask him to gently push the blade into the deck anywhere he likes. Riffle the top ends of the cards to make this action easier for him.

Ask the participant to keep his hand on the knife and remember the card next to it. But as you apparently show him this card, you will "force" the top card of the deck. To do this, riffle your left thumb along the top left corner of the pack. Your thumb will stop at the knife.

❷ Roll the cards above the knife into your right hand. To do this, tip your left hand down and to the right slightly, allowing the packet to lever into the fingers of your right hand. The packet falls faceup, so roll it once more so that it is oriented facedown.

continued ☞

3 Once the packet in your right hand is facedown, two things must happen. First, the knife must remain partly held by the participant and partly on top of the packet of cards in your left hand. Your right hand holds the real top of the deck, but you hold this packet slightly lower and to the right of your left hand. When this maneuver is done smoothly, it appears that the top card of the right hand's packet actually came from the center of the deck. This is called the *roll force*.

4 Hold the knife against the deck with your left thumb while you slide the face card (the Three of Clubs) toward your participant with your right thumb. Ask him to look at it and remember it. Ask him then to put the card back into the pack and take the knife again. Shuffle and ask the spectator to tap the knife on the deck.

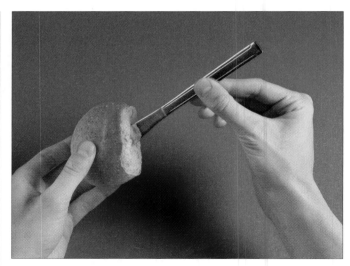

5 Now toss the deck, facedown, onto the basket of rolls. (Watch out for lit candles!) This makes a mess of faceup and facedown cards—and that's good.

6 Stare intently at the rolls. Show that your hands are empty and slowly retrieve the loaded dinner roll (be sure to grab the right one). Ask for the table knife and pretend to cut the roll. Actually, stick the knife into the secret incision to destroy any evidence of the secret.

7 Table the knife and start to pry the bread apart to reveal the card.

Stop for a moment and offer the roll to your participant asking, *"Here, why don't you do it?"* This creates the impression that he opened the bread without your help. Say, *"Perhaps the table knife is better used for bread. But it makes a pretty good magic wand."*

Your participant will discover a folded card inside. Ask him which one he chose before allowing him to unfold the card. He'll be amazed. And he'll be halfway done buttering his bread.

MASTER CLASS

A piano teacher once told me something that has significantly informed the way I present magic, even now. She said that individual notes are just noise—but the pauses between the notes make it all music.

The same is true in magic. Presentations are a combination of what you say and what you *don't* say when you're performing. Magician David Blaine uses silence very well. He performs effects with very little dialogue and sometimes none at all, saying only what's absolutely necessary to accomplish an effect. The silence offers a sense of mystery and focus. When you perform in silence, it's like hitting the "mute" button while someone is watching television—everyone reacts only to what they see.

I'm certainly not condoning constant silence. What magicians say during an effect is what makes it theirs.

CREDIT: A version of this trick, omitting the use of a knife, was invented by Tony Kardyro.

MODERN MASTERS

COPPERFIELD, BLAINE, AND ANGEL

David Copperfield, David Blaine, and Criss Angel permeate modern culture—their magic is visible everywhere, from network television specials to tabloids to rap lyrics. They are superstar magicians with larger-than-life effects and personas.

Copperfield's magic is informed by his love for theater, and this is evident in the theatrics and choreography of his work. He pioneered mega-illusions, and is best remembered for his feats involving major landmarks: he vanished the Statue of Liberty (and, I'll add, he returned it in pristine condition), walked through the Great Wall of China, and escaped from a raft over Niagara Falls. Copperfield still performs more than 500 shows a year.

David Blaine burst onto the magic scene in 1997 with the airing of his first television special. Blaine performed powerful, stripped down effects on the street. His major innovation was to emphasize the audience's reaction to the magic over the effect itself. His specials focus on his participants and how they are affected by his magic—so that viewers at home become part of David's show. Blaine also performs feats of superhuman endurance, including being buried alive and withstanding three days in a block of ice.

Criss Angel is a cross between Houdini and Slash, performing impossible escapes and magic effects with a heavy metal edge. Angel has an ongoing television series in which he walks up building walls, disappears a Lamborghini, and levitates passersby on the Las Vegas strip. He also performs in Believe, his own Cirque du Soleil show running at the Luxor Hotel.

Bewitched Banana

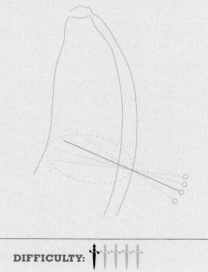

THE EFFECT You invite a participant to choose any piece of fruit from a basket and isolate it from you. You explain how New Orleans voodoo witches practice their own kind of magic. "We'll demonstrate," you say, "on this banana . . . we don't want anyone getting hurt."

You pick up a butter knife and mime the action of peeling and cutting a banana into five pieces—this invisible banana is the banana's "soul" (and apparently it was a bad banana). "What affects the soul affects the body," you say, inviting the participant to peel the real banana. When he does, he discovers that the five slices have become real. **It's voodoo with fruit. You've sliced the banana inside its peel . . . without even touching the fruit!**

THE SECRET Unbeknownst to the participant, he is forced to select a specially prepared banana. Using a pin, it's possible to cut a banana from the inside without visibly tampering with its peel.

THE PERFORMANCE

Your first objective is to force the banana. Suppose the fruit bowl holds an orange, a lime, and the banana. You'll use a forcing technique known as equivoque (we use equivoque in a different structural form but for the same purpose in "Trick Shot," page 26). In short, it appears that you will allow the participant to choose a piece of fruit. But actually, the choice is yours. It might go something like this:

❶ *"We need just one target for this experiment and there are three pieces of fruit. So we need to eliminate two. I'll let you decide."* You tell the participant only truths, but you're vague. You tell him that he will choose the fruit and that he needs to eliminate two pieces of fruit. But you don't tell him the rules.

❷ You say, *"Pick up any piece of fruit with your right hand."* Two things can happen here. He'll either pick the banana or he won't. If he picks the banana, say, *"Marvelous! Hold it in your hand and don't let me touch the target fruit."* Your participant will feel he has had a free choice. Indeed, he has.

But if he chooses the lime, you continue, undeterred. *"Excellent! Now pick up another piece of fruit with your left hand."* Again, two things can happen. Your participant will pick the banana, or he won't.

Suppose this time he picks up the orange. Recall that you told him earlier that he had to eliminate two pieces of fruit. Now you play that up: *"So you've eliminated the lime and the orange. That leaves the banana as our target. Excellent! Don't let me touch that banana."*

❸ Suppose the participant chooses the lime first, and then the banana. Once again, you're in control. Say, *"You've narrowed it down to two choices. We need to eliminate one. Hand one to me."* Do you see the trend? We're talking a lot without saying anything (car salesmen and tarot readers will find this part easy). You tell your participant that he needs to eliminate one more piece of fruit. But you don't tell him whether to hand you the piece he wants to use or the one he wants to eliminate. That is *your* choice.

❹ If he offers up the banana, say: *"Great. We'll use this as our target. Hold it and don't let me touch it."* If he offers the lime: *"Great. We've eliminated the lime, and that leaves us with the banana. . . . "*

In performance, the whole force takes about ten seconds. But because the equivoque (the process of eliminating options, see page 27) is a branching system, there are a lot of "what ifs." Don't let the lengthy description scare you away. The concept is one of the most powerful tools in a magician's arsenal; it is *literally* mind control.

❺ The rest is presentation. Pick up a table knife and mimic the actions of cutting an invisible fruit. *"I'm cutting the banana's soul,"* you say, trying to keep a straight face. *"And what affects the soul affects the body."* Invite your participant to peel the banana and discover that the banana has mysteriously been cut into four pieces. Remind him that you never touched the banana.

CREDIT: **The structure of forcing one of three items is attributed to Theodore Annemann.**

MASTER CLASS

A good magician examines her work by asking one question: "What's important here?" Let's think about the important points of "Bewitched Banana."

First, it's important that the participant believe the fruit is unprepared. How can this be arranged? The best way is to use a clever force, like equivoque (outlined above). But what else? Perform at your participant's house? Or prepare the fruit bowl before everyone arrives?

If possible, steer the conversation toward voodoo and then offer this experiment as a "spontaneous" demonstration. This attitude dispels the notion that you took time out of your day to cut a banana *through* its peel with a pin (which is illegal on weekends in Bismarck, North Dakota . . . but I digress).

It's also important that you do not touch the banana once the effect starts. Since you tampered with the fruit hours ago, this one is a freebie. You take advantage of the method by capitalizing on the hands-off approach: *"I promise I won't touch that banana at all,"* you might say before you begin. Afterward, recap by saying, *"And I haven't touched that banana, right?"*

PEPPER'S GHOST

On a stage in 1862, John Pepper debuted an astounding illusion unlike anything audiences had ever seen. During a scene in Charles Dickens's play *The Haunted Man*, an apparition appeared and faded before a live audience.

Pepper had adapted an idea by Henry Dircks called the Dircksian Phantasmagoria—but because Pepper was the first to achieve commercial success with it, the concept is often referred to as *Pepper's Ghost*.

Dircks's idea is that a plate of glass placed in front of a stage or room can change from transparent to translucent to opaque, depending on the light source. We experience this phenomenon every day. Imagine looking through a store window during the day, when the store is lit from inside. You can see through the glass and into the store. But at night, when all the lights inside the store are off, you see only your reflection in the store window. It becomes almost as reflective as a mirror, and you're unable to see what's on the other side.

Henry Dircks and John Pepper developed a way to shift the light source fluidly, so actors and props could materialize and fade away before a live audience. Today, the same principle changes women to gorillas in many sideshow exhibits and brings spirits to life in Disneyland's Haunted Mansion.

THE TEN GREATEST CARD TRICKS OF ALL TIME

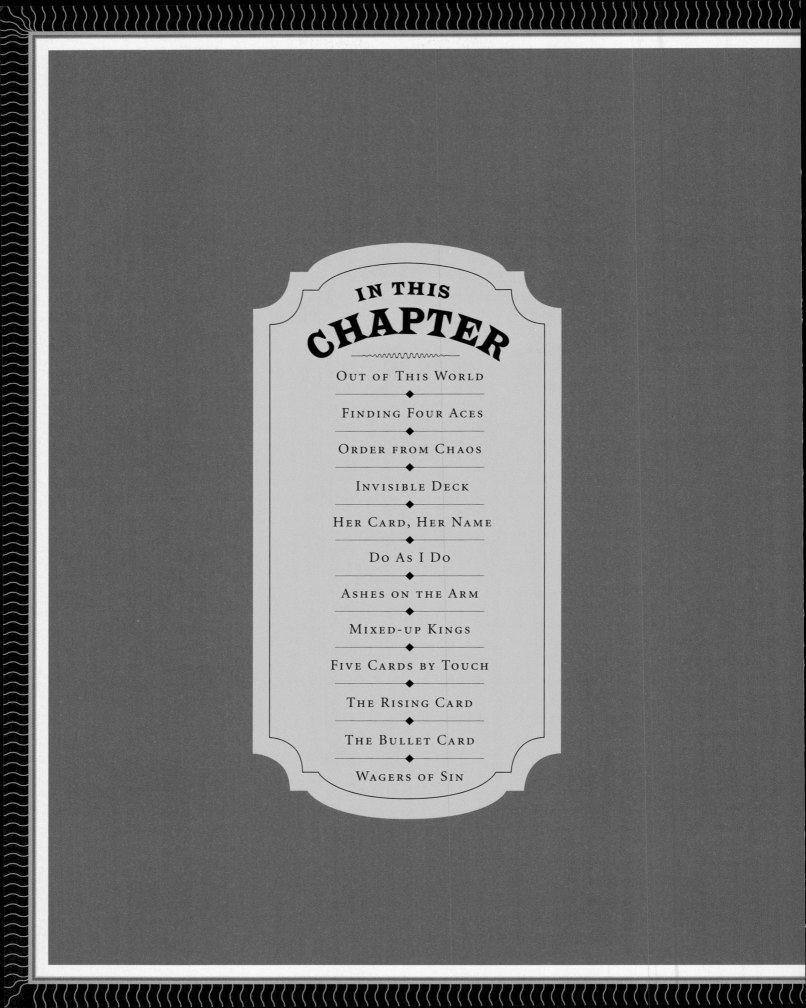

BECOMING A CARD EXPERT

Johann Nepomuk Hofzinser called card conjuring "the poetry of magic." Watching someone use an ordinary pack of cards to accomplish the impossible can affect an audience more strongly than any other magic performance.

But there are bad card tricks. Lots of bad card tricks. We've all suffered through at least one: Deal this many piles here, count that many cards there, spell your name—no, spell your card—wait, spell your card's name. . . . Beginners books are filled with these tricks: easy to teach and easy to do. But they're lousy card tricks.

That stops now.

Since I make my living inventing and performing card magic, I'm in a unique position to buck this trend. I've scoured the world and magic's vast literature. Here, then, are the best of the best, all in one chapter.

By the end of this section, you'll be able to find four Aces from a shuffled deck, cause a chosen card to levitate, and create order from chaos.

And that's not all. You'll soon discover that the strongest card effects are those in which the *participant* does the magic. "Finding Four Aces" and "Her Card, Her Name" are this rare kind of magic. Your participant finds four Aces; your participant finds her own card. It's spooky.

And then there's "Out of This World." Subscribers to the prestigious *Hugard's Magic Monthly* voted on more than half a millennium of card magic and chose "Out of This World" as the greatest card trick of all time. And it's coming right up! First, let's get your fingers nimble and primed.

THE WARM-UP

The Anatomy of a Card Trick

As a card magician, you need to know your way around a pack of cards.

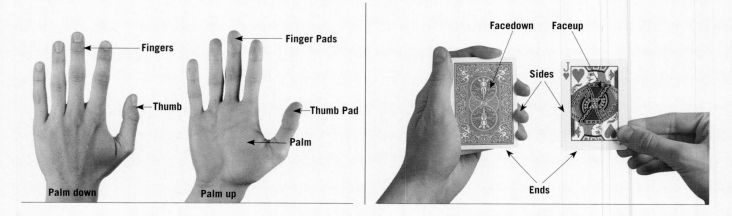

Thumbing

Several times in this chapter I will instruct you to "thumb over" a card or cards.
This is a magician's term for dealing the top card of the left hand's deck into your right hand.

❶ Holding the deck facedown in the palm and fingers of your left hand, press the pad of your left thumb onto the top card.

❷ Push the card gently so it slides off the deck to the right. This is known as "thumbing." Retrieve the card with your right fingers.

How to Shuffle: Tabled Riffle Shuffle

Any explanation of card shuffling will seem elementary to some, but as a professional magician, I often deal with participants who never learned how to shuffle a deck. As you can't claim to be a card magician unless you can competently shuffle cards, here is a crash course.

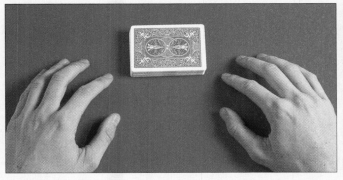

1 Seat yourself at a table and place your pack of cards on a soft surface, like a tablecloth. Position the pack facedown, with the sides parallel to the table's edge.

2 Grip the upper half of the deck at the right corners between your thumb and first fingers of your right hand.

3 Lift about half of the deck with your right fingers and place this packet of cards on the table directly to the right of the bottom half of the deck.

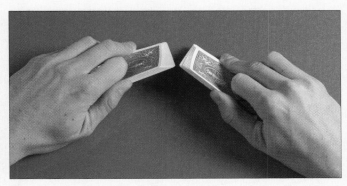

4 Grip one packet of cards in each hand, as shown, with your fingers pressed against the far sides of each packet and thumbs holding the near corners.

5 Slide the center corners of each packet near each other. Press downward lightly with the first fingers of each hand and gently riffle upward against the edges of the deck with your thumbs. As you riffle, continue to move the packets toward each other until the corners overlap and cards from both packets interweave. Note: Your first fingers help to regulate the speed of the shuffle and give the thumbs some opposition as they riffle through the cards.

Then push both packets completely together and square the edges.

How to Shuffle: Overhand Shuffle

This is perhaps the most common shuffling technique, and it has the added benefit of requiring no table.

1 Hold the deck "facedown," nearly perpendicular to the floor, gripping the ends palm up between your left thumb and fingers.

2 Position your right fingers beneath the deck with your right thumb pad resting against the left (and highest) side of the deck.

3 With your right thumb, peel a small packet of cards from the top of the deck and slide them into your awaiting right fingers.

4 Move your hands apart until the small packet clears the deck. Once the packet has fallen securely and completely into your right hand, move the hands back together, allowing the right hand's packet to slide beneath the left hand's deck.

5 Peel another small packet of cards from the left hand and into the right and repeat in this fashion until the deck is sufficiently shuffled.

A Card Force

Forcing a card is magic jargon for "forcing" a participant to choose a particular, predetermined card. She will swear she had a free choice, but you, the magician, will know which card she chose. This is a skill you will need for several effects in this chapter.

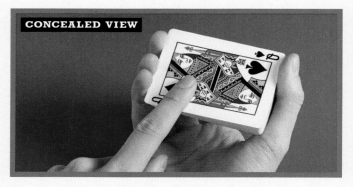 

1 First, secretly determine which card is on the bottom of the deck. Remember this card. It's your "force" card.

2 Hold the pack facedown and bevel the sides about two inches toward the left. Hold the deck from above with your right hand, supporting the end with your fingers.

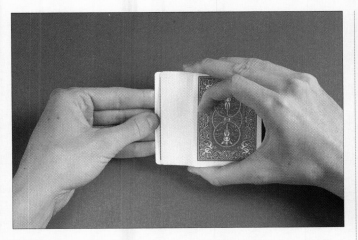

3 Pinch the bottom card at its left side between your left thumb and fingers.

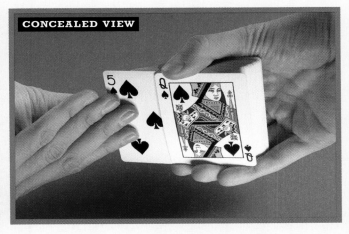

CONCEALED VIEW

4 With the deck facedown, push that bottom card to the right about an inch so that it's supported by your right hand finger pads.

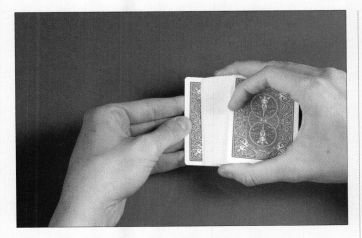

5 Deal through the cards. When you're performing the force, explain to your participant that you will deal cards from the bottom of the deck one by one, until you "find" the card she's chosen.

Take each card from what looks like the bottom of the pack. Actually, you're accessing the cards above the force card (the Queen of Spades) with your left finger pads.

Deal each card from the "bottom" of the deck and turn it faceup on the table. The force card remains concealed and undisturbed as you deal through the pack card by card.

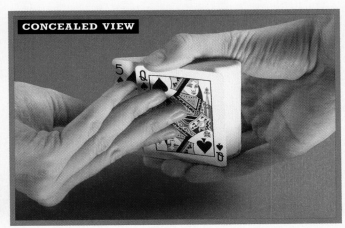

CONCEALED VIEW

6 When the participant tells you to stop, extend the finger pads of your left hands to the concealed force card and pull it to the left. Take this card into the your hand and deal it faceup onto the table. As they are viewing from above, your participants cannot tell that you are accessing a card misaligned with the bottom of the deck.

You have just learned the *Sid Lorraine glide force*. In the upcoming chapter, you'll use this easy sleight to find four Aces, make cards appear, and predict the future!

Out of This World

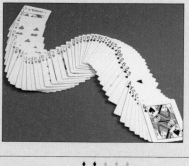

MATERIALS:
Pack of cards.

SETUP: Separate the colors in your deck and place all the reds (hearts and diamonds) on top of the blacks (clubs and spades).

DIFFICULTY: ✝✝✝✝✝

THE EFFECT "Without looking and without thinking about it too much, deal cards into two piles, here and there." You indicate two places on the table. "If you think the card is red, deal it here. If you think the card is black, deal it there." The participant complies and deals through about half the deck. You then invite another participant to deal through the other half. **The two participants have unknowingly separated the red cards and the black ones!** This one is so named for its devastating effect on audiences.

THE SECRET The deck is stacked with the colors already separated.

THE PERFORMANCE

"**M**y grandmother used to say she had a sixth sense," you start. "I told her snoring isn't a sense. But she was referring to a woman's intuition. That's what I'd like to try right now. Since I'm not a woman, would you help me?" (Obviously, adapt your patter appropriately according to you and your participant's gender.)

❶ "Take the pack," you invite your participant. "Without looking and without thinking about it too much, I want you to deal the cards into two piles, here and there." Indicate two places on your working surface, side by side. Specify that she deal the red cards to your right and the black cards to your left. Make sure she deals the cards one by one, but encourage her to deal rapidly, "without over-thinking it." When she has gone through about half the cards, stop her.

❷ "Let's try someone else's intuition . . . . Would you please deal the rest?" Have the first participant hand her undealt cards to a different participant.

"To differentiate where she stopped and you began," you say, "I'd like you to deal the blacks here, on top of her reds, and your reds there, on top of her blacks." You point, indicating that you want the second participant to deal opposite from the first. When all the cards are dealt, say, "Statistically, there should be an equal number of successes and failures. If there are more successes than failures, you both may have a sixth sense. If there are fewer than ten mistakes, I'd say you've performed the impossible. If there are fewer than five , you're coming with me to Vegas!"

3 Pick up the leftmost packet and invite a participant to pick up the other one and spread it on the table faceup. With your packet, spread it so all the cards face you and separate at the juncture of colors. Take the fan of red cards into your right hand and spread them faceup on the table. Place the spread of black cards on the table in a different spot, isolated. Encourage the participant to do the same.

"Pack your bags. We're going to Vegas!" The participant will discover that she, like you, holds a pack of cards perfectly separated according to your procedure.

MASTER CLASS

When you complete this effect, your audiences won't applaud wildly. They will be silent, still. Fear not—this is the ultimate compliment. This effect *slays* audiences; it's so unbelievable that it often scares the participants silent. It's a beautiful thing to watch, and to perform.

Some beginners don't understand how to process an effect like "Out of This World" because the participants—not the magician—do the magic. Let me assure you that although the participants do get the credit for having a sixth sense, there is never any question as to who the performer is. When your friends want to see something incredible, they'll ask *you* about *"the one where I separate the colors."*

Remember that our goal is to leave our audiences with an incredible story. You'll find that the experience of magic is paramount to who, specifically, holds the magic wand.

CREDIT: "Out of This World" was created by one of the 20th century's most brilliant magical thinkers, Paul Curry. He first published this outstanding effect in 1942, and it became an instant classic.

THE IRELAND SHUFFLE

"Out of This World" is considered the greatest card trick of all time. But if you can shuffle the cards before you begin this effect, you can make the greatest effect even greater. Even though the pack is stacked, this special shuffle won't disturb the arrangement.

1 Alter your starting position so the black cards are on top of the red cards.

2 Perform an Overhand Shuffle normally, taking small clumps of cards from your left hand into your right.

When you approach the deck's midpoint, peel cards *singly* with your right thumb pad. You must ensure that you peel each card individually until you are safely past the juncture of colors (between the twenty-sixth and twenty-seventh position). After that, continue to shuffle normally, taking small groups of cards and placing one packet on top of the next.

That's it! The shuffle should look real . . . because it is. You're changing the order of the cards, but you're maintaining the color separation.

CREDIT: Chicago magician Laurie Ireland popularized this innovative shuffling technique. It was first published in 1919 by Charles Jordan in *Thirty Card Mysteries*.

Finding Four Aces

ON DVD

MATERIALS:
A pack of cards.

SETUP: Place four Aces on the bottom of the deck and one indifferent card beneath the Aces. This way, you can show the top and bottom of the deck without exposing an Ace.

DIFFICULTY: †††††

THE EFFECT You deal through the deck, asking someone to call "stop" four times. Each stopped-at card is an Ace: **Your participant has "found" four Aces but doesn't know how she did it.**

THE SECRET Four Aces are hidden on the bottom of the deck and switched into play, one by one.

THE PERFORMANCE

"*O*ur subconscious minds are capable of more than you think," you say. Hold the pack of cards at chest level in your left hand, faces toward your participant.

❶ Riffle the ends with your right fingers, allowing each card to flick off the pads of your fingers. This gives the participant an impossibly quick slideshow of the deck's order. Take care not to riffle the first five cards or you'll expose the Aces. "*You saw the entire pack,*" you announce. "*Your eyes took in every card, but the cards passed too fast for you to process the order in your conscious memory. I'm interested in tapping into your* subconscious *mind to retrieve this information.*"

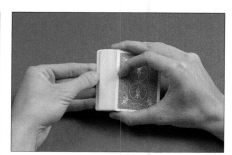

❷ Turn the deck facedown and bevel the sides so the bottom extends two inches toward the left. Hold the deck from above with your right hand, supporting the ends with your fingers.

❸ Tell your participant, "*Think Aces. Don't think about where they are. Just think 'Ace' and say 'stop' four times as I deal through the deck.*" As you speak, pinch a small packet of cards (at least five) from the bottom of the deck with your left thumb and fingers.

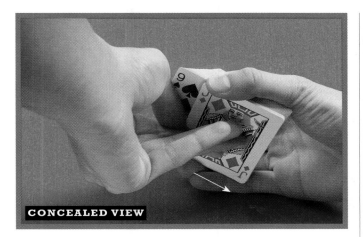

CONCEALED VIEW

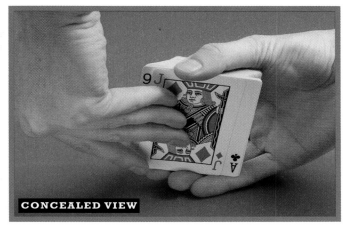

CONCEALED VIEW

4 With the deck still facedown, push this packet to the right about an inch so the right fingers support this concealed packet beneath the deck.

5 Begin dealing from the bottom of the deck by extending the finger pads to the concealed packet and pulling the indifferent card (Jack of Diamonds) to the left. Take this card into your left hand and deal it faceup onto the table.

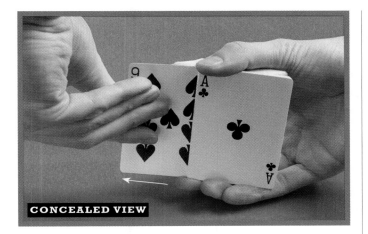

CONCEALED VIEW

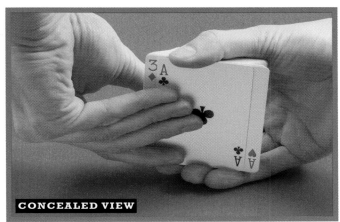

CONCEALED VIEW

6 You have removed the indifferent "cover card," leaving only the Aces jogged to the right.

Continue to deal through the remaining cards (avoiding the Aces) by taking each one from the bottom of the deck with the left finger pads. The concealed packet remains hidden as you deal out the pack, card by card. Layer each dealt card faceup on the table.

7 Whenever the participant tells you to "stop," take the next card from the concealed packet. Amazingly, it will be an Ace. Viewed from above, it's impossible to tell that the fingers are accessing a concealed packet misaligned with the bottom of the deck.

continued 👉

8 You can reveal each Ace as you go; this has a certain immediacy that is shocking to participants. But I prefer to deal the Aces facedown and reveal all four together, at the end.

MASTER CLASS

Finding four Aces from a deck of cards has built-in appeal for anyone who plays cards. The problem is, lots of folks don't. The presentation outlined above, about subconscious memory, appeals to everyone.

I use this presentation because it gives the effect *context*. The cards aren't magical here; they're used to illustrate a more intriguing topic: subconscious memory.

But if you think "memorizing" the position of four Aces is difficult, try the whole pack! Tom Groves did.

On November 3, 1994, Tom Groves memorized a shuffled deck of cards in 42.01 seconds without a single error. (But rumor has it that after the event, he couldn't remember where he had parked his car!)

On November 26, 1993, Dominic O'Brien memorized 40 decks of cards (2,080 cards total) in a single sighting with only one mistake, setting the world record.

CREDIT: **This is Sid Lorraine's force done four times with four Aces. His brilliant force is essentially a modernization of a classic sleight called the Glide. I've opted not to explain this awkward, antiquated sleight in favor of Lorraine's slick, natural variation.**

IN THE QUEEN'S HAND

A good magic show is about peaks and valleys. You can't perform all the card effects in this chapter in the same show or for the same group; the tricks are all too strong. But here's a quickie that audiences love.

Remove the Queen of Spades from your deck and examine it carefully. It's likely you're using Bicycle or Bee brand playing cards, and the artwork on the Queen of Spades depicts her holding what appears to be the Six of Spades. This little detail can make for a unique card effect.

THE EFFECT The participant selects a card—the Six of Spades—and shuffles it into the deck. You offer to find the card and remove the Queen of Spades. Your participant informs you that she did not choose the Queen. But you show her that the Six of Spades is, in fact, within the Queen of Spades' hand.

THE PERFORMANCE

To perform this effect, secretly place the Six of Spades on the bottom of the deck. Force the Six of Spades on the participant using the Sid Lorraine force, explained in both "Finding Four Aces" (page 78) and "Her Card, Her Name" (page 88). Allow the participant to bury her selected Six into the pack and shuffle.

Take the deck back and remove the Queen of Spades with confidence. Your participant will be tickled to tell you that you're wrong.

"I couldn't find the card," you say, *"because the Queen has it in her hand!"*

Order from Chaos

ON DVD

MATERIALS:

A pack of cards.

SETUP: Remove the Hearts and stack them at the bottom of the deck in the following order (from the bottom upward): *Q, J, 2, 6, A, 5, K, 10, 9, 4, 3, 7, 8,* rest of the deck.

DIFFICULTY:

THE EFFECT The thirteen Hearts are removed from a pack and thoroughly shuffled . . . and then instantly order themselves, Ace through King.

THE SECRET The secret setup takes care of everything. Though the shuffle sequences appear random, you are simply moving cards from one predetermined order to a different predetermined order.

THE PERFORMANCE

" *I saw a show on television last night about Chaos Theory. The experts describe chaos as a confused or disorganized state. But Chaos Theory, also known as the Butterfly Effect, asserts that even chaos is deterministic. There is some larger order for everything, and everything is affected by its initial conditions. I'd like to establish chaos in this deck of cards."*

❶ Split the deck in half and execute a tabled riffle shuffle (page 73). If someone watching you knows how to shuffle, you can even let him riffle the packets together. Your stack of Hearts on the face of the deck is still intact (there is just a chain of indifferent cards now dispersed between them).

Split the deck again, but this time cut only about a third off the top. Allow another participant to riffle the cards, or do it yourself. As long as the shuffles are *riffle shuffles,* you're fine. Your stack of Hearts is still in the order they started in, but they're spread throughout the deck.

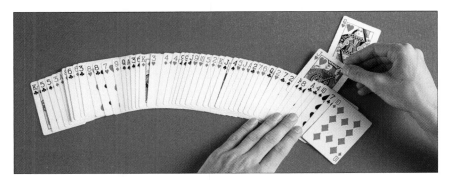

❷ *"Let's use Hearts,"* you suggest. Turn the deck faceup and spread through it, left to right. Starting on the right side, remove each Heart as you come to it and place each one faceup in a pile on the table. This reverses the order of the Hearts (when the deck is turned facedown, so that the 8 ends up at the bottom of the deck and the Q is at the top). The participants see each Heart coming out of the deck in an order that appears to be completely random. Be sure to remove each Heart in the order in which you come to it because while the arrangement appears random, this setup is imperative. Once you have removed all thirteen Hearts, set the rest of the deck aside.

3 Pick up the packet of Hearts, fan it out, and show the cards to the audience. *"An order you determined by your shuffles—it's chaos in a pack of cards."*

4 Turn the packet facedown and hold it in your left hand by the ends, in readiness for an overhand shuffle. *"Let's increase the randomness—the disorder—and see what happens."* You will overhand shuffle this packet in a pre-calculated, precise way. The trick is to make it look casual. Peel two cards singly with the right thumb pad, taking each card on top of the previous one. Once you have peeled

two cards, throw the remaining left-hand cards on top of those in the right hand.

Regrip the packet by the ends in the left hand. Now overhand shuffle three cards singly, peeling each one into the right hand. Again, put each card on top of the previous one. Then throw the remaining left-hand cards on top.

Repeat, this time running four cards singly into your right hand. Finish by throwing the remaining left-hand cards on top. You run different numbers of cards each time (two, three, and four) to simulate a random shuffle. This is creator Lew Brooks's brilliant idea: prearranging the cards, and then "unshuffling" them.

Situation Check: Let's make sure we're still together.
You're holding a facedown packet of Hearts. From top to bottom, the order should be:

4♥ 3♥ 7♥ 8♥ J♥ Q♥ A♥ 6♥ 2♥ 9♥ 10♥ K♥ 5♥

6 *"That's called an overhand shuffle. You might know that one. Another way to establish chaos in a pack of cards is using*

a shuffle I saw a little kid do between solitaire games. It looks like this." Thumb over the top three cards into your right hand without reversing their order. Toss the three cards, as a group, facedown onto the table. Now spread over two cards and take them in the right hand. Toss this pair on top of the tabled trio. Continue in this fashion, alternating between three-card packets and two-card packets. You start and end on a three-card packet. As you toss the packets, you can flash the faces of these groups to your audience. The order still looks like "chaos."

Situation Check: This can get confusing, so let's do another quick check. Your order, from top to bottom, should be:

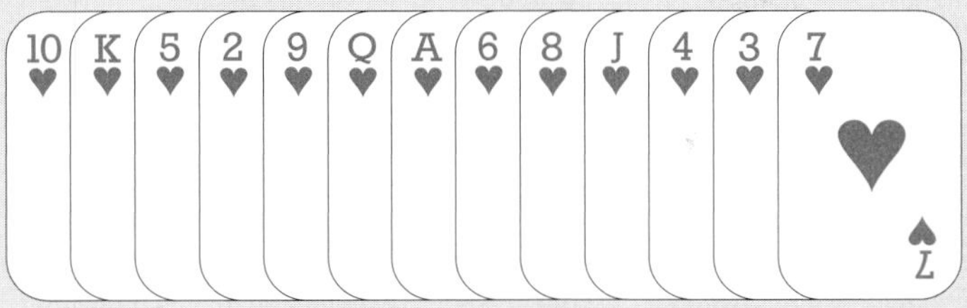

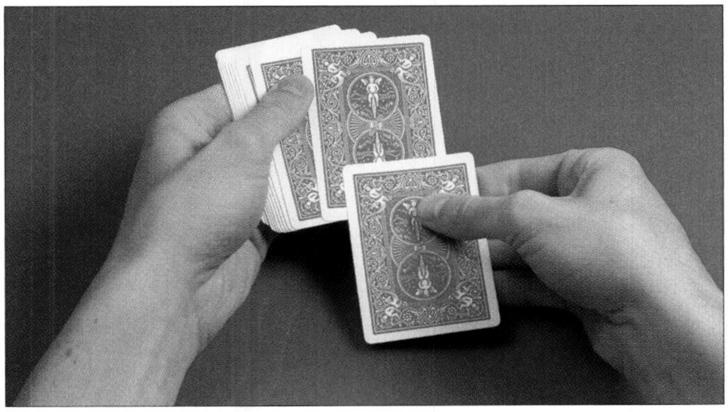

7 Say, *"I showed you the overhand shuffle and the kiddie shuffle. Now let me show you the famous unshuffle. Rather than mixing cards by shuffling them into one another, the unshuffle mixes cards by shuffling cards out of one another."* This doesn't really make sense, but it sounds good.

The unshuffle sequence is easy. Spread the cards between your hands, thumbing them over from your left hand, and outjog (push forward) every other card, starting with the second card from the top.

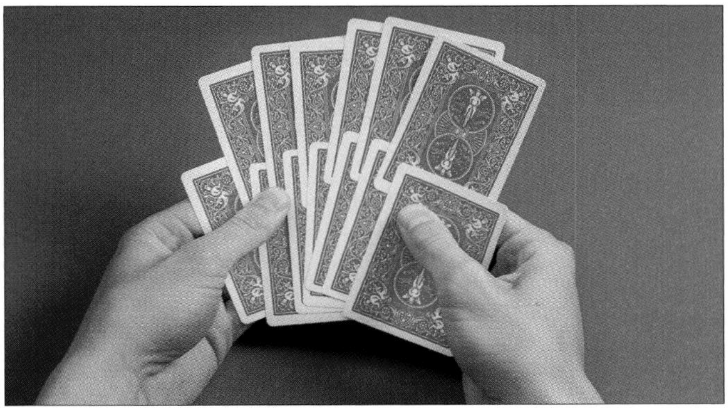

8 Use both hands to display the alternated packet, and then square the sides. The alternating condition of the cards is maintained, even when the cards are squared by their sides. Strip out all the outjogged cards, pulling them free of the inner packet. Drop this outer packet on top of the inner one. Magicians call this shuffle a *Reverse Faro.*

Situation Check: One last time, from top to bottom:

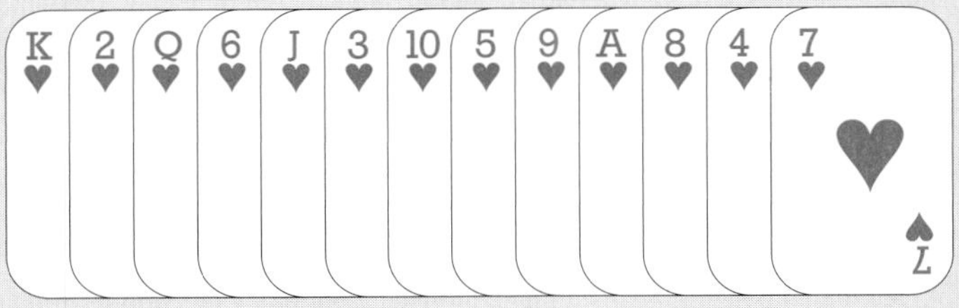

6 *"And last, there's the famous Down Under Deal."* Deal the top card facedown onto the table. This card goes "down." Take the next card into your right hand and place it on the bottom or "under" the deck. That's the Down Under dealing procedure. You alternate between dealing cards down (on the table) and under (beneath the packet). Continue in this fashion until the entire packet is on the table. (See also the Australian Shuffle, page 244).

If you peek at the tabled packet, you'll find it is now in numerical order. But we're not going to reveal it just yet.

"That's chaos. But if you try this at home and your shuffles are perfect, your cuts exact, then you, too, can create order from chaos!" Deal the cards one by one faceup onto the table to reveal the Ace, Two, Three . . . through King.

MASTER CLASS

This is a masterpiece in the hands of its creator, Lew Brooks. Brooks designed a simple but powerful effect with an intriguing story about chaos and order. Although there's not a single sleight in the entire routine, this will take practice. You'll have to practice to *remember* the different phases. Here's an outline to help you:

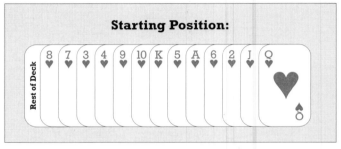

Cut deck in half and riffle shuffle.

Cut one-third from the top and perform another riffle shuffle.

Remove all the Hearts one by one, placing them in a faceup pile on the table.

Overhand Shuffle: Peel 2 and toss, then peel 3 and toss, then peel 4 and toss.

Kiddie Shuffle: Cut packets in 3, 2, 3, 2, 3 groupings.

Unshuffle: Unshuffle packet, pushing forward every second card, stripping out the outjogged cards, and placing them on top.

Down Under Deal: Alternate dealing cards down onto the table and under the deck.

Two more tips: If you're performing this effect and you don't have a table handy, you can perform the cuts and deals into a participant's hands.

If there are no competent shufflers watching, shuffle the cards yourself but allow a participant to push them together, squared.

CREDIT: Lew Brooks created "Order from Chaos." I've altered his handling to eliminate some sleight of hand and lengthen the shuffles, but the routine is basically the same. We have English magician C. O. Williams to thank for discovering how to maintain a packet's order throughout two riffle shuffles; he calls this principle *interlocking chains.*

Old Dog, New Trick: Using an Invisible Deck

Invisible Deck

MATERIALS:
An Invisible Deck, a regular card box, a small paper bag.

SETUP: Before the production, insert the Invisible Deck into a regular card box. Fold over the brown paper bag (the kind you pack your lunch in) three times and tuck the Invisible Deck inside the opening. Situate this bag on the table, in plain view.

DIFFICULTY: †††††

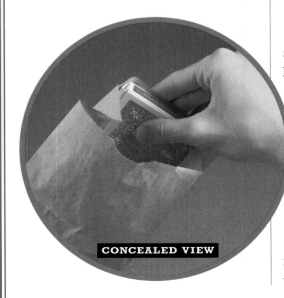

CONCEALED VIEW

THE EFFECT **Predict a thought-of card—one of the true classics of magic.** You propose an experiment with an invisible deck of playing cards. You pretend to hand an invisible deck to a participant. He is instructed to fan through the cards, pick one, and reinsert it facing the other way. When he complies, he throws the "deck" back to you. When you catch it, the pack becomes visible. And true to your participant's charade, his card is reversed in the pack.

This is, in my estimation, one of the five strongest magic effects you can perform. Period. Even though it's included with most beginner magic sets and sold in novelty shops around the globe, there is a simplicity—a clarity—that audiences are drawn to. Normally, some mathematics are involved in computing which pair of cards to separate. I've eliminated the math for you. I've also added a new way to produce the deck at the beginning.

THE SECRET What is an Invisible Deck? It's a trick deck of playing cards that exploits the "Rough and Smooth" principle. In summary, pairs of cards are gently stuck together, back to back. With a light grip, you can spread an Invisible Deck and each pair will remain together, like a single card. But when light pressure is applied to a particular card, it splits easily from its mate. This results in what appears to be the only reversed card in the pack.

THE PERFORMANCE

"*A*nybody know what this is?*" you ask, holding your empty hand above your head. "*This, ladies and gentlemen, is an invisible deck. Do you know why you can't see it?*" Pause. "*Because it's invisible!*"

"*Jean-Eugène Robert-Houdin, the famous nineteenth-century magician, once remarked, 'A magician is an actor playing the part of a magician.'*" (That's right. I've found yet another way to work in Robert-Houdin's famous quote. But, come on, it fits.)

"*I'd like to test your acting abilities now. Here, catch this invisible deck.*" Pretend to toss the invisible deck of cards to a participant. "*Please, shuffle the cards.*" Allow her to begin, then interrupt, "*It's easier if you take them out of the box first.*" This line is a classic, but in situ, it's hilarious.

❶ "*Now fan through the deck and take out one card. Got it? Show it around but don't let me see it.*" Allow her to play along. "*Put the card back into the center of the pack upside down. Put all the cards back in the box and throw them to me.*" While you talk, retrieve the paper bag. Unfold it, secretly holding the hidden deck with the fingers of your left hand, against the inner side of the bag, near the opening.

❷ When the participant tosses the invisible deck back to you, follow it with your eyes, moving your head like a spectator who's watching a tennis ball sail over the net. Hold the bag out to catch the invisible pack, and then release the concealed deck.

❸ It will fall to the bottom of the bag with a thud. The bottom of the bag will crinkle and buckle around the dropped deck. It's the perfect illusion of the invisible deck becoming real as it enters the bag.

Without hesitation, reach inside the bag and remove the deck; now it's visible. First applause cue.

"You did an excellent acting job. But let's see just how well you did. You shuffled an invisible deck, removed a card—any card—and reversed it into the center of the deck. For the first time, tell us—what card did you reverse?"

Allow her to respond. Remember the name of the card, and note whether it's odd or even (Jacks and Kings are odd, with values of 11 and 13, respectively, while Queens, with a value of 12, are even). Assume the participant names the Four of Clubs.

❹ Remove the Invisible Deck from the box, and take notice of the card on the side facing you. Is this card even or odd? Invisible Decks are assembled with all the even cards facing the same way and all the odd cards facing the other way. You must ensure that the participant's card is *facing you.*

Since the Four of Clubs is an even card, you must ensure that an even card—any even card—is facing you. If an odd card is facing you, as you remove the deck, turn the box around before you remove the deck.

Spread the cards gingerly at chest height, taking care not to apply too much pressure (or else the pairs will spread). You're in an interesting position. From the audience's point of view, it appears the cards are spread with the faces toward them. But you're also looking at a spread of faces.

As you spread the cards, sight the participant's selection. All the cards are even, so you must only discern the selection from the half of the deck that is facing you. When you find it, split the pair between your fingers. From the audience's viewpoint, a facedown card will show in the spread.

5 Invite a participant, perhaps someone in the front row, to remove this card and reveal its identity. *"I'd say you are a great actor, and thus a great magician!"* Second applause cue.

MASTER CLASS

You've seen this effect on television countless times, and all your favorite magicians have used it. Why? Because this isn't a card trick; this is magic with cards.

I've provided you with a professional-caliber presentation, which you can vary to suit your style and venue. The Invisible Deck is the prop—and the source of the magic effect—but there's priceless audience interaction, a script I've honed with over a decade of use, and a noteworthy production of the deck itself. The only component missing? You!

One last point: There are thirteen values in each suit, which means there are more "odds" than "evens." Thus, the Kings are paired together, back to back. You can either memorize which Kings face which way, or do what I do: *"Now take any card and reverse it in the pack—but don't take an obvious one, like a King, Instead, make it more difficult."* Problem solved!

CREDIT: Joe Berg created the Invisible Deck in the thirties. Originally called the Ultra Mental Deck, Eddie Fields is said to have come up with the invisible presentation after watching a patient in the psychiatric unit of a hospital shuffling an imaginary pack of playing cards.

DO-IT-YOURSELF INVISIBLE DECK

Invisible Decks aren't expensive—only about ten bucks. U.S. Playing Card Company brand makes one of excellent quality. But you can also make your own from any complete deck.

In addition to a complete deck of cards, you'll need a reusable glue stick—a useful product you can buy at any office-supply store. By design, this glue has a weak bond with a minimal residue. It also has the unique property of being repositionable, over and over again.

Take out the pesky Kings and then separate your deck into odds and evens (minus the Kings, there are an equal number of odd and even cards; we'll deal with the Kings last). Apply a thin strip of reusable glue to the back of all the even cards, near one end. Match up each even card with any odd card and then firmly press the pairs together, back to back. Apply the glue stick to two of the four Kings and create two pairs of back-to-back Kings. Gather all the cards and put them into the card box. You're looking at a homemade Invisible Deck.

Her Card, Her Name

ON DVD

MATERIALS:
A pack of cards and a bold permanent marker.

SETUP: How you discover a participant's name is entirely dependent on setting. If it's someone you know, this is a nonissue. But the effect has more impact if you use a stranger. If you know you'll be performing at a party, ask someone you know who he's bringing, or what the host's brother's cousin's name is. The more obscure and "impossible," the better. You want to use someone you simply *couldn't* have known beforehand.

Assuming her name is Sarah, write "Sarah's Card" clearly across the face of the Two of Hearts with a black permanent marker. A red card works best with black ink, and I suggest using a low card, like the Two of Hearts, because it has plenty of white space. Place this card on the face of the deck.

DIFFICULTY: 🗡️🗡️🗡️🗡️🗡️

THE EFFECT You bring up the subject of names and the meanings behind them. A participant, Sarah, is asked to choose a card. Without looking at the deck, you are able to determine Sarah's card: The Two of Hearts. But a card can be about more than personal choice—it can be personalized. **You turn over the chosen card and "Sarah's Card" is written across its face.**

THE SECRET You ascertain the participant's name in advance and write it on the Two of Hearts. That card is then forced on the participant.

THE PERFORMANCE

❶ You're going to use the same easy sleight used four times in "Finding Four Aces" (page 78). To do this, bevel the sides of the deck so the bottom extends two inches to the left. Hold the deck from above with your right hand supporting the ends with your fingers.

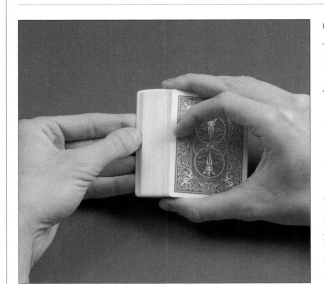

❷ *"What's in a name?"* you ask. *"All names carry meaning. These are playing cards, but each one has several names. It has a value name, like Seven or Ten or Queen, and it has a suit name, like Spades or Hearts."* As you speak, use your left thumb and fingers to separate the bottom (force) card from the deck and push it to the right about an inch.

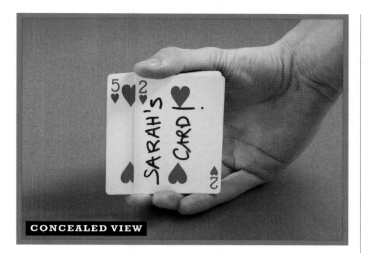

CONCEALED VIEW

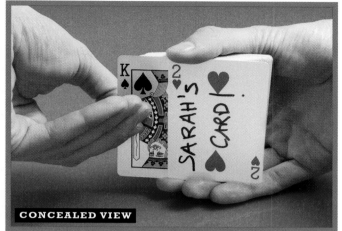

CONCEALED VIEW

❸ Support the concealed force card beneath the deck with your right fingers. Choose a participant and ask her to choose a card, saying, *"As I deal through the cards, just say 'stop' to find your name card."*

❹ Deal from the bottom of the deck by sliding each card one by one with the left finger pads, and placing it faceup in a pile on the table. You can deal comfortably from the bottom without disturbing the force card (your participant's card) jogged to the right.

❺ When the participant says "stop," extend your left fingers a little further to take the force card with your left fingertips and slide it to the left. From above (the participant's perspective), this action is indistinguishable from how you have been dealing. Place the forced Two of Hearts facedown in the participant's hand. Say, *"Don't look at your card just yet."*

The rest is build-up. *"Every one of these cards has a different name: Seven of Spades, Three of Hearts, Nine of Clubs. . . ."* Deal through the cards in your hand, calling off a few names and simply displaying the others. Then spread out the tabled cards. Your objective is to show that the other cards have nothing written on them. But you can't *say* that, of course, or you'll spoil the ending.

Place your fingers on your temples and concentrate. *"I'm going to think of the name of the card. . . . I've got a name! The Two of Hearts!"*

Before allowing the participant to check, add, *"But this card has another name."* Invite her to turn over the card and discover her personalized message.

MASTER CLASS

A Two of Hearts with "Sarah's Card" written across the face is useless to you; let the participant keep the card. Leaving a participant with a souvenir of your show is powerful, and it serves one of this book's primary objectives: to create *a lasting memory.* This amazing card effect isn't one your audience will soon forget. But Sarah will remember it forever because she's got proof!

I have been performing "Her Card, Her Name" for years. I recently ran into someone who saw me perform at a party more than seven years ago. When she saw me, she lit up and rummaged through her wallet. Behind the pet pictures and the credit cards, next to her license was—her chosen card! She had kept her card with her all that time; her card had become her story.

CREDIT: **This is yet another application of Sid Lorraine's forcing technique.**

THROWING CARDS

Howard Thurston, America's foremost magician at the dawn of the 1900s, could throw promotional playing cards into the audience at incredible speeds and distances—even into theater balconies. In the 1970s, Master Magician Ricky Jay gained renown for scaling cards into the skin of a watermelon. Today, magician Rick Smith Jr. holds the world's card-throwing record. Smith used to be a pitcher at Cleveland State University, and this training helped earn him the record for tossing (also known as "scaling") a card: 216 feet.

Thrown playing cards can even be used for self-defense (at least in the movies). Historically, scaling cards has almost always been reserved as a display of skill.

1 Begin by holding a playing card in your right hand: The pad of your index finger rests on the top right corner while you pinch the card from top and bottom between the thumb and the middle finger.

2 Curl your right hand in toward your body and flick the card forcefully, as you would throw a Frisbee.™

3 The card must rotate off the index finger.

Once you've got a working formula for throwing the card, try putting a little more force into the throw: Specifically, use more arm strength and focus on "snapping" your wrist as you release the card.

Troubleshooting

Scaling cards is completely a matter of trial and error. If your card flutters to the ground just inches from your body, you either aren't getting enough rotation during the release or you're throwing the card unevenly (always try to toss the card parallel with the ground). When you scale a card properly, you'll know it immediately; the card will whiz by at a speed disproportionate to the amount of force you applied. Just make sure you aim away from other people: Playing cards can draw blood!

Do As I Do

MATERIALS:
Two decks of cards, two chairs, and a table.

SETUP: Neither deck requires preparation.

DIFFICULTY:

THE EFFECT Two packs of cards are used and both are shuffled thoroughly by the participant. He keeps one deck and hands you the other. Both you and he proceed to remove a card and bury it in your respective decks. **When the chosen cards are revealed, you find, miraculously, that you both chose the same card!**

THE SECRET You use a "key" card, a magician's term for a card that indicates the participant's selection. It sounds complicated, but follow along and you'll see how easy this is.

THE PERFORMANCE

Say, *"Let's play a game. Please, move your chair directly across the table from me, and face me."* Allow the participant to comply. *"Actors play the 'Mirror Game' a lot to hone their physical acting skills. They try to become the person they're playing, and to do that they study the smallest tics and gestures that make someone unique. I want to play this game so we can get in sync with each other. I'll start by mirroring you."*

Now try your best to imitate physically every action and movement your participant makes. When he smiles, smile. When he blinks, blink. When he scratches his head . . . you get the idea. This is hilarious for your participant.

1 *"Now you imitate me,"* you say, presenting both decks of cards. Remove a deck from its case and wait for your participant to remove his. Shuffle your deck thoroughly and allow him to do the same with his deck.

"Now, to be as fair as possible, we should switch decks." As you hand your deck to the participant, glimpse the card on the bottom of your pack and remember it. This your "key" card because this card is the key to the effect. Assume it's the Five of Diamonds. Take the participant's deck in your hands and spread the cards toward yourself at chest height. Instruct the participant to mirror you and do the same.

❷ *"I'm going to remove any card from the deck,"* you say, picking one card as you do so. Allow the participant to remove one, too. Place your deck facedown on the table and make sure he does the same.

   "Remember your card." Now look at the card in your hand, but do *not* remember it. That's right; forget your own chosen card. The participant needs to remember his card, but you simply stare through your card, remembering only your key card (in this case, the Five of Diamonds).

❸ *"I'll put my card on top of my deck and then cut it into the middle."* So saying, place your card facedown on top of the facedown deck and cut the cards. (Lift about half of the deck, place it to the right of the bottom half of the deck, lift the bottom half of the deck and place it on top of the top half of the deck.) Make sure the participant mirrors these actions with his deck.

   When your participant cuts the deck, he unknowingly situates the key card directly above his selection.

   "Let's trade packs again, to keep things fair." Switch decks with your participant and fan your new deck toward yourself. Say, *"I'm going to remove my card from your deck. I want you to remove your card from my deck."*

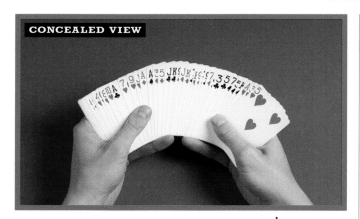

❹ Fan through the deck and apparently remove the card you selected earlier. Actually, you find the Five of Diamonds, your key card, and take the card directly to the right of it. This is your participant's chosen card.

❺ Hold the chosen card against your chest so it's kept a secret. Set the deck on the table and allow the participant to mirror this action. Keep your card against your chest.

6 *"That was an amazing example of mirroring. I really feel like we're on the same wavelength. Wouldn't you say?"* As you turn the face of your card toward the participant, he will turn his card toward you. Both cards match!

MASTER CLASS

"Do As I Do" is one of the preeminent card classics. It's often described in beginner books because it's easy to do. But one component is almost always missing: a presentation. Here, there's a premise for this automatic card effect, in the form of a game.

Effects that deal with synchronicity and coincidence are believable to audiences, but only if framed in the proper context. All the mimicking and mirroring might seem superfluous, but this game serves two important purposes. First, it's fun. It's stupid fun, but that's engaging.

This presentation's other purpose is to add believability to the climax. There's a trick to "Do As I Do," but only you know that. To your audience, this is a persuasive illustration of how two people can be of the same mind.

CREDIT: Robert-Houdin's trick, "The Sympathetic Cards," though not identical, is the foundation of this effect.

SIMON ARONSON

Chicago's Simon Aronson is one of magic's ingenious creators. A lawyer by trade, Aronson has a passion for magic, and he is responsible for creating some of the most memorable card tricks ever devised.

Aronson has played an influential role in my magic, and I try to adhere to his philosophy on constructing effects: "There is a world of difference between not knowing how something's done versus knowing that it can't be done."

With some magic effects, the stakes simply aren't high enough. Here Aronson encourages us to raise the stakes. If a magician deals through a packet of cards and stops on the one you selected, you might be fooled. You might even be impressed because the odds of your finding the right card among all the others are improbable.

But there is a world of difference between improbable and impossible. If the name of the card appears in ash on your forearm (see "Ashes on the Arm," page 94), your reaction will be much more intense because that is *impossible*.

Ashes on the Arm

ON DVD

A deck of cards, a tube of Chapstick, a pencil, a scrap of paper, an ashtray, and a lighter.

SETUP: Choose a card and place on the bottom of the deck. Let's use the Two of Diamonds as an example.

Prepare your arm by writing the card's abbreviated "name" (use the number "2" and the outline of a diamond shape) with your Chapstick. The substance is invisible but slightly sticky.

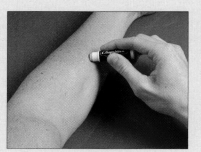

When ashes are rubbed on your arm, they will adhere to these secret initials. (Don't let participants see you write on your arm with Chapstick. They'll either know how the effect is achieved or they will think you have chapped arms. Neither is good for your rep!)

DIFFICULTY:

THE EFFECT A participant selects a card and writes its name in pencil on a scrap of paper while your back is turned. You turn around, light the paper on fire, and rub the cooled ashes on your forearm. **Presto! The name of the participant's chosen card is revealed written across your forearm.**

THE SECRET The card is forced; you control which one the participant chooses. A secret application of Chapstick is required to make the card's initials appear on your forearm.

THE PERFORMANCE

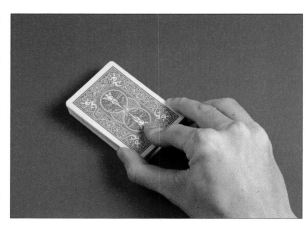

❶ You'll begin with a clever force called the Criss-Cross Force. Set the deck on the table facedown. *"Please, cut the cards at any point,"* you say, inviting the participant to cut the deck. He does so, setting the top portion of the deck to the right (your left) of the bottom.

❷ Pick up the bottom portion with your right hand as you say, *"Let's mark the place you cut to."*

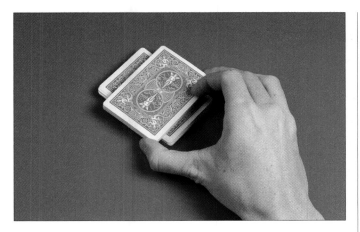

❸ Place the packet of cards in your right hand sideways on top of the tabled packet, to form a small cross. Now you need to implement some time direction; this simply means occupying the audience long enough for everyone to forget about the exact formation of the cards.

❹ Say, *"You could have cut the pack anywhere, but you cut it at a particular spot, on a particular card. In a moment, I'm going to ask you to focus on that card. To reinforce the image of the card, I'd like you to write the name of it on this piece of paper."* Hand the participant a pencil and paper.

Turn your head away and then lift the upper packet from the deck and aim the face toward the participant. You're actually showing him the bottom of the deck, but due to the cross formation, it appears you're showing him a card from the center, at exactly the point he cut.

❺ Ask your participant to remember this card and write it on the scrap paper provided.

Ask the participant to fold the paper to conceal the card's identity. Replace the packet on the table; you won't need the cards anymore. Say, *"Most magicians find chosen cards with their fingers. I'm not going to do that. Most mind readers find cards with their brains. I won't do that, either. I'm going to find your card with my muscles."* Roll up your sleeves and flex. This should get a laugh.

❻ *"You don't look impressed. Maybe the mood isn't right."* Offer to fix the mood, perhaps asking someone to dim the lights. Take the scrap of paper and light it at one end.

continued ☞

7 Drop it into the ashtray and allow it to burn completely. Wait about thirty seconds or until the ashes are cool (it doesn't take long). Please, be careful here. You'll need your fingers for several chapters following this one, so don't burn your hands now.

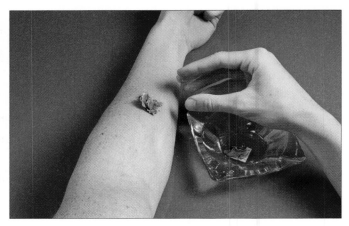

8 Pick up the flakes of ash and drop them on your forearm. Rub the ashes across your arm, allowing the Chapstick to do its thing: The ashes will stick to the invisible initials you've written on your arm.

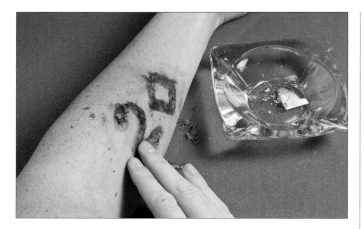

9 Within moments, the name of a card appears . . . and it's the Two of Diamonds.

MASTER CLASS

"Ashes on the Arm" perfectly illustrates the difference between card tricks and magic with cards. Nobody remembers this as a card trick; people remember that a card they thought of appeared on your arm. Although the presentation I've included is light, this can also be played as a dark, occult mystery. However you play it, this isn't card magic—it's magic . . . with cards.

CREDIT: The "Ashes on the Arm" idea was first published by Prevost in 1584. The Criss-Cross Force was invented by Max Holden in 1925.

Mixed-up Kings

MATERIALS:
A deck of cards.

SETUP: Begin with the four Kings reversed (faceup) on the bottom of the deck.

DIFFICULTY: ✝✝✝✝✝

THE EFFECT You cleanly divide the deck into two halves and turn one half faceup. You shuffle the two halves together, disorienting the deck. **With a snap, the cards all turn facedown except for four cards . . . the four Kings.**

THE SECRET The four Kings are already reversed on the bottom. The rest is just sleight of hand.

THE PERFORMANCE

❶ You start with a story: *"The other day a guy challenged me to find four Kings from a shuffled deck. We bet a drink on it. Since finding four Kings is one of my specialties, I agreed.*

"But before I had a chance to shuffle the cards, the man grabbed the deck out of my hands and did the unthinkable. He shuffled faceup cards into facedown cards, like this." So saying, hold the deck in your left hand in preparation for dealing, making sure to conceal the King's position at the bottom.

❷ Cut about half the cards, lifting them by the ends with your right hand.

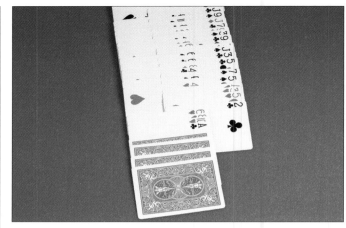

❸ Turn over both packets simultaneously. Turn the left hand palm down as you rotate and turn the right hand palm up. Move both packets to the table. If you move both hands toward the tabletop *as* you turn them over, nobody will notice that there were reversed cards on the bottom of the left hand's packet.

❹ The true condition of the cards is as follows: The cards in the left-hand packet are entirely faceup except for the top four, which are the facedown Kings. The right-hand packet is faceup. Perform a tabled riffle shuffle with the two packets.

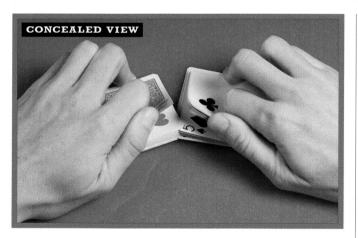

CONCEALED VIEW

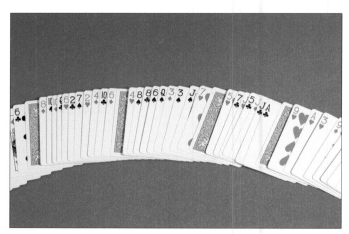

❺ The audience believes you're shuffling facedown cards into faceup cards. Actually, you're mixing only the facedown Kings into an otherwise faceup deck. *"How could I find the Kings now?"* you ask. *"This drunk guy stole my deck and shuffled faceup cards into facedown cards. This was quite a challenge."* Perform a few more shuffles and cuts to apparently show the mixed condition of cards. Actually, the facedown Kings contrasted with the faceup deck give the illusion that the entire pack is mixed faceup and facedown.

❻ *"But I had been practicing,"* you continue. Turn the deck faceup and spread it on the table from left to right. *"So I used sleight of hand to straighten every card in the deck!"* Wait for a participant to notice four facedown cards remaining in the spread.

7 "'*Don't forget,*' *I told him,* '*the challenge was to find the four Kings. So I did!*'" Remove the four facedown cards and reveal them to be the Kings.

MASTER CLASS

One reason some people hate magic is that they don't like being challenged or put on the spot. I don't blame them. "*Which shell has the pea? Wrong! Guess again? Wrong!*" It reminds me of being called on in class when my hand wasn't raised.

One way to take the sting out of a magic effect is to change the roles. In "Mixed-up Kings" *you're* the one put on the spot; the drunk guy challenged *you*. Framing an effect within a story eliminates the challenge to the audience without diminishing the impact.

CREDIT: Dai Vernon helped pioneer the plot described above; he called it "Triumph." He also came up with the storyline I've adapted for the script. The secret turnover move was invented by Japanese magician Tenkai Ishida.

DAI VERNON: THE MAN WHO FOOLED HOUDINI

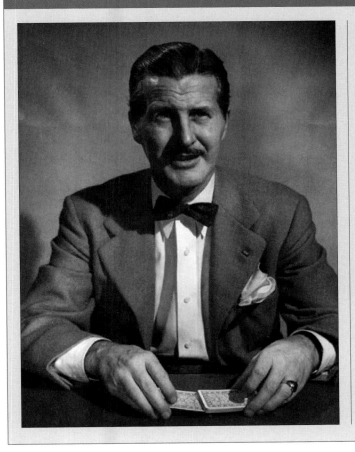

Dai Vernon was the twentieth century's most influential close-up magician. Born in Canada in 1894, Vernon adapted cheating techniques to magic and updated antiquated sleights. His style was completely fresh, and he turned the magic world on its head. He was a virtuoso.

Although Vernon passed away in 1992, his legacy lives on through his many students and writings. One of his students told me that Vernon used to remind magicians, "Confusion isn't magic." This is sage advice, particularly since magic effects can so easily become confusing. We must always remember that the *effect* must be clear in the audience's mind.

A young Dai Vernon once found an audience with Houdini. The famous Houdini billed himself as the "King of Cards," and bragged that if he saw any trick three times he would figure it out. Vernon showed him the same card trick eight times. Houdini was stumped. Vernon became known thereafter as "The Man Who Fooled Houdini."

Five Cards by Touch

MATERIALS:

Two identical decks of cards and the box for one.

SETUP: Retrieve the two identical decks of cards. Shuffle one deck and remove 26 cards. Remove the same 26 cards from the other deck and order the two sets of cards to match. Place one stacked group on top of the other so the top card and the 27th card down are the same, the second card and the 28th card down are the same, and so on. Place this special pack into the card box.

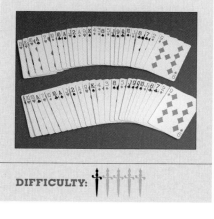

DIFFICULTY: †††††

THE EFFECT A deck of cards is displayed and cut by five participants. These people are invited to remember a different card, and each one is asked to bury it back into the pack. You place the pack in your pocket and ask each participant to call out his or her card. **"Five of Clubs," the first participant says. No sooner does she name the card than you reach into your pocket and pluck it from the deck. And you repeat this effect four more times!**

THE SECRET The deck is stacked and prepared.

THE PERFORMANCE

"*Have you heard the term 'muscle memory'?*" you start. *The concept is that our muscles—fingers, face, and toes—have a memory that works independently of our conscious thought. Breathing is a good example. We don't contemplate every breath we take; we just breathe. And when we're driving a car, we're not consciously thinking about the brake pedal or the steering wheel; we just drive. I've been working on the muscle memory in my fingers. Let's try an experiment.*"

❶ Remove your special pack and turn it faceup. Spread the deck between your hands. You can even allow the participants a cursory glance at the entire spread; nobody will notice that there are duplicates in play.

Square the deck and place it facedown on the table. Ask a participant to cut the deck and complete her cut (replace the lower portion on top of the upper portion). Invite several other audience members to cut and complete, too.

2 After the deck has been cut to everyone's satisfaction, distribute the top five cards facedown to five participants, in a left-to-right row.

CONCEALED VIEW

3 Turn your back and invite each person to look at his or her card. With your back to the audience, you take care of the dirty work. Quickly count 21 cards off the top of the pack and transfer them to the bottom. Since there are five participants remembering cards, you have about thirty seconds to complete your secret transfer. During this time you might occasionally speak to the participants, *"Remember your cards, please,"* or *"Don't let me see your cards."*

4 Due to the unique arrangement of the pack, duplicates of the five selections now reside at the top five positions. It works automatically, so you don't have to check this each time.

Turn to face your participant again and spread the deck. Invite each person to slide his or her card back into the pack. Take care that all the cards are placed *beneath* the top five cards in the deck.

5 *"Now I memorize the cards,"* you say. Hold the deck near your face and riffle the edges rapidly, staring into the makeshift flipbook of numbers and suits. Pretend to memorize the order of the deck in *"less than one second."*

continued 👉

6 Place the deck in a shirt or pants pocket and address the leftmost participant. *"Now for the muscle memory. I'd like you to name your card. The second you name it, I'll reach into my pocket. I'll retrieve your card using only muscle memory."* It's likely that the participant won't believe this; but now you prove yourself.

7 Whatever card she names, reach into your pocket and remove the top card as fast as you can . . . it will be the first selection. Go down the line from left to right, asking each participant to name his or her card. Each time, you remove the selection with superhuman speed and accuracy.

MASTER CLASS

Five participants. Five chosen cards. Five lightning-fast locations. This effect has all the components of good magic: audience involvement, an interesting presentation, and an astounding effect.

Remember that card effects aren't always limited to close-up situations. You can use "Five Cards by Touch" for large audiences—up to fifty people.

CREDIT: Jim Steinmeyer created this card effect and first published it in "The Real Magic Souvenir Program."

JIM STEINMEYER

Jim Steinmeyer is magic's Renaissance man, and he wears many (top) hats: lecturer, author, and effect creator. He has designed illusions for Doug Henning, David Copperfield, Siegfried and Roy, and countless other magicians around the globe. When Copperfield made the Statue of Liberty disappear in 1983, the effect was one of Jim's creations.

But Jim doesn't only think big; he has created many diabolical close-up miracles, including "Five Cards by Touch." Jim is also one of magic's most knowledgeable historians, and here he draws inspiration from magic's rich heritage—namely an effect by nineteenth-century conjurer Alexander Herrmann.

The Rising Card

MATERIALS:

A deck of cards with the box, and a craft knife.

SETUP: Cut a hole along the length of the logo-side of a card box. The hole should be less than an inch wide and about.

Place the cards inside the box and you're ready to begin.

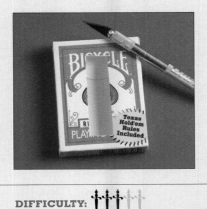

DIFFICULTY: ✝✝✝✝✝

THE EFFECT Your participant selects a card and you shuffle the card back into the deck. You replace the deck in the case and place Gunther, your invisible trained flea, inside. "Now tell Gunther the name of your card," you say to the participant. **A moment after she names her card, the card box opens of its own volition and her selection rises slowly from the container.**

THE SECRET After forcing the card you push it upward with your first finger, through a secret cutout on the back of the box.

THE PERFORMANCE

" **I** 've got fleas," you announce, then pause. This is one of my favorite effects to break the ice. "*Don't worry, they're trained fleas. They don't bite; they do magic!*"

Remove the cards from their case, taking care to keep the cut side of the box facing the floor and out of sight. Table the box and shuffle the pack. Spread the cards from hand to hand toward your participant and ask her to remove and remember one.

❶ Take nine cards into your right hand. The easiest way to do this is to thumb over groups of three, taking them into a right-hand spread.

❷ Ask the participant to replace her card on top of the cards in your left hand. Then place the spread in your right hand on top of her card in your left hand and square the deck. The participant's selection looks lost in the deck, but you know its precise location: tenth from the top.

❸ Perform an overhand shuffle to transfer the top nine cards to the bottom, as follows: Hold the cards in the left hand, by the ends. With your right thumb, peel four cards, one by one, into your right hand. Throw the cards from your left hand on top of the right hand's four cards. Repeat the process with three cards, and then with two cards. The participant's card will now be on top. But only you'll know that!

Place the cards faceup inside the card box, keeping the cutout on the box's underside hidden (so the back of the deck is in contact with the cutout).

❹ *"And now I need my flea magician, Gunther."* Hold your empty left hand palm up. *"Say hello to Gunther,"* you promise. When the participant does this, respond, *"That's actually not Gunther. That's his wife, Wilma. Gunther's over here now."* Reach into your participant's hair to search for your lost flea. *"Here he is!"* you announce, pinching your fingers together to mime pulling the flea from your participant's scalp. Look at your fingers and shake your head. *"Wait—never mind. I've never seen this flea before."* Place the "flea" back in your participant's hair and eventually find Gunther. Place him inside the card box and tuck in the flap.

CONCEALED VIEW

CONCEALED VIEW

❺ Hold the box vertically at the sides, between your right fingers and thumb. Position your first finger behind the box; curl your first finger slightly so the pad rests alongside the secret cutout.

❻ *"Tell Gunther your card."* When the participant responds, slowly and gently push upward on the card that is resting against the hole. The card will push the box's flap open; from the participant's perspective, this looks eerie.

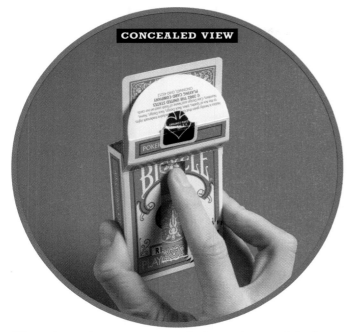

CONCEALED VIEW

7 But it gets better. As you push the card upward farther, it apparently rises from the box.

8 Remove the card with your left hand and show both sides to your participant and audience. Confirm that it is indeed the card your participant selected. Thank Gunther, then casually reinsert the card into the center of the pack.

MASTER CLASS

Michelangelo once said, "Details make perfection and perfection is no detail." Magic legend Dai Vernon expounded upon this notion and its application to good magic. "The Rising Card" is an excellent example.

At the end, I instruct you to replace the selected card back into the cased deck, in the center. Why? What difference does that make? The effect is over. You might think nobody is paying attention.

But the selected card rises from the top of the pack, and you want to give the impression it rose from somewhere in the middle. By removing the card and then casually replacing it in the center of the deck, you leave the audience with a specific impression: The card levitated from the *center* of the pack.

CREDIT: "The Rising Card" is a classic of magic dating back to the 16th century; the opening card case is an original touch I discovered as a kid.

Old Dog, New Trick: The Svengali Deck

The Bullet Card

MATERIALS:
A match, a pin, and a Svengali Deck with its case.

SETUP: A Svengali Deck is *the* trick deck of choice. As these cards are hocked at fairgrounds, boardwalks, and carnivals, you've probably got three packs in your desk drawer. If not, online and retail magic stores stock them.

In addition to having a Svengali Deck on hand, prepare a bullet hole in one of the duplicate cards: Take one card and blacken just the back with a lit match.

Poke a small hole in the center of the card with a pin. Place this card on the face of your deck and put the deck into its box.

Just before you're ready to perform, reach into the box and remove all the cards except the prepared "bullet" card, which you secretly leave inside the box.

DIFFICULTY:

THE EFFECT **A professional routine for the world's most popular trick deck.** You cut the Six of Spades into the center of the deck and it appears on top; this is repeated several times. Then, the entire deck changes into the Six of Spades. Finally, you form your fist into a gun and "shoot" toward the deck. One card is discovered with a real bullet hole: the Six of Spades.

THE SECRET A Svengali Deck is a trick deck composed of 26 normal cards and 26 duplicates (for example, it might have 26 Fours of Spades). The duplicates are shaved slightly on their ends, negligibly shorter than 26 normal cards. The duplicates are alternated with the other cards (long, short, long, short, and so on).

With this special pack of cards, it's an easy matter to show all the cards and have each one appear to be different. By spreading the cards in a different way, you can ensure that all the cards appear the same.

Begin by forcing whatever card your Svengali Deck forces. Mine uses the Six of Spades. There are many ways to force the card, but I like this one because in addition to the force, it subtly shows all the other cards as different.

PERFORMANCE

❶ Hold the deck by the ends in your right hand. Position your thumb above and fingers beneath, with the face card of the deck angled toward your audience.

❷ Curl your right first finger behind (on top of the deck).

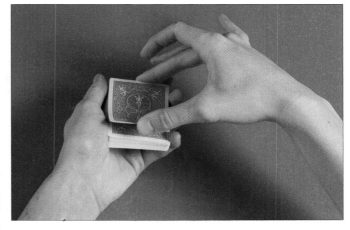

3 Apply light pressure with your curled right first finger and allow the cards to flick off your right thumb and riffle into your left hand. As the cards fall, invite a participant to insert his finger into the deck at any point. Make a joke: *"Choose any finger and insert it into the pack."* Look at his hands. *"Nice choice. People usually give me a different finger."*

Owing to the "Long/Short" principle of the deck, no matter where he inserts his finger, the card *beneath* it will be the Six of Spades. Separate the pack wherever the participant places his finger. Invite him to look at the card pinned underneath and remember it. Ask him to return the card to the same position. Reassemble the deck.

4 Invite the participant to cut the deck, and gesture so he cuts the deck holding it at the ends. Have him complete the cut. Whether he cuts deep or shallow, the Svengali Deck always ensures that his card (or a duplicate) will end up on top. Before you reveal the selected card on top, you'll prove it is *not* on top (even though it is). The Svengali Deck makes this easy. Just reach down and try to lift the top card from the deck, but grasp the card only by the ends.

5 Because the top card is shaved slightly, you'll automatically grip the second card from top. Lift both cards, as one, and show the participant that his card isn't on top.

Invite him to cut the cards again and complete the cut. Once again, show him that an indifferent card is on top. *"I want you to cut one more time. But concentrate when you cut this time. Really concentrate on your card."*

6 Invite him to cut and complete once more. This time grasp the top card from the sides and reveal that the participant has cut his card to the top.

continued ☞

7 Place the Six of Spades back on top and invite your participant to cut it back into the middle. Snap your fingers, peel off the top card and turn it over. *"It's ba-ack!"* Place the card on top and cut the deck yourself.

Pick up the deck and apparently take the top card in your right hand. But as before, take two cards by lifting at the ends. Show the indifferent card to the audience and drop both cards (as one) facedown on top of the deck. Immediately thumb over the top card a bit. Snap your right fingers and regrip the top card by the sides. Display it to the audience: It has changed into the Six of Spades!

8 Cut this Six back into the middle of the deck and hand the deck to your participant. Invite him to cut and complete a few times (just make sure he cuts from the ends). Then ask him to deal cards onto the table, one by one, stopping anytime he likes. As he deals, secretly count the cards as he deals them. If he stops on an odd card, instruct him to keep it facedown in his hand. If he stops on an even card, ask him to deal it to the table and take the *next* card into his right hand. (Either way, you're forcing the Six of Spades.)

9 Before letting him look at the card he stopped on, point out that had the participant dealt one card more or less, he would have stopped on a different card. As you explain this, turn over the top card of the tabled pile and the top card of the deck to show that they are truly different. After a dramatic buildup, invite your participant to turn over the card in his hand—the Six of Spades has returned!

10 Reassemble the deck by placing the participant's Six of Spades on top of the tabled pile and then placing the tabled pile on top of the cards in her hand. All the cards still alternate. Snap your fingers and announce that the Six of Spades has disappeared. Cascade the cards as you did in step 3, faces toward the audience. You'll again show the audience that all the cards are different (no Six of Spades will be visible). Tell the participant, *"All the cards are here except one . . . your Six of Spades."*

⓫ Place the deck faceup on the table and reach into the card box. Withdraw the scorch-marked Six of Spades, taking care to remove it with the face toward the audience. Place this card faceup on top of the deck.

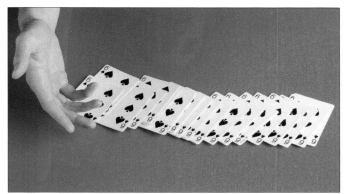

⓬ Offer to change the entire deck into his selected card. To effect this change, lift the faceup pack by the ends and hold it a couple inches above the table. Cascade the cards in a left to right spread to show that every card has changed into the Six of Spades. Actually, you'll notice the cascading cards fall in pairs, with the indifferent cards conveniently concealed behind the Sixes of Spades.

⓭ Pick up the cards, turn them facedown, and give them one complete cut. *"You've seen your card come to the top of the deck, you've seen a card change into your card, you've dealt to your card, you've cut to your card, you've seen the entire deck changed into your card. The only thing this trick is missing is an element of danger."* Form your hand into a fist and "shoot" his card through the deck.

⓮ Spread the deck facedown on the table to reveal one card, burned by your fatal shot . . . the Six of Spades.

continued ☞

MASTER CLASS

When using a trick deck, always remember that only you know it's tricked! The squeaky old line, *"I have here an ordinary pack of playing cards . . ."* almost always works counterintuitively. As soon as it's mentioned, participants start to wonder. *"But is it normal? He didn't show us all the cards. He didn't let me touch the deck."* Few people will question a deck's legitimacy *unless* you bring it up—so just don't broach the subject!

The Svengali Deck is an excellent stand-alone piece, but it has other applications, too:

A Forcing Deck

By now you know what a card force is: you apparently offer someone a free selection of any card, but actually force her to take a predetermined card. There are several ways of forcing a card with a normal deck (page 74), but the card force explained here (allowing a participant to insert her finger into the cascading deck) is a great one. You can force a card with this deck and later reveal that card with a written prediction: *"I knew you would choose the Six of Spades."*

Stabbed

❶ Force the Six of Spades (or whatever force card your Svengali Deck is comprised of) on a participant. Then borrow a table knife and ask him to insert the knife into the side of the deck at any point. Separate the deck at this juncture and casually turn the upper packet over. If the card on the face is the Six of Spades, you've got a miracle (and you can show that the card above and below the Six are different).

❷ If the card on the face is *not* a Six of Spades, you know a Six of Spades is below the blade. Turn over this card to show the participant has "stabbed" his own card.

CREDIT: Burling Hull created the Svengali Deck in 1909. We have Alan Alan to thank for the bullet card conceit.

MARKING YOUR GAFFED DECKS

Go get a pen right now. Seriously. I'm going to save you from an otherwise inevitable and embarrassing pitfall that happens to anyone who uses trick decks: using the wrong deck.

There are thousands of trick decks on the market today, and each one serves different purposes. Once you start buying them, they're hard to tell apart. At least once in his life, every magician confuses his Svengali for a normal pack. And it takes a *real* magician to fix that problem! Here's how to prevent it:

Magicians mark their stacked and trick decks on the boxes. The marks should be small and indistinguishable unless you know what to look for. And, the markings should always be in the same spot, so you can look at any box and immediately know what's going on inside it.

Every pack of cards has a sticker to seal it closed. Most of these stickers have a small white margin, ideal for a few letters. I mark my Svengali Deck by writing "SVE" in this margin. I mark my Invisible Deck "INV."

It's a minor inconvenience now, but it will save you from a magician's worst nightmare—getting caught.

Wagers of Sin

MATERIALS:
A pack of cards, a copy of the letter template (included), an envelope, and a pen.

SETUP: This sinister routine by Max Maven turns a simple card force into a routine that is at once eerie and hilarious.

The first step is to prepare the prediction. Simply copy down the poem (or simply to copy the template on page 270), written by Max Maven:

> *And so our little game is done;*
> *The cards are played,*
> *   the prize is won.*
> *My Four of Spades*
> *   belongs to thee . . .*
> *In turn, thy soul belongs to me.*

These make excellent souvenirs for participants so you may want to reproduce them in quantity using a copy machine.

Store a pen in your right front pants pocket.

DIFFICULTY: ⚔⚔⚔

THE EFFECT You ask a participant to sign and date a folded prediction—but not to peek at the message. You then invite her to remove eight cards from a shuffled pack. She deals seven cards back to you and keeps one for herself: the Four of Spades. **Not only does prediction foretell her chosen card, but it is revealed to be a signed contract with the devil for her soul!**

THE SECRET The Four of Spades is forced.

THE PERFORMANCE

❶ Begin with the prediction face up on your work surface, with the written prediction uppermost. Fold the bottom two-thirds up and crease sharply.

❷ Now fold one-third back toward yourself and crease sharply again. You've created an accordion fold so the prediction is entirely concealed within the folds. When the participant initials the exposed portion, she will unknowingly sign away her soul.

❸ Remove the Four of Spades from your deck and conceal it facedown beneath the prediction. Place the prediction and the card hidden beneath it into an envelope.

Hand the pack of cards to a participant and ask her to shuffle them thoroughly. "*How you shuffle,*" you say, "*will determine the outcome of the effect.*" Present the envelope and explain that you have made a prediction inside. With your right fingers and thumb remove the prediction (along with the Four of Spades concealed on the underside). Table the empty envelope.

❹ Retrieve the cards from your participant and hold them in your left hand, ready to deal. Place the prediction on top of the deck and hold it in position with your left thumb. Secretly slide the hidden Four of Spades onto the top of the deck. With your newly freed right hand, retrieve the pen from your pocket as you say, "*To preclude switching predictions after you've chosen a card, I'd like you to sign and date the prediction.*"

❺ Hand the participant the pen and the prediction. Ask her to sign and date it on the blank visible section and reiterate that she is not to peek just yet. You have secretly loaded the Four of Spades on top of the deck under the guise of introducing your prediction.

Say, "*I'll show you a piece that was shown to me by a stranger I met on a darkly lit road. He didn't tell me his name, but challenged me to a game of cards. I didn't know it at the time, but this man was the devil!*"

Continue, "*He asked me to remove eight cards from a shuffled deck. You mixed the pack already, so we'll use the eight cards you randomly shuffled to the top.*" Count eight cards facedown into a pile. This transfers the Four of Spades to the bottom of the packet.

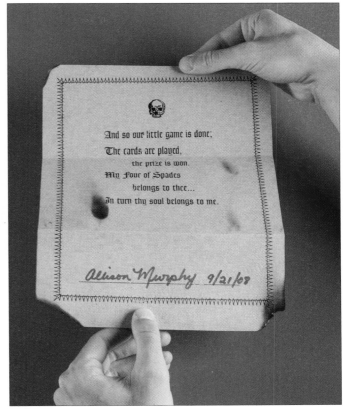

6 Invite the participant to pick up the packet. *"Do you know which card is referred to as the Devil's card?"* Most participants won't know. *"It's the Four of Spades. It's referred to as the Devil's bedpost because those who are dealt this card 'sleep' with the devil. In the game we're about to play, this is the card you want to avoid."*

Say, *"Deal one card to me,"* pointing to a spot on the table in front of you, *"and keep one for yourself by placing it on the bottom of your packet."* As she places the new top card on the bottom of the packet, instruct her to continue this way, dealing a card on the table to you and the next one to the bottom of the packet. She should continue distributing cards in this fashion, one down and one under, until only one card remains in her hand. As she deals, say, *"It doesn't seem fair that the opponent gets seven cards and you get only one."*

7 Invite the participant to turn over her remaining card . . . the Devil's bedpost card! Now retrieve the prediction and open it toward yourself. Read it aloud:

And so our little game is done;
The cards are played,
    the prize is won.
My Four of Spades
    belongs to thee . . .
In turn, thy soul belongs to me.

Slowly turn the prediction toward your participant. She will quickly realize it's a signed contract . . . for her soul.

MASTER CLASS

This effect is classified as bizarre magick. Bizarre magicians use their effects as a vehicle to illustrate dark parables. "Wagers of Sin" is a game of cards against the devil, with the ultimate swindle: the participant's soul. You begin by telling a story about playing cards against the devil. But, as the story unfolds, it becomes evident that *you* are the devil because the participant is playing cards against you. The deception comes full circle when the participant realizes she accidentally signed the ultimate I.O.U.

CREDIT: Max Maven first published "Wagers of Sin" in *The New Invocation* (issue 35, October 1986, pp. 416–419), a magazine dedicated specifically to "bizarre magick." "Wagers of Sin" is based on Maven's "Preoction" (see the October, 1982 issue of *Linking Ring*).

MAX MAVEN

Max Maven is one of the world's leading mentalists and magical thinkers. He has hosted and been featured on hundreds of television shows around the world. Orson Welles called him "the most original mind in magic."

Maven is also the most prolific magician in history. Max has created and published over 1,700 effects to date. He also pioneered interactive magic, where the magician performs magic on television for the home viewer or reads your mind over the phone. If interactive magic piques your interest, check out pages 241 through 258 where I devote an entire chapter to just this brand of mystery.

CHAPTER FIVE

KID CONJURING

MAGIC FOR KIDS, AND MAGIC BY KIDS

Think, for a moment, about what makes magic special. A coin disappears, and for a split second, we're children again. It isn't a magician's cummerbund or top hat that captivates people: it is the moment of true astonishment. Most moments of true astonishment are brief intervals right after an effect ends and before our rational adult minds apply logic. In the split second between these processes: a moment of childlike wonder.

And we spend our entire lives trying to get back to this state, or at least get glimpses of it. That's why we see movies and read stories—and that's why we watch magic. Whether you have kids or you are one, the magic in this chapter is designed to involve and inspire young people. These effects amaze young people, and so do the presentations attached to them.

I selected the magic for this chapter with great care because I actually started my career as a children's entertainer. I was the busiest twelve-year-old magician in the Greater Cleveland area—it even said so on my card! (To be honest, I was also the *only*

twelve-year-old magician in the area, but modesty and magic don't mix.) I learned quickly what works for kids and what doesn't. "Cutting Yourself in Two" is a great effect to teach a young aspiring magician, and it can be easily adapted to bisect a child volunteer. This wonderful illusion comes from one of our industry's leading thinkers, Jim Steinmeyer. He has designed illusions for today's most famous magicians, and he has agreed to share "Cutting Yourself in Two" with us in *Magic*. In this chapter, you'll also learn how to produce an endless supply of gum balls from your mouth and how to make a pet—rather, a picture of your pet—disappear.

There's a misconception that kids are easier to fool than adults. My experience shows quite the opposite. From a child's perspective, the world is a place filled with magic. You flick a switch and light fills the room. You turn a knob and water flows from a faucet. You press a button and change Mom's boring news into a cartoon. Every part of a child's life is magic, and by comparison, the effects performed by professional magicians can seem unremarkable. So, another

important lesson I learned as a twelve-year-old is that *how* an effect is presented is as important as the effect itself.

The secret to entertaining children is interaction. Kids love to be involved—so let them handle the props. Pull the coin from *his* ear; let *her* pull the handkerchiefs from the tube. Think about it: televisions, electricity, and faucets are all good tricks if you're a little kid. But they can't provide real interaction; a magician can. *You* can.

THE WARM-UP

How to Produce an Object

Whether it's a coin or a gum ball, plucking a real object from the air impresses kids—and former kids. But plucking an object from behind a kid's ear is even better because there's a participatory element. The key to producing palmed objects is in the rhythm and choreography of your hand.

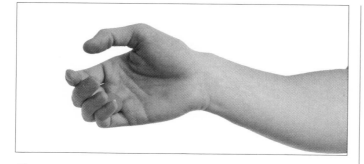

❶ Suppose you have a gum ball concealed in your hand—it should be nestled where your third and fourth right fingers meet your palm.

❷ Producing the object is technically simple: Just roll the gum ball into view with your right thumb. But this is an oversimplification.

❸ With your supposedly empty right hand, move your whole arm forward. Before your hand reaches its stopping point, focus your eyes intently at the area you will produce the object from. It's as if you see it before the participants do, and that helps them experience the magic.

4 When you reach the spot you want to pluck the gum ball from—an elbow, a child's ear—stop moving your arm. Roll the ball into view with your thumb and fingers by simulating the finger movements you would use to pluck a small fruit from a tree. Twist your wrist, turning your palm in and then up, and jerk your arm toward you sharply. These actions help blur the source of the object.

5 Present the gum ball between your right thumb and first or second finger.

Cutting a Child in Two

MATERIALS:
Two lengths of satin ribbon in different colors.

SETUP: Let's assume the ribbons you use are blue and yellow. Cut each ribbon to a length of about three feet. Tie a large knot at each end of the yellow ribbon.

DIFFICULTY: 🗡🗡🗡🗡🗡

THE EFFECT You present two lengths of ribbon, tied together. Wrap them around a child's body and give a sharp tug. **The knotted ribbons pass through the child's midsection, visibly cutting him in half.**

THE SECRET The specially knotted ribbons slide *around* the body, not through it.

THE PERFORMANCE

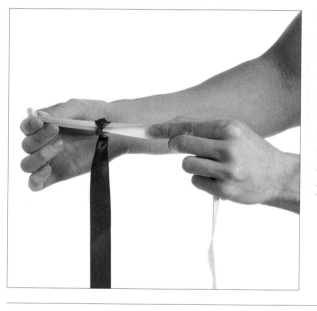

❶ Wrap one end of the blue ribbon around the yellow ribbon and tie this blue end in a loop. This loop must be loose enough to slide along the length of the yellow ribbon, but small enough to "catch" on the yellow knots at each end.

❷ Tie a knot at the other end of the blue ribbon and you're set to cut someone in half.

Display what appears to be two ribbons knotted together. Pull gently to prove they are tightly attached to each other. Actually, the ends aren't tied together at all—but the blue ribbon's sliding loop gives the perfect illusion of a double knot.

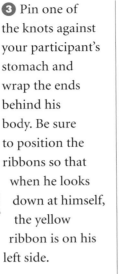

❸ Pin one of the knots against your participant's stomach and wrap the ends behind his body. Be sure to position the ribbons so that when he looks down at himself, the yellow ribbon is on his left side.

❹ Behind his back, openly switch the ends in each hand and come forward again. You should be holding the yellow end in your right hand and the blue end in your left hand. You can also turn your participant around and display the ribbons crossing against his back.

❻ At the same time, move both hands forward and apart. Done quickly, it gives the perfect illusion of pulling the ribbon *through* his midsection.

❺ Now you'll apparently pull the ribbons through your participant's body. As you pretend to pull the ends in each hand forward, move your right hand briefly in front of the knot against your participant's stomach. Secretly release the yellow end in your right hand and pull on the yellow knot against his body.

MASTER CLASS

Our words paint pictures even more vivid than our magic. What's the magic here? A small length of ribbon penetrates the body. Interesting, perhaps, but underwhelming. But cutting yourself in half? Now that's good.

Fortunately, what you say influences what your participants see. You announce that you'll cut your participant in half. Instantly the effect is more impressive, even if the magic is the same. Now your audience has a point of reference—a story—to hold onto.

And your story doesn't have to be the one outlined above. What if you announced that you would become a ghost for a moment, like a translucent apparition without form? The ribbon would seem to melt through your body. What if you claimed the ribbons were razor-sharp? Each of these presentations would change the *effect* without altering the *magic*.

Sawing Yourself in Half: You can adapt this effect to perform it yourself. Simply prepare the ribbon as described, but wrap it around your body.

CREDIT: **Legendary inventor Jim Steinmeyer created this ingenious effect. It was first published in "The Real Magic Souvenir Program."**

SAWING SEMANTICS

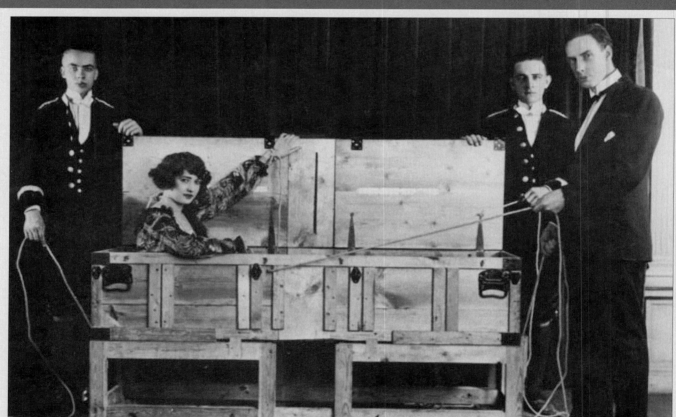

On a London stage in 1921, magician P. T. Selbit locked a woman inside a box, strapping her feet and head into place. Then he did the unthinkable: *he sawed through her.* Today illusion shows are filled with mutilations of beautiful showgirls. But in 1921, this was a provocative, controversial number. Selbit called it "Sawing through a Woman."

Selbit was an instant hit in England, and the news of his success traveled fast. American magician Horace Goldin heard about "Sawing through a Woman" and created his own version. He called it "Sawing a Lady in Half"

Selbit came to the United States in September 1921, but by that time bisecting women was old news. He returned to England and continued to create whimsical illusions until his death in 1938.

Gum Balls from the Mouth

MATERIALS:
Two gum balls of the same color.

SETUP: None.

DIFFICULTY:

THE EFFECT A classic grandfather trick that still wows today: **You produce an endless number of gum balls from your mouth.**

THE SECRET There are two simple moves involved. When performed concurrently, they give the illusion of an endless supply of gum balls.

THE PERFORMANCE

CONCEALED VIEW

CONCEALED VIEW

1 When nobody is looking, secretly place one gum ball in your mouth and keep an identical one "palmed" (see page 178) in your right hand.

2 When you're ready to start coughing up gum balls, maneuver the gum ball to the front of your mouth and pin it in view between your teeth and lips. (Welcome to the secret world of "sleight of mouth"!)

3 Keeping your palm turned toward your body (so the gum ball remains hidden in your hand), move your right hand to your mouth.

Cover your mouth with your hand for only a second, during which two actions take place simultaneously.

❹ First, retract your tongue slightly and allow the visible gum ball to fall back into your mouth. Seal your lips as this happens. Second, push the palmed gum ball into view in your right fingertips.

❺ Lower your right hand to waist height. Toss the gum ball you're holding into the air and catch it again; this attracts everyone's eyes to the gum ball. When the gum ball toss is done smoothly, nobody will detect the switch.

CONCEALED VIEW

❻ Pretend to put the gum ball in your right pocket. That is, openly "place" the ball into your right pants pocket, but instead of leaving it there, curl your fingers around it and palm it a second time.

7 With your right hand still inside your pocket, maneuver the gum ball concealed in your mouth back into view, pursed between your lips. Act puzzled here, as if you tried to speak and the gum ball appeared at the tip of your tongue.

8 Remove your right hand from your pocket, again concealing the gum ball behind your fingers. Pretend to remove the visible gum ball from your mouth again, secretly switching it with the palmed gum ball in your right hand.

9 This two-move sequence can and should be repeated several times with mounting levels of surprise. The effect isn't impressive when you remove only five gum balls from your mouth; I had a fraternity brother who really could do that.

10 But when you apparently remove, say, a dozen gum balls . . . well, that made Grandpa my hero.

MASTER CLASS

You'll notice that no script is offered. That's because your mouth is full throughout this effect.

But no script is not the same thing as no presentation. David Blaine launched his career performing magic without saying much at all. Here, you must rely on your inner monologue to guide you.

How would you feel if gum balls kept appearing inside your mouth? What would you do? Whatever your answer, *that* is your inner monologue. When I perform "Gum Balls from Mouth," I act surprised at first; wide eyes, raised eyebrows, good posture. As the gum balls keep appearing, I express frustration and perform the moves with more speed and aggression. This gives this static, repetitive sequence a dramatic arc that makes it deceptive and funny.

CREDIT: This effect is often attributed to Bellachini, who performed it in the latter half of the 19th century using eggs.

Old Dog, New Trick: Using a False Thumbtip

Poked

MATERIALS:
A magician's false thumbtip or finger (available in all magic or novelty shops.)

SETUP: Use a pair of scissors to trim the thumbtip so that it extends only to the first joint of your thumb. (A false fingertip will work even better, but these are harder to find.)

DIFFICULTY: †† †††

THE EFFECT You approach someone—preferably someone you've never met. You grab hold of his clothing and poke your finger right through his shirt. A moment later, the participant's shirt is restored. This is best suited for informal situations, as an icebreaker. **Don't underestimate this simple yet shocking effect of poking a hole in someone's shirt and restoring it.**

THE SECRET This clever illusion of penetration is possible only with a false thumb.

THE PERFORMANCE

❶ Begin with the thumbtip concealed in your left hand, curled inside your fingers. The thumbtip's opening should be facing upward (near your left first finger).

❷ Approach a participant and stare inquisitively at his shirt as if you've just noticed a stain. With both hands, pull his sleeve forward a few inches. (Do this slowly and without aggression, as your goal is to engage him in a magic effect, not a fistfight.)

❹ Just after you pull your right hand away, brush the outside of the shirt with your hand, as if wiping away the hole.

Now step back and enjoy your show. The shirt's owner will *swear* there's a hole in his shirt. He'll search the fabric for a few seconds, look up at you, search a few seconds more, look up at you again—all the while unable to reconcile what you did with what he sees. Now is a good time to explain that you're a magician!

❸ Move your right hand to the underside of the sleeve material. Poke your right first finger into the material and move your left hand to the outside of the material. Push your right finger through the shirt material into the thumbtip. The fabric will gather between your real fingertip and the inside of the thumbtip. Curl your finger upward, away from the shirt, and wriggle it quickly back and forth. This ensures the thumbtip is always a flesh-colored blur, and minimizes any discrepancy in its size and color, as compared with your real fingers. You'll create the perfect illusion having poked a hole through the fabric.

Pause just a beat in this position—enough to scare the shirt's owner. To repair the "damage," curl your right first finger downward and close your left fingers around the thumbtip. Retract your right first finger from the tip, allowing the thumbtip to be secretly carried away by your left fingers (as it was in step 1).

MASTER CLASS

I thought this was a weak use for a thumbtip until I saw Gregory Wilson astound dozens of strangers with it. It's performed more like a prank than a magic effect. When the fabric is restored, people are confused and *then* amazed. It's quite amusing to watch; it's even more amusing to perform.

MODERN MASTER

GREGORY WILSON

Gregory Wilson is one of magic's most skilled and entertaining close-up magicians. Before he moved to magic, he worked for years as a professional comedian—a talent he's since applied to his magic in what he calls a "Criminal Act." His whole presentation is based on the premise that he is a con man, and he takes the audience through a hilarious survey of some classic cons . . . with a magic twist.

The Vanishing Pet ON DVD

THE EFFECT Show a photograph of yourself with your dog, and then make the dog disappear from the picture.

THE SECRET There are two pictures involved, and a simple switch.

MATERIALS:

Somebody who can use a digital camera to take pictures of you, a printer, several printouts, a rubber band, scissors, and your favorite pet.

DIFFICULTY: †††††

SETUP: In this age of digital cameras and printers, the one-time preparation involved is no longer difficult. Get someone to take two pictures of you. In the first one, pose holding your favorite dog, cat, or iguana. Look happy here; after all, you're with your best friend. Have your coconspirator take a second photo almost identical to the first, but, without the animal. Shrug your shoulders and look confused (this expression comes naturally for most of us.) The background and lighting should be the same as in photo 1.

Print one copy of photo 1 (the one with "Sadie the dog") and about a dozen copies of photo 2.

Photo 1 (with dog)

Photo 2 (no dog)

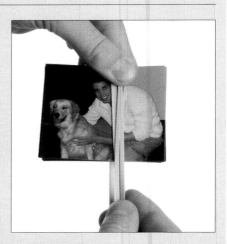

❶ Doctor the first photo by cutting off the portion of your body that remains the same (doesn't move) in photo 2; this won't hurt you or the photo one bit.

❷ Line up photo 1 (with Sadie the dog) on top of the multiple copies of photo 2 (no dog) to form a stack.

❸ Your head and body in the two uppermost photos should line up perfectly. Bind the stack of photos with a thick rubber band so it looks as though you have a bunch of photos of you with your dog. (The rubber band will mask the seam between the photos.) In truth, all the photos (except the top one) depict you *without* your dog.

THE PERFORMANCE

1 Present your stack of photos and offer to give one to a friend. Introduce them by saying, *"This is Sadie, my dog."* Hold the stack of photos toward your friend and allow him to enjoy your dog. It's important that he see the dog in the photo—otherwise its disappearance will mean nothing. You might point out a detail or two, like, *"Look at that tail,"* or *"Can you believe those ears?"*

2 *"Like most dogs, Sadie does tricks. Here's one of my favorites. 'Sadie, Roll over! '"* Turn the stack of photos facedown and wait for your friend to groan. Then ask your participant to hold his hand out, palm up.

3 *"Here's another one: Sit!"* Apparently remove the bottom photo (photo 1, with dog) and hand it to the participant. Here's where the secret switch comes in.

CONCEALED VIEW

❹ You actually remove the photo second from the bottom (that is, the photo without the dog). To do this, pull on the exposed end of the second photo—the area you trimmed away from the cover photo. Slide this picture from the rubber band and have the participant pull it completely (still facedown) from the packet.

"*Stay!*" you command, while you stare intently at the photo. (More groans from your friend.) Keeping your eye on the photo, you can casually pocket the stack of photos, eliminating any evidence of a switch.

❺ "*Here's my favorite trick. 'Sadie, disappear!'*" Invite your participant to turn the facedown picture right side up. When he does, he discovers that Sadie is gone (and that you are sporting the "duh" look). He can take the picture and the story with him, as a reminder of your vanishing pet.

MASTER CLASS

Nearly everybody loves animals, and people love to share animal stories. I keep a stack of photos on me so that whenever the subject is raised, I'm ready to perform this effect.

And this presentation isn't as awkward as you think. I was born in Canton, Ohio, and I had *several* neighbors who periodically gave out studio shots of themselves with their poodles. It was actually charming. Weird—but charming.

And you aren't limited to the pet theme provided. Here are some other ideas using the same gimmick:

The Vanishing Statue: Have someone take a digital picture of you in front of a famous statue or building, and then another picture without the landmark in the background. This works well with the Eiffel Tower, Brooklyn Bridge, and so on.

The Village Idiot: Is there someone annoying in your circle of friends? Take one picture with him and one picture without him, and then demonstrate your ability to make him completely disappear.

Making Money: Prepare by having someone take two pictures of your hands: one with your hands empty, and one with them full of cash. Now you can tell the story about *"the time I made money appear at my fingertips."* And show people the photo to prove it!

CREDIT: The gimmick you constructed is based on what magicians call the "Out to Lunch" principle. Clare Cummings and Bob Ellis gave it this name in the 1940s. The principle dates back to the nineteenth century, and in 1923 William Larsen Sr. published a version with paper.

Sleeves and Sneezes

THE EFFECT This is a time-tested children's classic, revamped. If you are young or teaching magic to someone young, this is a great effect to work on—the simple yet seemingly impossible production of tissues or confetti and silly novelties. **You will produce a seemingly endless number of tissues.**

SECRET You conceal a tube within a tube, creating a secret compartment for all the items you'll continue to produce throughout the performance.

MATERIALS:

A bunch of tissues and a large piece of cardboard.

DIFFICULTY:

SETUP: First you'll construct the tube—which you'll call your "sleeve." Cut two approximately 20-inch-square pieces of cardboard. You can vary the size depending on both the size of your venue and the size of your production items, but this is a good starting point.

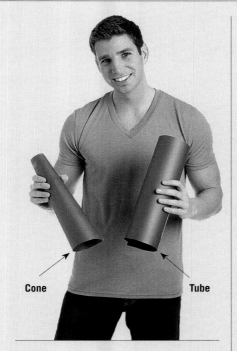

Cone   Tube

① Roll one cardboard square into a tube and secure it in place with a strip of tape along the seam.

Roll the second square into a thinner tube and insert this smaller tube into the larger one. Reshape the inner tube into a gently tapered cone.

② One end of the inner tube should rest against the outer tube. The other end of the inner tube should be a bit smaller, leaving a couple of inches of empty space between the inner and outer tubes.

③ Fill the space with whatever you want to produce. Tissues, handkerchiefs, confetti, small toys, squeakers, party favors, candy, or a mixture of all these. Pack the items tightly into the tube and fill all the available space.

PERFORMANCE: This effect is best performed to music because, after all, how much can you say about silks and confetti?

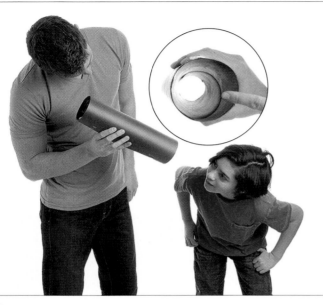

❶ Before producing the items, display the tube. Insert your hand into it and call it your "sleeve." You can tell your participants about how magicians use their sleeves, and here you'll show them how.

Point the "wide end" toward your participants and allow them to look through it, at you. The illusion is deceptive; the participants see into one end of the tube and out of the other. It appears empty. But due to their limited perspective, they will be unable to tell that there's a hidden chamber.

❷ Aim the wide end of the tube toward the floor (orienting the secret chamber at the top) and begin retrieving your production items. Pull out a few silks and toss a few pieces of candy to your audience, then show the tube empty again.

❸ Retrieve a few more tissues, and continue in this fashion until you have produced all your items.

MASTER CLASS

I volunteer at a women's shelter in my hometown, where I teach magic to children who come from abusive households. Magic is a potent confidence builder, and this is always part of the curriculum. I show the kids how to construct the sleeve, and then how to perform the effect. This is an excellent "workshop" item for classrooms, and it's easy enough that everyone present can perform it.

CREDIT: English magician Jules Danby invented the "Silver Tube Illusion" in 1919.

WORKING MIRACLES

MAGIC AND MISCHIEF IN THE OFFICE

This is a collection of presentations designed to amaze and inspire businesspeople.

Wouldn't you like to "see" an employee's thoughts? Bend metal with your mind? How about predicting the stock market? Until now these desires were the stuff of dreams and movies. But effects like "Groupthink," "Telekineticlip," and "Psychic Stocks" will make these dreams come true, if only in the minds of your coworkers.

What separates *your* corporate presentations from everyone else's? Magic! When you deliver your quarterly reports, you include humor, audience interaction, and amazing ways of communicating information. Look no further than "Mental Money" to make a lasting impression.

This chapter explores magical ways to make a statement for your audience. You'll learn mysterious effects that promote teamwork and interoffice communication. And you'll prove that *anything* is possible when you present the classic "Mathemagic"—

arguably the most astounding numbers stunt ever devised.

Each piece of corporate conjuring is completely self-working—many can be done on your first try. Each one uses items you already have at your desk: tape, scissors, sticky notes, and paper clips. And each effect is customizable to your newest product line, or the theme of next month's meeting.

This chapter proves that magic motivates. There is a *message* behind these mysteries. Let's use them to amaze. Let's use them to *inspire*.

THE WARM-UP

The Big Action Covers the Small Action

The idea that a larger, overt action covers a smaller, secret action is the principle behind some of magic's most useful sleights and effects—and a form of misdirection. In this chapter, several effects are based on this simple axiom. Here's an example to illustrate the principle.

CONCEALED VIEW

keep your audience on your left side

1 Turn your body, angling your left side toward your participants, effectively eliminating their view of your right side. Hold a pen with the fingertips of your right hand and extend your left hand, palm up.

This vanish relies as much on direction/redirection as it does on technique. And the direction is in your words: "*I'm going to cause a quarter to appear in my hand on the count of three.*" Show your left hand empty and, with the pen in your right hand, make an indication toward your left palm.

Now everyone is expecting an appearance—not a vanish. With this presentational direction, you can get away with murder . . . and you can certainly get away with ditching the pen behind your ear.

2 Here's how it works. Raise the pen with your right hand in an upward gesture, in preparation to tap your left hand on the count of "one." Raise the right hand until the pen touches your right ear. The members of your audience can't see precisely where the pen is situated at this moment because your right side is angled away from them. And they won't be focused on your face because their eyes will be locked on your left hand, in anticipation of the quarter you've just promised to produce.

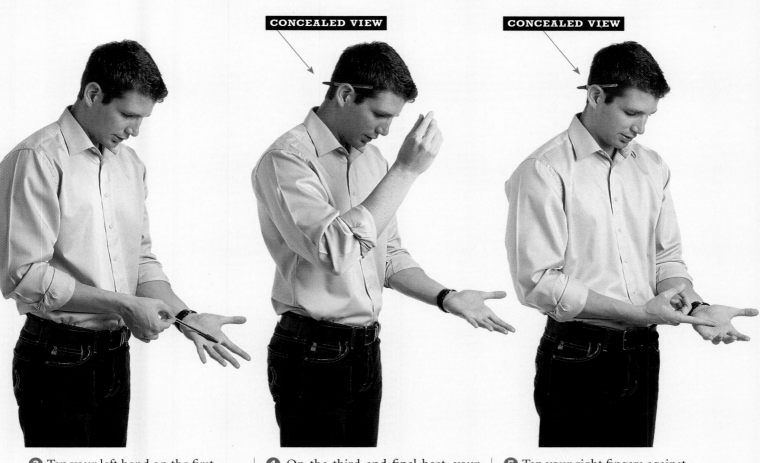

CONCEALED VIEW

CONCEALED VIEW

3 Tap your left hand on the first beat. Repeat this gesture on the second beat, counting "two."

4 On the third and final beat, your right hand's action will remain the same, but this time you will deposit the pen *behind your right ear*. Remember that nobody is focused on the pen, let alone your ear. You have all the cover you need for this bold but effective sleight. Just leave the pen behind your ear and continue moving your empty right hand downward as if it is still holding the pen.

5 Tap your right fingers against your left hand and pause. Then say, *"Wait, the pen vanished!"* Let your participants appreciate this unexpected surprise, and then turn your head toward them and wait for them to notice the pen's ridiculous reappearance . . . behind your ear.

The big action of tapping your left palm covers the small action of placing the pen behind your ear.

PEN-etration ON DVD

SETUP: The sticky note and pen should be borrowed. To prepare the bill, place it portrait side up on a carpeted surface. Push a pen point through the bill near the right end, along the line where the white space ends and the border begins. Widen the hole just enough to accommodate the pen's entire thickness. Remove the pen.

Now fold the two ends toward each other, keeping the portrait on the inside. Don't fold the bill exactly in half; instead, allow the left end to extend just beyond the secret tear. Unfold the bill and keep it tucked in your wallet. Remember not to spend it!

DIFFICULTY: ✝✝✝✝✝

THE EFFECT You create a hole in a dollar bill by pushing a pen through it. Then you perform "psychic surgery" to close the hole and heal George Washington's wound instantly.

THE SECRET The pen does go through a pre-punctured hole in the bill, but through an optical and auditory illusion, you'll give the impression the hole is at the center. It's actually near the end of the bill.

THE PERFORMANCE

A conversation about doctors or medicine makes a nice segue into this routine. It's also a great way to brighten an actual hospital patient's day, or to help someone who's nervous relax about needing an operation. Whatever your lead-in, direct the conversation toward psychic surgery.

The topic of psychic surgery is raised. *"You know these people, right? They're the ones who make incisions and remove organs, without ever piercing the skin."* Most folks are familiar with the concept, particularly if they lived through the seventies. *"These guys aren't practicing medicine—they're practicing deception. Allow me to demonstrate."*

hidden tear will be about here

❶ Remove the prepared bill from your wallet and ask to borrow a pen and a sticky note. Both of these items are easy to find in an office setting or can easily be planted in a hospital room. Hold the bill with both of your hands with the portrait of George Washington facing your participant. The fingers of your left hand block the hole from his view. You can invite him to examine George and make sure all appears normal.

❷ *"George will be our psychic surgery patient."* Fold the bill along the pre-folded line. *"Nurse,"* you say as you crease the fold, *"the patient is prepped."* Take the sticky note and adhere half the sticky strip along one side of the folded bill, and then adhere the remaining portion of the strip to the other side so it folds around the bill's crease. As you apply the sticky note, say, *"And*

this is George's hospital gown—don't laugh, once I had to wear one this size." By configuring the paper this way, you ensure that it will cling to the bill without the aid of your fingers. In this position, you can casually display both sides of the covered bill in your left hand. Simply cover the hole on the underside with your fingers as you let your audience look over the props.

❸ Retrieve the pen. Set the pen cap aside and mime using the pen like a syringe. Hold the pen in your right hand and insert the tip between the "open" ends of the bill. Secretly slide the pen through the pre-punctured hole. Although the participant will clearly see you slide the pen inside the bill, the tip will actually poke out beneath the bill, concealed from view.

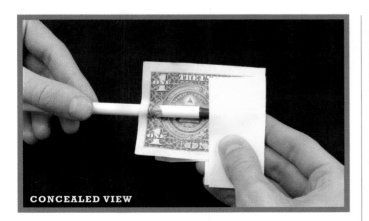

CONCEALED VIEW

❹ Continue sliding the pen toward the fold of the bill, taking care that the tip goes between the underside of the bill and the sticky note that's folded around it. *"Psychic surgeons,"* you begin, *"claim to make real incisions."* So saying, reposition your hands so that they grip both the sticky note and the bill from the sides, near the fold.

❺ Slowly push the end of the pen against your body. Use your body as the force that apparently pushes the pen through the bill.

As you push slowly, you accomplish a rare achievement in magic: an illusion that is simultaneously visual and auditory. The participant sees the pen go between the folds of the bill and come out the folded end. He *sees* the pen tip puncture the sticky note. At the same time, he *hears* the sound of a one-dollar bill tearing (he actually hears only the sound of the sticky note tearing, but what he sees misinforms what he hears).

continued 👉

6 Push the pen tip through the sticky note about an inch. Pause here and allow your participant to scrutinize the scene. Show him the visible top side of the bill.

7 Allow your participant to look closely at the torn hole in the sticky note.

8 Now peel back the sticky note, giving him the "gory" view of the surgery. This view is a particularly convincing display of a pen penetrating a bill.

Pull the pen all the way through the sticky note. Say, "*What makes psychic surgery so amazing is that no incisions are ever really made.*" Table the pen and remove the sticky note from the bill.

9 Display the hole in the center of the sticky note. Now unfold the bill, covering the tear on the side with the fingers of your right hand (so George faces out). Before the audience can zoom in on his portrait, cover him with the fingers of your right hand.

Execute a kneading action, as though you're "psychically healing" the hole in the bill. Move your fingers away from the center of the bill and brace the note between your fingers, so your hands mirror each other. Now you can invite the spectator to feel George. He won't discover a hole in the center because there isn't one. And he won't find the hole under your left fingers because he isn't expecting there to be one.

"*Just remember: It may look like I magically healed this bill. But just like psychic surgeons . . . it's all just an illusion!*"

MASTER CLASS

There is a direct correlation between audience impact and audience involvement. I'm not insisting everyone at a magic show needs to pick a card. I'm talking about involving someone on several levels. "PEN-etration" is an uncanny illusion because the participant uses three of the five senses.

First he *sees* the pen penetrate. He *hears* the bill tearing. Then he *feels* the restored bill. Add to that a cultural reference he has always wondered about—psychic surgery. Your participants shouldn't just watch the show. They should be part of it.

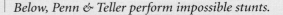

CREDIT: Penetrations like this one have been explored by great creators like Jay Sankey, David Harkey, and Steve Fearson. This trick, however, was invented and first published by Japanese magician Johnny Hirose in 1984.

SKEPTIC?

When you perform this trick you're carrying on a magician's tradition. Since the rise of Spiritualism in the 1840s, magicians like Harry Houdini have been the mythbusters of their day, making sure that magic tricks are used to create real smiles, not scam religious hoaxes. Skeptic James Randi and magicians Penn & Teller continue the tradition today, performing "psychic surgery" to illustrate how "real psychics" are *real* fakes.

Performing magic makes you a bearer of powerful secrets. And with these secrets comes a responsibility to your audience. You'll feel the temptation to claim your magic as real, but resist the urge. Instead, use your amazing powers to entertain and *educate*. Houdini would be proud.

Below, Penn & Teller perform impossible stunts.

Telekineticlip

MATERIALS:

A box or dish of paper clips.

SETUP: Make sure a handful of paper clips is handy.

DIFFICULTY:

THE EFFECT **A miraculous spoon-bending-like trick using the standard office paper clips.** It is a slow day at the office and everyone is convened in your cubicle, wishing they could will the clock hands forward five hours. You hand a coworker a paper clip and ask him to unfold it so it is a straight piece of wire. You take the wire between two fingers and hold it completely still. At first nothing happens. Then, while you remain motionless, the ends of the wire begin to curl slightly. The paper clip curls upward; a slow twist forms in two places. You immediately hand the bent paper clip back to your coworker. "Too bad," you say, pushing everyone out of your office, "pity that doesn't work on clock hands."

THE SECRET Grab a metal paper clip and straighten it as much as possible. You'll immediately discover that it's impossible to get all the kinks out—and that's the secret. Hold the straightened clip near one end between your left first and second fingers. Roll the wire across your left thumb pad with your right first finger. Roll the clip *extremely slowly* so that it isn't apparent that you're moving. You'll notice that as you rotate the straightened clip, even the tiniest kinks cause the length of the wire to bubble, rise, and gyrate. The raw secret is underwhelming and obvious, so let's add some smoke.

THE PERFORMANCE

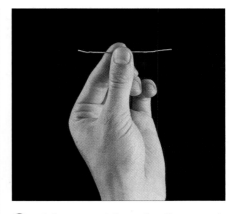

1 Creator Daniel Garcia developed some hilarious byplay before the actual effect, and this bit requires a handful of identical paper clips, preferably in the plastic containers they're sold in. Display the paper clips in their container, remove the lid, and extend the clips to a participant.

Say, in your most obnoxious carnival barker voice: *"Pick a clip, any clip."* Allow the audience to react, but encourage your participant to actually remove a paper clip. *"Remember your paper clip,"* you say, *"and don't let me see it."* Extend the plastic container toward your helper again and ask her to place the paper clip back into the container. When she has complied, replace the lid and say, *"Now I'll shuffle."* Pause one beat here, and then violently shake the container of paper clips. Without saying a word, remove the lid and then grasp one paper clip from within. Hold it up to chest height. *"Thank you very much!"* When the laughs and faux applause have subsided, invite the participant to remove another paper clip.

2 Ask her to straighten the clip as much as possible. As discussed previously, it is physically impossible to completely remove the three kinks where the wire originally curved. Reassure her that the wire need not be perfectly straight.

Take the wire back in your right hand, holding it near the right end between your thumb and fingers. Display the wire at chest height and transfer it to the left hand. Take the wire between the thumb (from below) and the left first and second fingers (from above). Display the straightened wire in your left hand.

CONCEALED VIEW

push with your thumb
to gently crimp

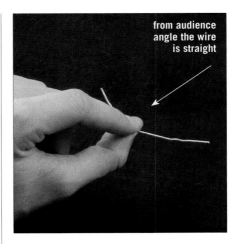

from audience
angle the wire
is straight

3 Now you'll execute two actions at the same time: Turn your body to your left to apparently display the wire to the leftmost spectators. As you do this, gently crimp the wire by pushing the left thumb between the left fingers. The crimp should measure less than one centimeter and should be a gentle curve, not a sharp angle. Both your body turn and the positioning of the left fingers help cover the crimping action. Once you have made your secret bend, remove the left second finger and regrip the wire so that it is held at the crimp's apex between only the first finger and thumb.

4 Roll the wire so the bend is angled forward, parallel with the floor. From the audience's position, the wire still appears straight.

continued 👉

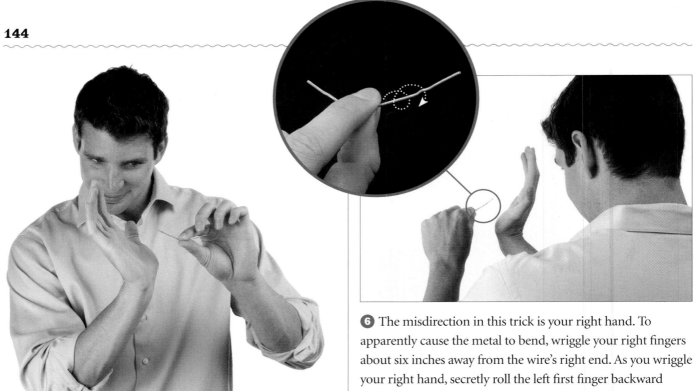

5 From above, the bend is obvious; thankfully, most offices don't have balcony seating, so your angles are fine. Your right hand helps distract audience attention from the secret actions of your left fingers.

6 The misdirection in this trick is your right hand. To apparently cause the metal to bend, wriggle your right fingers about six inches away from the wire's right end. As you wriggle your right hand, secretly roll the left first finger backward *very, very slowly.* Put together, it appears that the ends are curling upward slightly. Wriggle your fingers slowly at first, and pretend to bend the wire with your mind only slightly. Because there are two kinks and a crimp, even the tiniest turn of the wire results in an animation feast for the eyes.

7 Pause for a moment, holding your left hand completely still. Move your right fingers to your temple, close your eyes and fake your best Zen-like pose.

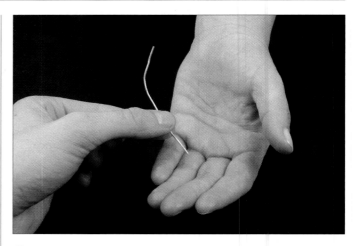

8 Now open your eyes and reposition your right hand a few inches from the wire.

Wriggle again, this time faster. As your right hand wriggles, turn the clip a little more, until the ends point upward.

Hand the bent clip to your spectators as an examinable souvenir. Feign exhaustion after the bending, as if your mental powers have been drained.

MASTER CLASS

This demonstration has all the components of memorable magic. It's impromptu; you can perform this effect anywhere you find a paper clip. It's easy; the hardest part of the trick is straightening the paper clip wire (and the *participant* does that part).

The effect is also visual. People respond better to animations they see than to animations they must infer. This effect would be substantially weaker if you placed the straightened clip in your pocket, snapped your fingers, and then removed the wire in a bent condition. In "Telekineticlip," nothing is left to the imagination.

If possible, your presentation should be topical. Do this effect in response to comments like *"I saw a guy bend spoons with his mind on TV,"* or when a subject like ESP, the Force, or Uri Geller is raised.

You will find good uses for "Telekineticlip" because it's very visual. It plays equally well for one other guy in your cubicle or for the entire advertising department.

Finally, this effect is *commercial*. This is a word magicians use to describe effects that promote audience interaction and byplay. You can play it scary or for laughs.

CREDIT: Houston's Daniel Garcia developed this effect during class when he was in grade school. Now twenty-four and a professional magician, he still uses it and has graciously allowed me to share it here.

THE MAGIC GESTURE

It seems silly, but in "Telekineticlip" I want you to take the right hand's "wriggling" seriously. Contrary to what you might think, the right hand's actions are as important as the left hand's. The right hand directs attention away from the method (the left fingers' secret rolling action). But the right hand's actions also determine how the audience perceives "Telekineticlip." The wriggling action shows that *you* make the clip bend and shows the audience explicitly how the magic looks.

To suspend disbelief, the audience must sense a magical moment. That's why magicians use magic wands and magic words. *Think like your audience.* The wave of the wand causes the rabbit to appear in the hat (not the trap door in the table). The coin doesn't get behind your nephew's ear by sleight of hand; it appears when you snap your fingers and say "Abracadabra!"

You certainly don't have to wriggle your fingers throughout your entire act. But in every trick, you have to do *something*. Instead of a wand, misdirection master Al Goshman sprinkled a saltshaker over his props! Arthur Brandon said it best in *Milo and Roger*: "Magic is really just a lot of bull*#%!. But you've got to know just how to shovel it."

Mathemagic

MATERIALS:
A pen or permanent marker and a piece of paper.

SETUP: While this routine can be done on the back of a business card or cocktail napkin, I'm going to explain a memory-free way to present it to a large group. You'll need to trace a four-by-four grid on an easel or poster board with a permanent marker. The lines need not be perfect.

Here's where the memory cheat comes in. With pencil, lightly write in the following numbers at the upper left corner of each square:

8	11	N	1
N-1	2	7	12
3	N+2	9	6
10	5	4	N+1

Fill in these numbers like you would a cheat sheet: small and light. Remember, the audience (and any surrounding teachers) should not be able to see your writing. If you envision making this effect part of your permanent repertoire, it's worth committing the above table to memory.

DIFFICULTY: †† †††

THE EFFECT Superhuman math calculations that look like magic!
Using any named number, say 51, you fill in a grid with numbers that appear to have been chosen at random. But now you point out a bizarre coincidence: Every row adds up to 51. So does every column. And the diagonals. And each quadrant. You get 51 when you add the numbers more than sixteen different ways! Oh, I almost forgot—you fill in the chart in less than thirty seconds.

THE SECRET You have to do a few easy computations, but almost all the numbers in the grid *are the same every time.* Thus, you can either rely on a "cheat sheet" or commit them to memory. The only numbers that change with each performance are the equations involving "N" (there is one in each row).

You calculate **N** by subtracting 20 from the named number. All the other calculations are as easy as pie (the edible kind).

So, once the participant names the number, subtract 20 and remember the result. Using a permanent marker, begin copying the numbers from your cheat sheet into the top row, left to right. When you approach the third column, fill in **N**. Continue this process throughout the grid, pausing only to feign concentration.

Since the other twelve numbers are simply copied from your crib sheet (or from memory), even if you hesitate on the simple equations, you can still complete the chart in less than thirty seconds.

Now let's talk about the fun part: taking credit. The Magic Square (as it is often called) is one of the incredible wonders of mathematics. Now you know how it works, but you'll still be amazed at how it *always* works.

The following sums total the named number:

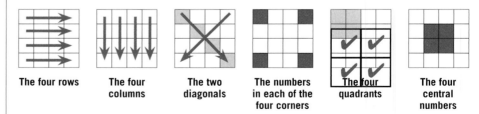

| The four rows | The four columns | The two diagonals | The numbers in each of the four corners | The four quadrants | The four central numbers |

Sixteen in all. It's mighty impressive. But here's the absurd part: There are even more sums (the two cross-diagonals, the two side-centers) too obscure to point out in performance!

Now you know how to do a Magic Square. But without a presentation, a number square will always be math—a puzzle at best. One part of the equation is still missing . . . you!

THE PERFORMANCE

A t a corporate presentation, say: *"Our business—any business, really—is like an enormous equation: the right product plus the right clients, multiplied by reliable, friendly service, minus the competition and divided by a dozen donuts and two decafs equals success. And in any business, the math has to be perfect. But math also shows us that, with hard work, anything is possible.*

"In the spirit of the human equation that is our business, I'd like to show you some of my own hard work. And that anything is possible."

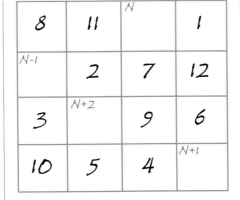

CONCEAL YOUR CALCULATION OF N

Number given is 38

38
−20
18

N = 18

1 Reveal the blank grid to your audience. (It may have your memory charts written in the grid.) Call on someone: *"Mike, do you have a second hand on your watch?"* Assume he does. *"In a moment I'm going to ask Sheila to name any number under 100 and I'm going to use that number in sixteen rapid-fire calculations. And you are going to make sure I do it in less than thirty seconds. When I say go, I want you to follow the second hand for thirty seconds—that's halfway around the big circle."* The audience will laugh here. *"But listen carefully. I'd like you to count down the last ten seconds aloud, like, 'ten, nine, eight'... okay?"*

2 Remove the marking pen and hold it near the upper left square on the grid. *"Sheila, name any number."* Assume she shouts 38. *Immediately* subtract 20. Your secret number N is 18. *"All right, Mike. Go!"* NOTE: If someone should name a number less than 20, just tell her *"Oh, 11 is too easy ... make it a bigger number!"*

The moment you say go, start writing as fast as possible.

3 The first row is cake—you already know all the numbers: 8, 11, 18 (your secret number), and 1. The second row's first square is N-1, or 18 - 1 = 17. After that: 2, 7, and 12. Continue in this fashion as fast as you can. You'll always beat thirty seconds. After all, almost all the answers are there in pencil. When you're done, your "38" board will be full.

"What I've tried to do is fill in this grid so that every row adds up to your thought-of number, 38. Let's check."

continued ☞

8	11	18	1
17	2	7	12
3	20	9	6
10	5	4	19

||||

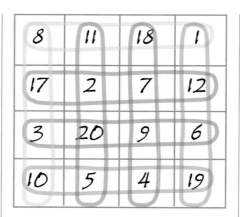

8	11	18	1
17	2	7	12
3	20	9	6
10	5	4	19

卌 |||

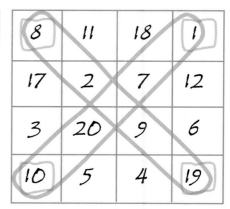

8	11	18	1
17	2	7	12
3	20	9	6
10	5	4	19

卌 卌 ||

❹ At this stage, *slowly* go through all four rows so that everybody can follow your addition.

"8 and 11 make 19, and 19 plus 18 is 37, plus 1 is 38!" Never fear, because all the rows eventually total 38; you can't be wrong as you add aloud.

A nice way of highlighting each sum is to circle it with a different colored marker. Keep a tally of sums above your grid to reinforce how many times the board totals the named number. Add up the columns a little more quickly as you go, skipping over the interim math, saying for the first column: "8 and 17 and 3 and 10 is 38!"

❺ When you're done with all the rows and columns, the board will look like this. Note the eight tally marks. Remark, *"Anything is possible."*

Here's a great gag I use whether or not I actually have any change in my pocket. In a rush, I shove my hand in my pocket and take out a handful of change (or I cup my hand so it looks like I'm holding a few coins). I mumble, as if to myself, *"Six pennies, one nickel . . . plus 4,"* and I look up, as if tabulating the result. Then I smile and say, *"And that makes 38!"* This gag breaks up an otherwise intense routine, and provides an excellent, light moment for an applause cue.

❻ *"But what made those calculations so difficult was making sure I got the diagonals correct."* In turn, circle both diagonals and announce that they, too, add up to 38. Add two tally marks to your total.

"Even the numbers in each corner add up to 38." Circle the four corner numbers. *"8 and 1 and 10 and 19 make 38!"*

MASTER CLASS

Math is an inevitable part of everyone's life and business. Whether you're calculating tips or deriving pi, this stunt is an instant Pythagoras starter kit. What's more, you can do this the first time you try. And yes, you can even perform "Mathemagic" after a full cocktail hour or at the next company party.

The key is finding the right forum for your performance. For example, after someone calculates a restaurant tip, you might demonstrate your own lightning calculations on the back of the receipt. Or if your job involves budget meetings, use this to garner interest.

I took a business math class in college, and I did "Mathemagic" on the chalkboard a few minutes before the first class. My eighty classmates were stunned at first, and then convinced they had signed up for the wrong course! My math professor—a renowned statistician, actually—was so impressed with this stunt that he: *(a)* thought I was a young Einstein, and *(b)* insisted I teach it to him so he could impress his other classes.

Categorically, this is not a magic trick. Why? "Mathemagic" accomplishes the *opposite* of a magic effect. It shows skill. The very essence of artistic magic is the concealment of skill. Here, the magician isn't doing the impossible: She's doing a demonstration that is possible—

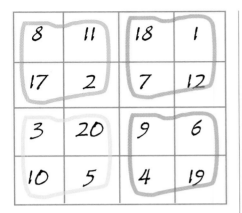

8	11	18	1
17	2	7	12
3	20	9	6
10	5	4	19

~~HHT~~ ~~HHT~~ ~~HHT~~

7 *"Even the quadrants add up to 38,"* you announce. *"8 plus 11 plus 17 plus 2 is 38! 18 plus 1 plus 7 plus 12 is 38!"* Outline each quadrant before adding it aloud, so your audience can follow along. Pick up the pace considerably here. Even though you're in no rush, "Mathemagic" requires enthusiasm and even a feeling of urgency to play well. Since this is a "beat-the-clock" premise, it's in your best interest to turn up the intensity near the end. And the four quadrants are near the end.

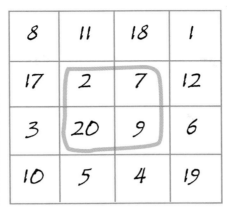

8	11	18	1
17	2	7	12
3	20	9	6
10	5	4	19

~~HHT~~ ~~HHT~~ ~~HHT~~ |

8 *"I've saved the best for last. The center square—the inner numbers."* Circle the center quadrant. *"Please, add with me: 2 plus 7 plus 20 plus 9. That's* sixteen *ways to make 38. Anything is possible!"*

PAUL GERTNER

Motivating with magic works—and it pays! Paul Gertner makes his living as a corporate magician (a self-billed "Infotainer"). He performs a "Magic of Thinking" show for private companies, in which he shares "magic" brainstorming techniques used by Houdini, Einstein, Edison, and Da Vinci. He works with his clients' senior management on ways to integrate products or slogans into his show, and he performs powerful magic that applies meaning to their program. Speaking about a company's ability to change, he visually transforms a borrowed twenty-dollar bill into a genuine *thousand-dollar bill.*

　"Every successful presentation entails an element of magic," says Gertner. "There must be something that holds the attention of the audience as the information is delivered. Magic has the unique ability to grab the attention of the audience while communicating a message."

but difficult. If you see a card hidden in the magician's palm, the illusion is shattered. She exposed her *skill* (or lack thereof). But when you see someone make sixteen calculations in less than thirty seconds, the performer's skill is no secret. This is why magicians and mentalists have wowed audiences with Magic Squares for hundreds of years: It's our chance to step away from the trap doors, roll up our sleeves, and get *real* credibility.

　The presentation outlined above is designed to attract interest in a business setting. "Anything is possible" is the theme—it's the emotional hook that grabs the audience and pulls people into your performance. "Mathemagic" is pretty abstract, and it begs for a human element.

That's where you, the operator, come in. You could spin a story about your "other" job at NASA, or explain to your accountant that you "work with numbers a little, too." There are lots of ways to make math come alive: the presentation you use, the setting you perform in, the interaction with the timekeeper and participant, the panache with which you reveal the sums, the pocket change gag. You remember how boring algebra class was? The only difference between sitting in class and a standing ovation is the emotional hook.

CREDIT: The Magic Square dates back nearly 2,700 years.

Disappearing Ink

MATERIALS:
Any pen with a cap. You also need to wear an outfit that includes a jacket, blazer, or pants with easily accessible front pockets.

SETUP: Just make sure you've practiced a lot in front of a large mirror (bathrooms are great for this!).

DIFFICULTY:

THE EFFECT **Make a pen and its cap disappear . . . right before your coworkers' eyes.** You remove the cap from a pen and display it on the palm of your outstretched left hand. You tell the participant that you are going to make the cap disappear, but you actually make the pen disappear. A moment later, you look to your left and reveal that the pen has reappeared *behind your ear*. And true to your word, the cap has now dematerialized.

THE SECRET You *put* the cap in your pocket. That's it! But while the method is simple, this effect is a master's course in misdirection. You'll use physical and mental direction to divert attention from otherwise blatant actions.

THE PERFORMANCE

1 Ask, *"You've heard people say 'the hand is quicker than the eye,' right?"* A lead-in question is one of the best ways to establish interest and interact with your participant. Listen to your participant's response, then offer to make the participant's pen cap disappear. This statement is the mental direction; you are giving her an expectation of what is about to transpire. She is conditioned to believe the pen cap will vanish, but not the pen (we work on this in the "Warm-up" section at the beginning of this chapter, page 136).

Position the cap of the pen on your outstretched left palm and hold the pen in your right hand. Gesture toward the cap with the tip of the pen.

2 It's likely that your participant won't look away from the pen cap, no matter what you do or say. This is the physical direction. She is focused on the pen cap—maybe on your entire left hand. But she is certainly *not* focused on your right ear.

3 Your participant should be to your left. Begin by making a slight body turn toward your right. Just before each of the three beats you count (*"One, two . . . three!"*), raise the pen in your right hand up and toward your head, so the bottom tip almost touches the top of your ear.

4 On each of the first two beats, bring the pen downward.

5 Touch it to the pen cap in your palm, as if wielding a magic wand.

continued 👉

CONCEALED VIEW

CONCEALED VIEW

6 On the last count, move your right hand up and back as before. But this time, simply tuck the pen behind your ear. Speed isn't important here; remember, nobody's looking.

7 Without stopping, move the right hand down toward the cap. Fluidity should be your goal. Take care to keep your right fist clenched as though it still held a pen. Pause here and let the effect register. At first, your spectators will think you have failed; the pen cap remains in the palm of your left hand. But eventually they'll notice the pen itself has disappeared.

CONCEALED VIEW

8 Relax your body and square your shoulders toward the participant. She may not notice the pen behind your ear at first, and it's actually funnier if it takes her a while to do so. Moments like these make magic exciting. Don't rush through them. If a small group is watching, some spectators may notice more quickly than others.

9 As you retrieve the pen from behind your ear, turn your body toward the left. By turning in this way, you allow everyone a better view of the pen behind your ear. But there's more going on here than meets the eye. By turning, you render your left hand (and the cap it holds) conveniently *out of view*.

As you openly retrieve the pen with your right hand, your left hand silently drops the cap into your left pocket.

⑩ In a continuing action, reposition yourself so your shoulders are squared to the audience. As your left hand comes back into view, remember to curl your fingers gently, as if they still hold the cap.

Offer to repeat the demonstration. Count to three again and gesture with the pen as you did before. This time, note that your left hand must remain in a fist.

⑪ On the third beat, open your left hand to show the cap has disappeared.

MASTER CLASS

When a pen and a cap disappear visually, everyone in your audience is sure to think the hand is quicker than the eye. But as you've realized by now, the key isn't to move the hands quicker than the eye. The key is to keep their eyes busier than your hands.

Magic lecturers often use "Disappearing Ink" to illustrate two powerful concepts. We've already explored the concept of physical and mental direction (and how they can be used congruously). As discussed in "The Warm-Up" on page 136, the other concept is simple: Big actions cover small actions.

In "Disappearing Ink," a sweeping body turn is the "big" action. Ditching the pen cap in your pocket is the "small" action. Whenever two actions occur simultaneously, remember these two points:

1. The audience's eyes follow the bigger action.

2. The audience's eyes follow the first movement.

To illustrate, let's reexamine "Disappearing Ink." Are you getting caught ditching the cap in your pocket? Here's the fix: Minimize the distance between the left hand and your pocket before you drop the cap.

This makes the "small" action smaller. When you're ready to do the move, make a larger body turn to the left. Finally, make sure you execute the body turn *before* you move your left hand toward your pocket. This way, the people in your audience will zero in on your body, not your left hand.

CREDIT: **The choreography involved in "Disappearing Ink" belongs to Harry Crawford, with help from Lou Tannen and Harry Lorayne.**

Post Bent

MATERIALS:
A pen or marker and a sticky pad.

SETUP: Tear off a small piece from a single sticky note, taking care that you use the portion without the sticky strip along the edge. The strip you tear off should be about one and a half inches long and half an inch wide. Adhere one end of this piece to the sticky strip on the back of another sticky note. The tab works best if it's centered.

To prepare for performance, lightly place the prepared sticky note back on top of the pad.

DIFFICULTY: ✦┼┼┼┼

THE EFFECT This is yet another take on the classic spoon bending trick. You draw a spoon on the top page of a Post-it® pad and you then peel the page from the pad and hold it near your eyes. **You remain completely still as the spoon drawing bends by the will of your mind—Telekinesis for the twenty-first century.**

THE SECRET Your thumb does the bending. Your thumb bends a hidden piece attached to the back of the sticky note. But a little cheating and a little gimmick go a long way in this easy stunner.

THE PERFORMANCE

❶ Approach an associate at her desk and ask to borrow a stainless steel spoon. Assuming her desk isn't at the checkout of a cafeteria, she won't have one to lend. *"That's fine,"* you say, *"then just imagine that* this *is a spoon."*

Take out your sticky note pad (sticky strip on top, uppermost) and marker, and draw a simple spoon on the middle of the top page. *"I saw this Uri Geller guy on a talk show once. He bent a spoon without touching it. Have you ever seen anyone do that?"* Acknowledge the response.

2 *"Well, I've been practicing."* Peel the prepared page from the pad and hold it in your right hand, fingers in front and thumb at the back. Move your left first finger to your temple and breathe deeply, feigning concentration.

To make the spoon bend, pull down on the end of the tab with your concealed right thumb *as slowly as possible*. You have less than an inch to work with. If you rush the pulling action, the trick will be over too soon. Let the page bend subtly at first, and then pull further for a more dramatic bend.

3 From your participant's perspective, the illusion is perfect.

To restore the bent spoon, hold the sticky note in front of your eyes and blink rapidly. As you blink, slowly push the tab upward with your thumb, allowing the page to straighten.

4 There are two options for making the page examinable. If the participant isn't too close or too concerned with examining your spoon drawing, then pull down on the tab

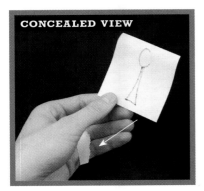

with your left thumb, this time quickly. This will cause the tab to break free of the sticky strip it was attached to and fall into your left hand. Hide the extra piece in your left fingers as you pick up the page with the fingers of your right hand, and then give it to the participant.

But what if she is watching too carefully? Just use this blow-off: *"Do you want to see me break a spoon with my bare hands?"* Now tear the page several times. *"Here, a broken-spoon souvenir."* Hand the pieces to your participant. Now the secret tab is indistinguishable from all the other torn pieces.

MASTER CLASS

Remember that a magic effect happens in the participant's mind. Bending a piece of paper is meaningless. But add a spoon doodle and a pop culture reference like Uri Geller and you've got magic. More importantly, the participant has a story.

It is helpful to think of the magic we do in terms of stories or experiences. Here, the participant's story is that you bent a spoon without touching it. Sure, the spoon was a drawing, and yes, you were touching the paper, but these details drop away when the effect is over. Only the experience remains.

The famous Las Vegas magician Lance Burton once told me that his last trick, the floating Corvette, is *not* one of his best tricks. Why does he keep it in his show? And why does he *close* with it? The story! Tourists go home from Vegas and tell their friends an unbelievable story: "Lance Burton levitated a Corvette. I was there!"

CREDIT: Alain Nu, creator of "Post Bent," is one of the world's leading mentalist entertainers.

Groupthink

THE EFFECT You gather friends around you in your office and present three objects from your desk: a book, a pen, and scissors. You hand a coworker your tape dispenser and ask him to place it on top of any of the three objects: the book, the pen, or the scissors. Your associate hesitates on the pen but eventually places the dispenser on the book. Your associate removes a bookmark from the book and reads a handwritten note with his name and a personalized message. **You have predicted your coworker's choice before he even decided to play the game.**

THE SECRET "Groupthink" is based on a principle known as "Multiple Outs." The strength of this method is that it is *absolutely impossible to figure out.* Not even Einstein could solve this one definitively. There simply isn't enough information. But when you have secretly loaded *multiple outs,* you will always be correct—no matter what gets picked.

MATERIALS:
A tape dispenser and a pad of paper, along with any three objects from your desk (such as a book, a pen, and a pair of scissors), and a marker.

DIFFICULTY: † | | | |

SETUP: Use any three objects on your desk. Make sure there are also other items on your desk, including a pad of paper. For example, assume you use scissors, a pen, and a book.

You'll need to write down three predictions. Later you'll reveal whichever one corresponds to the participant's decision. This means you must also remember which prediction goes where.

Choose your participant ahead of time and address him or her in each scenario. For example, write, *"David, you will choose the pen,"* in large print on the back of a notepad. Position this notepad on your desk; it will serve as the mat or "stage" for the other objects.

On a small piece of paper, write, *"David, you will choose the scissors,"* and tape this prediction to the underside of the tape dispenser.

Cut another piece of paper into the approximate length and shape of a bookmark, and write, *"David loves red so he will choose this book!"* Put this prediction between the pages of the book. Now put the book on a shelf, your scissors in a drawer, and the pen in your pocket. Invite everyone into your office and you're ready to perform.

THE PERFORMANCE

❶ *"Communication is the key to any successful project,"* you start, motioning to all your coworkers. *"The members of a team should always communicate with one another. In fact, when teammates work together enough, they begin to notice trends, strengths, weaknesses, and even anticipate decisions."*

You point to one person and say, *"I'd like to try this experiment with you."* As you speak, produce the three objects and place them in a row.

Say, *"In a moment, I'm going to ask you to think of one of these objects,"* gesturing toward the table. *"You can change your mind as many times as you like, but when you settle on one object, place this tape dispenser on top of it."*

"Now you might choose the book, because it's the biggest." Now start talking like a used-car salesman. *"Or maybe you think I want you to choose the book, so you might choose the pen. The pen is closest. But then again, maybe I placed the pen so you would choose it. Maybe you'll choose this pair of scissors, because it is the easiest to convert into a weapon."*

Your audience laughs.

The participant picks up the tape dispenser and then hesitates before placing it on the pen. *"Do you want to change your mind?"* you ask. Surprisingly, he does. He moves the tape dispenser on top of the book.

❷ *"Pick up the book,"* you instruct. *"I knew you were going to choose the book. I knew you would first pick the pen, and then change to the book. That's my job: to know what my teammates are thinking. I put a prediction in that book before we started this experiment—before you even came into the room."*

He removes a bookmark and reads a printed message: *"(His Name), after a long, hard decision, you will choose the book!"*

❸ If the participant chooses the scissors, don't mention anything about the book. Instead, call his attention to the tape dispenser which he used to indicate his selection. On the bottom, he'll find an amazing note that correctly predicted his free decision. Notice that in this scenario, you call attention to the tape dispenser. But if the participant chooses the book, you don't even mention the tape dispenser.

❹ If the participant chooses the pen, move all the objects aside and capitalize on otherwise unimportant truths. *"This pad has been in your sight the entire time. I haven't touched it. Would you please read my prediction on the back?"* Here, a prop you didn't even *mention* beforehand becomes the central element of this effect . . . but only *after* the participant chooses the pen.

MASTER CLASS

Audiences sense fear. Through posture and eye contact, a good magician exudes *confidence*. He's in control at all times. "Groupthink" challenges our confidence as magicians because we must think on our feet. What if I say the wrong thing? What if he sees the writing on the bottom of the tape dispenser? What if I forget something? If the performer calls attention to the wrong prediction or even hesitates near the end of the effect, the illusion is shattered.

Confidence is the solution, and the only way to achieve confidence is practice. Run through the routine five times in your office, alone and aloud (pretend you're on speaker phone). Then try it on a few friends. And a few more. Every time you do it, you'll become more comfortable starting an illusion with an ending that always changes. After a couple of performances, your fear of failure will morph into an unspoken confidence. This confidence affects your posture and delivery and it reinforces the idea that you are using the one (and *only*) prediction in play.

Psychic Stocks

MATERIALS:
A newspaper, scissors, Chapstick, an ashtray, and a lighter.

SETUP: Prepare the secret stock message (I suggest a two-letter symbol, like GM), by writing it legibly with Chapstick across the inside of your forearm. If you're

wearing a long-sleeved dress shirt, you can re-button your cuff, covering your arm until you perform. Otherwise, just keep your sleeves rolled. Don't worry about someone noticing the writing on your arm; smearing Chapstick on your body isn't typical behavior, so no one is looking for it.

Have the newspaper with the stock listings, scissors, matches, and an ashtray nearby. You will need to use caution with the matches and scissors, and take note of where you are; most businesses are smoke-free environments with touchy smoke detectors. Remember: If your participants jump out of their seats because of a fire alarm, that does *not* count as a standing ovation.

DIFFICULTY: ╪╪╪╪╪

THE EFFECT You hold up a clipping from *The Wall Street Journal* listing the daily performances of about a thousand stocks. The participant chooses any stock from the newspaper clipping, say General Electric. You ask her to concentrate on its symbol, GE. You take the newspaper clipping and burn it completely. Next, you pinch the ashes between your fingers and smear them on your forearm. As you rub, you ask your participant to concentrate on the letters, **the thought-of stock symbol magically appears on your forearm!**

THE SECRET While it appears your participant has a choice of any stock listed in the newspaper, you will force a predetermined company symbol on her. How do you get the initials to appear on your arm? The same method we used in "Ashes on the Arm" (page 94). Chapstick! It is as invisible as it is sticky. Using the Chapstick like a marker, write the force symbol (or any secret message). When the time is right, ashes can be rubbed over the message and it will appear in an eerie manner.

THE PERFORMANCE

"**S**ince the stock market's founding in 1792, analysts have been searching for a winning system or equation. Imagine if someone could foresee a winning stock. In fact, let's imagine together."

This intro establishes your credibility and piques the audience's curiosity. At the same time, you never claim actual abilities. You're "imagining together."

Cut just above your chosen stock

❶ Turn to the newspaper's stock listings and cut out a column about twelve inches long. Nonchalantly cut the column precisely above your "force" stock.

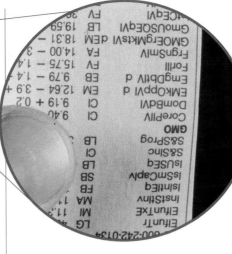

2 Display the newspaper clipping and allow a participant to examine it. Ask her to confirm that all the stocks are different and that there are literally hundreds to choose from. Retrieve the clipping and turn it so it is facing your body. Pass the clipping from your right hand into your left. As you transfer the newsprint,

reorient it so that the stocks face you and read upside down. Retrieve the scissors with your right hand.

3 Open the scissors and position the newsprint between the blades, near the uppermost edge. *"I'd like you to think of a stock,"* you direct. *"But everyone always thinks of something obvious, like Google or Yahoo. So, I'll let you choose one at random."* This is, of course, all smoke.

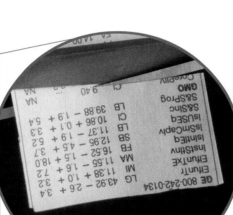

No matter where you cut, your chosen stock is at the top

4 Ask the participant to call "stop" as you run the scissors down the length of the clipping. *"Call 'stop' whenever you like."* When she does so, stop moving and ask if she would like you to move the scissors up or down. It really doesn't matter, so feel free to emphasize the fairness.

When she is satisfied, snip through the clipping.

5 Allow the lower portion to flutter to the floor. *"Please pick up the clipping and remember the stock symbol—the one just below where I cut. I promise I won't peek."* Look away and allow the participant to comply. *"We'll think of this stock as a winner. And I'll try to pick it up through Extra Sensory Perception, or ESP."*

continued ☞

6 When she retrieves the clipping, she'll automatically orient it writing-side up and remember the uppermost stock listing. Unbeknownst to her, you have forced GE. Encourage your participant to remember the stock's abbreviation, not just its full name.

Now extend the ashtray toward the participant and ask her to tear up the "evidence." Have her drop the newspaper pieces into the ashtray (tear up your half of the clipping and dump your pieces in, too).

7 Now light a match and drop it on top. While the paper burns, say, *"So—you've got a stock symbol in your mind. We're destroying the only evidence. I'll use what's left to help me divine your stock."*

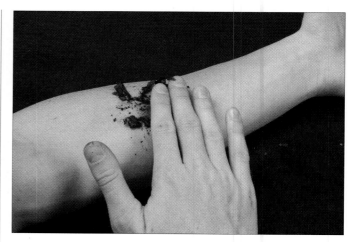

8 The paper will burn quickly and cool almost immediately. Once the ash flakes are safe to touch, pinch some between your right thumb and fingers.

9 Slowly rub the ash across your forearm. Lightly spread it around, and don't be in a hurry to cover your transparent message. The ashes will stick to the invisible initials you've written on your arm. Let its appearance "fade in" slowly, as you say, *"Concentrate on your stock . . . keep repeating the symbol over and over and over in your head."*

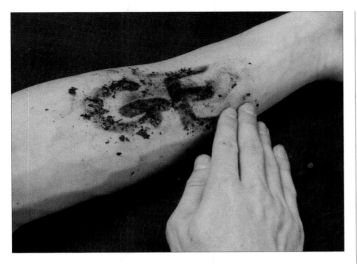

10 Eventually dust away the loose ash and reveal the stock symbol. Ask your participant to confirm her thought-of symbol. Try it once and you'll agree: This pick is a winner.

MASTER CLASS

Money magic has built-in appeal, and this theme taps into something that countless people have lost money trying to do: predict a stock.

The point is this: everyone is connected to the 300 trillion-dollar U.S. stock market (particularly in an office setting), so there is something for the participants to identify with. Long before you engage in any magic, you've got to engage your audience.

"Psychic Stocks" is actually two classic pieces of mentalism. The first one is the newsprint force and the second one is the revelation on your forearm. You can easily separate the two. For example, after forcing the stock, you might choose to reveal your prediction from within a sealed envelope. Or, you might drop the stock force and ascertain a piece of secret information—perhaps your boss's embarrassing middle name—and reveal that from the ashes of a cigarette.

CREDIT: "Psychic Stocks" is a routine I developed with fellow magician Joel Givens. We originally designed the routine for use in a trade show for the Sony Corporation. The stock force comes from an idea called the "Newspaper Text," a newspaper force invented and published by Albert Spackman, in 1964, and ash revelation, dating back to Prevost in 1584.

ADELAIDE HERRMANN PAVES THE WAY FOR WOMEN

In the late nineteenth century, magician Alexander Herrmann was a massive success in the United States. He performed alongside his ballet-dancing wife, Adelaide, and subjected her to typical illusionist feats: she was apparently decapitated, levitated, and burned on a nightly basis. But when her husband died in 1896, Adelaide did something truly unexpected at the time. She did magic.

While Adelaide wasn't the first female magician, she achieved unprecedented success as a female star of magic. And by all accounts, she was excellent. She produced live animals of all sizes and even performed magic's most dangerous effect, the Bullet Trick (see page 186). Years earlier she cringed every time her husband posed in front of loaded muskets. Now she rose to the occasion and performed the feat with grace and agility, withstanding the fire of six bullets without injury. Forty-two years old when her husband died, she spent the next thirty years in the spotlight, relying on her determination and skill before retiring from the stage at 75.

Coffee Conjuring

THE EFFECT "Do the coffee thing," your associate pleads during a break. You retrieve a creamer. "Step one is pouring the creamer into my fist." You peel back the lid on a creamer and slowly pour cream into your left fist without a drop leaking from your fingers.

"Step two is turning the creamer invisible and dropping it in my coffee." You open your fist and pantomime pouring the cream into your cup of black coffee. As you stir you say, "Step three is turning it visible." The cream slowly appears in milky clouds, causing your coffee to lighten.

"And the last step is not to waste a single drop." You table your coffee cup and call attention back to the opened creamer. You rub the top of it and concentrate. When you move your hand away, the creamer is *sealed again.* "But look," you say, holding the creamer up to the light. "Even though the creamer is sealed, it's only half full!" **Your friends are astonished to see you turn cream invisible, then visible, then see you reseal the opened creamer package.**

THE SECRET The method is mostly science, and plays on two audience assumptions. The first assumption is that this is an impromptu miracle; actually, there is some secret preparation. The second assumption is that coffee creamers are sealed full. They're not. Cream is packaged only half full, and a pocket of air occupies at least as much space as the cream.

The science of "Coffee Conjuring" involves depositing creamer into the *bottom* of a full cup of hot coffee. Since the creamer is cold and the coffee is hot, the creamer will remain on the bottom of the cup, separated. Like oil and water, the two won't mix until stirred by the spoon. Until it is stirred, the coffee appears black, despite having a healthy portion of cream at the bottom.

MATERIALS:

A table set for lunch, including coffee cups, spoons, and a small bowl of chilled coffee creamers; black coffee and a straw.

SETUP: To perform, you'll need two containers filled with creamer, a cup of hot coffee, and a straw.

❶ Open one creamer by peeling the foil top off all the way. The foil tops typically have two tabs for ease of opening.

DIFFICULTY: ⚔⚔⚔⚔⚔

SETUP, CONTINUED:

2 Carefully place this extra top over the second, sealed creamer container and align the two tabs. Since the underside of the extra top was in contact with the creamer, it will likely be wet and tacky. This helps it adhere to the top of the sealed creamer container. As an added precaution, align the two tabs with the sealed tabs, and fold them over. Place this prepared creamer among the other creamers, but take note of where the prepared one rests.

3 Next, open a different creamer and carefully suck its entire contents into a full-length straw. One slow, steady slurp will get the entire creamer into the straw. The minute you taste cream, press your tongue against the straw's end, plugging it. This creates an airtight seal, ensuring that the cream will now stay in the straw. Carefully transfer the seal from your tongue to a fingertip, taking care not to lose any of the cream out of the other end. (You may remember doing this when you were a kid—keeping a finger over the end of a straw and then releasing milk all over a sibling's head.)

4 Insert the straw into the coffee cup so that the end touches the bottom. *Slowly* (over a period of about thirty seconds), release your seal on the other end of the straw, letting the cream leak into the cup. When you do this slowly, the cream will sink and rest at the bottom of the cup.

5 Situate a spoon in the cup so you can stir the coffee at the appropriate time. All this preparation must take place before you sit down, and out of audience view.

continued ☞

THE PERFORMANCE

CONCEALED VIEW

1 Now you are ready to do "the coffee thing." Pick up the prepared creamer and hold it in your right hand. With the fingers of your left hand, carefully peel back the extra foil lid. Peel toward your participants so the back of the flipped top will cover the supposed opening. Now make a fist with your left hand and hold the creamer near the fist. Pretend to pour the creamer into your left fist. Pause after a few seconds of pouring to wipe the bottom of your left fist with your right wrist, as if smearing away some leaking creamer. This part, of course, is all acting.

2 Slowly open your left hand to show that the creamer is invisible. Mime tossing it into your coffee. Now you'll reap the benefit of your preparation. Slowly stir the coffee with the spoon.

3 Be sure to stir slowly, so the changing color is gradual and theatrical. When the reappearance has set in with the audience, draw attention back to the empty container in your right hand.

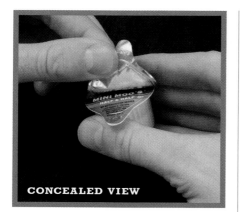

CONCEALED VIEW

4 Show your left hand empty and then cover the top of the container, secretly placing the upper, peeled tab of the extra top between your left thumb and the base of your first finger. As you wave your left hand

over the creamer container, simply steal the extra top away, keeping it concealed in the palm of your hand. Drop your hands into your lap and invite the participants to examine the resealed creamer. While your hands are out of view, toss the creamer cover to the floor, hiding the evidence.

MASTER CLASS

Magicians refer to pieces like "Coffee Conjuring" as situational magic. These effects are designed for specific audiences and locations. There's nothing more sacred to an employee than coffee—unless it's a coffee

break—so it's easy to find an ideal time and setting for this effect.

"Coffee Conjuring" is also a good effect to *underplay*. This stunt must seem off-the-cuff, and this is why I haven't written a script. Most of the effect is performed in silence, letting your actions speak for themselves.

CREDIT: **This effect was created by** *Magic*'s **chief consultant, Joel Givens.**

Mental Money

THE EFFECT You're about to start a meeting and already your employees look bored. "Alright everyone, please put your notepads down for a minute." You hold up four small envelopes, numbered 1 through 4. "Three of these envelopes contain what we offer our customers," you say as you mix the envelopes. "The other one contains what they give us in return."

You offer three of the four envelopes to people in the room. "Choose one, please. And remember, you get to *keep* whatever is inside." You're left with one.

You instruct one person to open her envelope. She removes the contents: a piece of paper. It reads, *Friendly Customer Service.*

The next person opens his envelope and finds another paper: *Exclusive Products.*

The last person opens and reads the paper inside: *Fair Return Policy.*

The question on everyone's mind is, what's inside *your* envelope.

"Congratulations," you say. "The three of you had a completely free choice, and you chose three ways we serve our clients. And when we offer good service, exclusive products, and a fair return policy, this is what we get in return. And remember that I said everyone could keep the contents of the envelope he or she chose." **You open your envelope—the only one your participants didn't select—and remove a hundred-dollar bill.**

THE SECRET The participants can choose any of the four envelopes. All four have paper inserts. How do you get the money? The hundred-dollar bill is hidden *behind* the four envelopes. At the end, you only pretend to take the money out of your envelope.

The effect is easy to accomplish because of a metal clip that holds the envelopes (and money) in place.

MATERIALS:

Four envelopes, a metal clip, a permanent marker, and five slips of paper.

DIFFICULTY: ✝✝✝✝✝

SETUP: The metal clip used can be found in the cash drawers of most offices. If you don't have a key to the cash drawer, you can buy a clip for less than a dollar at good office supply outfits. You'll need one about three inches long.

"Mental Money" also requires four small envelopes. Manila coin envelopes are easy to find in an office, but any small envelopes will do the trick (literally).

❶ Using a thick permanent marker, number each envelope, 1 through 4.

❷ Place a prediction in each envelope and slip it into the money clip.

continued ☞

SETUP, CONTINUED:

3 You must supply your own cash reward. How much you use depends on the business you're in (and, I suppose, the success of that business). Let's assume you're using a hundred-dollar bill. Fold that bill into fourths and tuck it into the clip, behind the envelopes.

THE PERFORMANCE

1 Display the clipped envelopes to the audience, keeping the whole unit close to your body so you don't expose the hidden money. You can hold the entire outfit with just the left hand, fingers in front and thumb behind. Go through the presentation, allowing each participant to call an envelope's number.

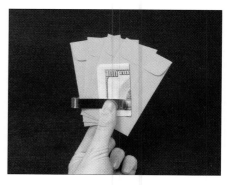

2 Slide each numbered envelope from the clip and hand it to the corresponding participant. After sliding one out, adjust the others so they cover the concealed bill from view. Between selections, slide the bill left and right with your thumb, so it is always safely hidden.

What happens if a participant wants to switch? Just reinsert her envelope into the clip *before* removing her new choice. In this manner, you can always hide the money behind the remaining envelopes.

3 When three envelopes have been distributed, you'll be left with just one, still under the clip and with a bill concealed behind it. One by one, allow each participant to open his or her envelope and reveal the contents. This is the time to elaborate on your corporate message, or play up the gag items you placed inside.

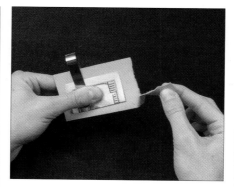

4 When you're ready to magically conclude, tear open the top of your envelope with the fingers of your right hand.

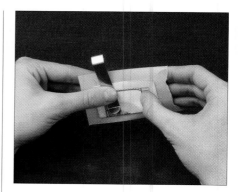

5 Insert your fingers into the envelope's opening, but allow your right thumb to slide behind the envelope. Place your thumb on top of the concealed money.

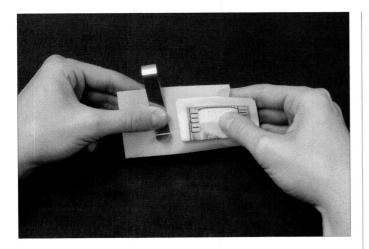

6 In one motion, withdraw your hand from the envelope, sliding the bill away from the clip with your right thumb. (Be careful not to pull out the planted prediction in the envelope as well.) This action gives the perfect illusion of removing money from inside the envelope. Unfold the money and pocket your "winnings."

MASTER CLASS

This effect is based on a classic called "Bank Night." But most magicians get "Bank Night" all wrong, particularly those who teach it in books. The danger here is creating animosity in those we wish to entertain. Nobody likes to lose, and let's face it: In this trick they lose.

To solve this problem with presentation, you've got to replace suckers with winners. Position everyone on the same side. Reread the "Effect" as outlined above and you'll notice that "Mental Money" is not presented as a game or challenge. Also notice that *you* don't win the money; everybody wins the money. Your staff wins the money, metaphorically.

You can use any number of predictions when performing this effect. Find a theme that suits your audience. Here are some suggestions:

Free Gift: Offer a gift to three participants. Explain that everyone gets to keep the gift in his or her envelope. Stuff the envelopes with the nuttiest gifts you can think of: a ketchup or salt packet, an earplug, a coupon for 10 percent off fabric softener. Each of these gifts is funny, but not as funny as their expressions will be when you reveal your own gift . . . a hundred bucks!

Predict-it: Write "You will choose this envelope," on each of the predictions. The participants will be underwhelmed at your predictions, but duly impressed at how you managed to keep the C-note.

Motivational: The presentation above is just one example of how to tie in magical entertainment to your daily business routine. Perhaps you're unveiling new slogans or products. Unveil each one on a different prediction, and then explain that because of these "exciting new products, we're left with . . . the money!"

You can adapt the presentation and predictions from the script outlined above. Remember that, regardless of your performance, you need *four* predictions—one for each envelope. The audience will only see three of these predictions, and you cannot control which three they see. Seal each prediction inside an envelope and situate all four envelopes inside the clip. Note that the envelopes are fanned slightly, so that the numbers are visible.

CREDIT: The plot for this presentation is by Tom Sellers, who published it in the United Kingdom in 1935 as "It's Only Chance." In the United States, Floyd Thayer marketed the trick in 1936 as "Bank Night."

Karate Clip

MATERIALS:
Two paper clips.

SETUP: Prepare by inserting your right first finger into the gap of a paper clip. Depending on your finger size, you may need to widen the clip's center opening.

Before approaching your audience, curl your right first finger toward the inside of your palm so the clip is hidden from view. Be sure you have a matching paper clip handy.

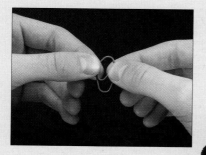

DIFFICULTY: ⚔️⚔️

THE EFFECT "When you're bored with paper football or 'Pin-the-Tail-on-the-Accountant,' here's an office game you can try." So saying, you pick up a paper clip from a neighboring desk and toss it in the air. **As the tossed paper clip descends, you jab your finger at it and catch it on your fingertip.**

THE SECRET Magicians refer to superhuman demonstrations like this one as pseudo-skills, because although they are not presented as magic, they do have a covert method. This stunt builds audience trust in your talent. The secret here isn't eighteen years of grueling practice. It's a second paper clip.

THE PERFORMANCE

1 To apparently "stab" the paper clip in midair, simply display the duplicate in your left hand. Be sure to show the left hand otherwise empty. Toss the paper clip in the air a few times to "practice," allowing the clip to fall back onto your left palm.

When you're ready to show off, toss the clip into the air. As it descends, you'll perform two actions simultaneously.

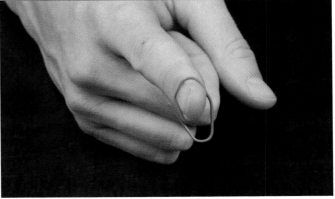

❸ When your fingers stop moving, a paper clip is clearly skewered on your first finger. Participants will assume it is the same paper clip they saw you toss into the air, and they will attribute you with great (albeit useless) skill. The most important part is keeping a straight face, even feigning difficulty. Legends are made of this stuff.

MASTER CLASS

This is the anti-magic trick. That is, to really make this stunt believable, you've got to convince your audience (and yourself while you're executing it), that stabbing a paper clip in midair is an acquired skill. Your audience must never even suspect that there is a "trick" to it other than hard work.

To make the illusion perfect, practice your stabbing action a few times. Use your body and thrust your right hand forward, almost like a karate chop. Also, practice stopping *completely* after you catch the paper clip. If you really could catch a paper clip on the tip of your finger, you would use a similar action.

CREDIT: "Karate Clip" is based on a trick that appeared in Ponsin's *Novielle Magie blanche dévoillée* in 1835, which David Roth adapted for the "Karate Coin," published in the 1980s.

❷ First, you'll extend your right first finger out and into the path of the falling clip. As this happens, catch the descending clip in the other fingers of your right hand. The tossed clip falls directly into the top of your closing fingers as they form into a fist.

The catching and stabbing actions happen so fast that the audience is unable to distinguish the midair switch that takes place.

Virtual Magic

MATERIALS:
Any computer with Internet access.

SETUP: When you're ready to perform the effect, log on to *www.joshuajay.com/magicbook/virtualmagic* with your participant. But before you do that, I'll teach you how to "talk" to the computer without saying—or typing—a word.

DIFFICULTY: ♱♱♱♱♱

THE EFFECT You call your coworkers from their cubicles and invite them to surround your desk so they can see your computer screen. You access a website and invite someone—anyone—to name a card. **Without typing or talking, you click START on the web page and within seconds, the named card appears on the screen.**

THE SECRET This computer program is sneakier than it seems. You'll encode the participant's thought-of card to the website based on where and how you move the cursor.

THE PERFORMANCE

The starting point is the website www.joshuajay.com/magicbook/virtualmagic. You perform the trick while logged in there. The address is no secret; you can invite your participant to check out the site later. Without knowing how to encode the card to the program, however, he will be unable to make thought-of cards appear on the screen.

1 When you arrive at the site, your screen looks like this. Begin by letting the Card Engine know that you're a magician. Logging in (identifying yourself as a magician) is actually a two-step process, ensuring that there is no chance a curious spectator can accidentally engage the program.

The first step is the how you click the ENTER button. While regular users will simply click anywhere on the word ENTER, you must click below the word, on the black blob beneath the letter *T*.

2 You are taken to a new screen that shows several links, including START THE MACHINE. Click anywhere on that icon to arrive at a screen that has an abstract background of moving shapes.

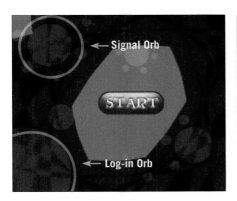

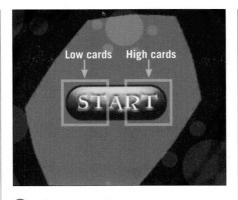

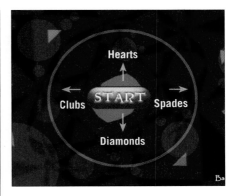

❸ To complete the second step required to log in, casually position the cursor on the large "orb" (circle) in the lower left corner of the screen for a few seconds. It is not necessary to click on the orb. The program confirms your presence when six small circles appear around the "signal orb," the large rotating circle in the upper left corner.

Once the machine recognizes you as a magician-user, it is ready to receive the encoded information about your participant's thought-of card. Your participant can continue to look over your shoulder without ever noticing your covert actions.

❹ Ask your participant to name a card. *"Imagine a full deck of playing cards spread out in front of you,"* you say. *"Run your finger through the air, as if you're running your fingertip along the faces of the cards. Stop anytime. What card is your finger on?"* This is just a fancy way to ensure that your participant realizes he has a completely free choice.

When he names a card, your next action is determined by whether the card is low (Ace through Six) or high (Seven through King). If the card is low, click the left side of the START button. If the card is high, click the right side of the START button.

As soon as you click either side of the START button, your cursor becomes invisible. Don't worry, it's still there and still under the control of your mouse; you just can't see it. Instead, a "dummy" cursor appears on the screen. This fake cursor is nothing more than a movie loop, with subtle movements that reflect an idle mouse hand. For anyone watching your screen, it appears that your mouse hand isn't moving much at all. You're in stealth mode, baby.

❺ Now it's time to code the suit and value of the card. These are communicated to the computer at the same time, in an invisible action.

The suit is cued by the *direction* in which you move the now-hidden cursor. It helps to think of the suits in the familiar "CHaSeD" order: Clubs, Hearts, Spades, Diamonds. If your participant named a Club, move the cursor to your left; a Heart, move the cursor upward; a Spade, move the cursor to your right; a Diamond, move the cursor downward. You won't be able to see the cursor moving, but it's moving just the same.

The value is cued by the *distance* that you move the cursor. Here you have a guide: Watch the "key orb," the small circle in the upper left corner of the screen. The farther you move the cursor toward the edge of the screen, the more dots will appear around the key orb. Each dot indicates a card value (three dots equals a Three, four dots equals a Four, and so on).

continued 👉

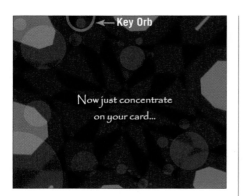

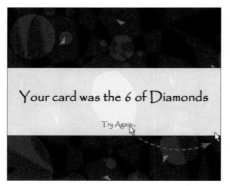

6 If, at the beginning of the coding sequence, you clicked the *left* side of the START button, you communicated to the computer that the card is a low-valued card, Ace through Six. Moving the cursor to the left until five dots appear around the key orb would encode the Five of Clubs. If you clicked the *right* side of the START button, you indicated to the computer that the card is a high-valued card, Seven through King. In high-value mode, no dots around the key orb indicate a Seven (7 + 0), one dot indicates an Eight (7 + 1), two dots indicate a Nine (7 + 2), and so on.

When actually performing this effect, you'll move the cursor less than an inch to code an entire card. Within seconds of completing the secret coding process, several prompts appear on the screen ("Stare into the center of the screen…", "Now just concentrate on your card…"), followed by a message correctly naming the selected card. As the message appears, your invisible cursor and the dummy cursor merge. After that, the cursor responds normally.

7 "Let me try," your participant says. And he *will* say this. Now the magician has an opportunity to take the mystery deeper.

Immediately after performing the effect, you're offered two options: TRY AGAIN and BACK. When your participant asks to give the Virtual Magic Card Engine a try, invite him to switch places with you. Click on TRY AGAIN and then, before standing up, *move the cursor to the far right edge of the screen.* Leaving the cursor in this position for a few seconds cues the Card Engine that a guest-user will be seated at the computer. In this mode, the card will not be signaled to the computer by moving the cursor, but a magical result will still occur!

8 Your participant sits down and takes control of the computer. You say, *"This time, I get to think of a card."* Pretend to choose a card in the same way your participant did, by running your finger through the air and stopping at an imaginary card. You actually calculate a card based on the one your participant named. Let's say your participant's card was the Six of Diamonds. Add three to the value and use the next suit in the ChaSeD sequence. Among magicians, this formula is known as the Si Stebbins system for determining the order of cards in a stack; however, the idea is over 400 years old. Add three to the Six in your participant's Six of Diamonds to arrive at a new value of Nine, and take the next suit after Diamonds in CHaSeD order is Clubs. You announce that the card you've chosen is the Nine of Clubs.

Your participant clicks START, you stare at the screen. A message appears, naming the Nine of Clubs!

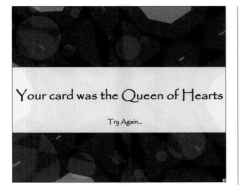

9 If your participant wants to remain in the command chair for one more try, he can click the TRY AGAIN link. All you have to do is say the next card in Si Stebbins order (in this case, the Queen of Hearts); after he clicks the START button, that's the card that will appear in the message. It's probably not a good idea to allow your participant to be the magician more than a couple of times or he may catch on to the card sequence.

10 To resume command of the Card Engine, hover your cursor over the large orb in the lower left corner of the screen and wait until all six circles appear around the signal orb. Now you're once again set to code cards to the computer. If you want to let your participant explore the site on his own, just click the BACK button and walk away. Without knowing how to log in, he will be unable to discover the secret of the Card Engine.

MASTER CLASS

Both magician and guest mode can be repeated over and over, provided you log in each time. Even with virtual magic, some practice is required. But the more you rehearse and perform this effect, the more you'll reinforce your memory of the code and the procedure for curing the computer.

The method above is quite involved, so it's easy to forget the most important part: the presentation. Don't just go through the motions! When the program asks you and your participant to concentrate or focus on the center of the screen, do it in

earnest. Even though your computer is the acting magician, you're still the performer.

CREDIT: **Curtis Hickman is a professional software developer and an amateur magician. Only someone well versed in both areas could have devised "The Card Engine." Says Hickman: "I wanted to fuse my two passions, magic and computers, and create a lasting impression with everyone who came through our office." And for all the technology, Hickman reminds us that it's still magic: big action covers small action, camouflage masks secret, and people are still astounded.**

Perhaps the participant names the Queen of Clubs. This is a high card, so click the right side of the START button.

Clubs are coded by moving leftward. So move the cursor slightly to the left.

Your participant chose the Queen, so you coded a high card. Therefore, the orb's dots indicate cards Seven and higher. This means that two dots would indicate Nine (7 + 2). And five dots indicate the Queen (7 + 5 = 12, or Queen).

Stop moving the cursor leftward when five dots appear around the key orb. Within seconds, the prediction, Queen of Clubs, appears.

THE TURK

"Thinking" machines have always been rooted in magic. In 1783, Benjamin Franklin played a chess match against a bizarre opponent billed as "the Turk." Franklin lost. In 1809, it was Napoléon Bonaparte's turn. Bonaparte played chess with the Turk in Vienna. He lost, too. That the Turk was not human makes these victories even more impressive. The Turk was a clever device that captivated the imaginations of royalty and readers all over the world.

Magic inventors from the eighteenth century would often craft automatons, small machines that could carry out such complicated tasks as baking, firing a quiver of arrows, or performing gymnastic stunts.

But the Turk was the most sophisticated machine of its time. Built by Baron Wolfgang von Kempelen, it was filled with levers, wheels, and pulleys. Oh, and a human operator. The Hungarian showman von Kempelen debuted the Turk in 1769 and allowed human challengers to play chess against his mechanical marvel. The Turk won most of the time.

But the secret to this particular automaton was not in the turning of gears, but in the concealment of its human operator. Someone controlled the Turk from the inside (and he had to be a great chess player!), but owing to von Kempelen's clever construction, the operator was concealed from view.

MONEY MAGIC

CONJURING WITH CURRENCY

I reach behind your right elbow and produce a bottle cap. You're pretty impressed. Maybe you even crack a smile. But when I reach behind your left elbow and produce a hundred-dollar bill, the hair on your neck rises. Why? Because, in magic, like anything else, money talks.

When someone finds out you're a magician, people often respond by asking: "Can you make money appear out of thin air?" This is rather telling. People rarely ask us to saw a lady in two or pull a rabbit from a hat. In people's minds, producing money is the ultimate magic effect.

So when they when ask, "Can you make money appear?" (and they will) with "Bank Roll" and "Grandpa's Coin Trick," your answer is, "Yes!"

With "Table Trouble," I'll share an uncanny illusion in which your participants see and hear an ordinary coin penetrate a tabletop. You'll learn how to restore a torn bill with "Trash to Treasure," and with "Penny Pressed," you'll visually smash a borrowed penny.

Money magic fulfills our greediest (but most common) desires: making it, doubling it, concealing it, spending it. This chapter will transform you into a walking bank. Money will appear and disappear at your fingertips. You'll turn paper to cash and cause money to appear in people's pockets. This isn't your uncle's quarter-from-the-ear stuff (no, that was in kid magic); this is money magic.

The Switch

The false transfer dates back to the very origins of magic, and it provides the framework for nearly every sleight-of-hand effect out there, from the venerable "Cups and Balls" to the disappearing coin. There are many variations, but the switch is an all-purpose application of the false transfer.

❶ Secretly conceal an object in your left hand. For example, loosely curl a doggy biscuit in your left hand (that's right, a doggy biscuit). Display another object—let's say a coin, in your right hand, holding it between your right thumb and first finger. The right second, third, and fourth fingers rest beneath the coin, extended. Ask a friend, *"Is it okay if I feed your dog?"*

❷ Before he has a chance to answer, you execute the switch: With your left hand, cover the coin from the audience's view and pretend to take it into your left hand by closing your left fingers into a fist. At the same time, secretly slide the coin between your right second and third fingertips. These fingers are used as pincers, and their grip should support the coin independent of the right first finger and thumb.

❸ Under cover of the left hand, curl your right second and third fingers toward your right palm, securing the coin. Continue to close your left hand into a fist and to move it away, apparently holding the right hand's coin. Be sure to stare intently at your left fist as if it contains the coin.

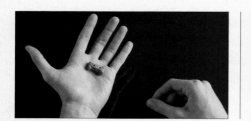

❹ Open the left hand to show that the coin has changed into a doggy biscuit. Your friend will like the trick. His dog will love it Drop your right hand to your side casually. When nobody is looking, allow the coin to fall onto the curled right fingertips, where it remains concealed in finger palm.

The Complete Vanish

Magicians refer to a "complete vanish" as any sleight that enables you to end with both hands completely empty.

As described above, the false transfer or switch leaves you with a coin in finger palm. If you're standing, you must simply retain the coin in palm position until you can casually ditch it in your pocket. If you're seated, you can turn this into a "complete" vanish. After executing the false transfer, rest your right hand on the edge of the tabletop so your fingers extend just beneath the tabletop. Release the coin into your lap without moving your right hand. First show your audience that your left hand is empty and *then* raise your right hand to chest height to show that it, too, is empty.

The Miser's Dream

MATERIALS:
An opaque coffee mug, a quarter, and a handful of change (a mixture of 8 to10 different coins is best).

SETUP: A coffee mug works perfectly for the produced coins, though an opaque glass or bucket will work, too (showing a transparent mug for clarity here).

The routine begins with a quarter-in-right-hand finger palm.

Just before the performance, cup the coins in the fingers of your left hand and then pin the coins against the inside of the mug. Notice that the left fingers are extended, pinning the coins in a flattened column against the inner side of the mug while concealing them from view. With the left thumb, brace the mug from the outside.

DIFFICULTY:

THE EFFECT This is the classic quarter-from-your-ear . . . completely revamped. **You produce *dozens* of coins from nowhere, cause invisible coins to materialize, and even let a participant produce a coin.**

THE SECRET "The Miser's Dream" uses a variety of principles: palms, productions, switches, and timing.

THE PERFORMANCE

"T he Miser's Dream" is really just a continuous production of the same coin (now concealed in your right fingers). Each time it is produced, you switch it for one of the coins concealed by your left fingers.

❶ Hold the mug (and concealed coins) by the lip with your left thumb and fingers and begin by reaching into the air and producing the right hand's coin. To do this, push the palmed coin into view with the right thumb.

continued ☞

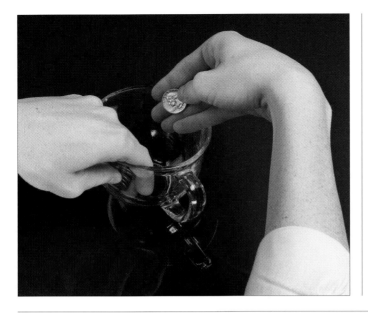

2 Display the coin for a moment and apparently drop it into the mug. Here you'll execute the first switch: Move the right fingers inside the mug, as if to deposit the produced coin. Under cover of the mug, slide the coin back into finger palm with the right thumb.

At the same time, loosen your left fingers' grip and allow one of the concealed coins to fall to the bottom of the glass. There is no technique here; you simply loosen your grip until you feel (and hear) one of the coins fall. When you time it correctly, it appears that the coin you produced dropped into the mug with an audible "clink."

If more than one coin should fall, don't despair. The audience can't see inside the mug, and the audible difference between dropping one or more coins is indistinguishable. Retract the right hand with the quarter concealed inside it.

3 Repeat the same procedure for all the remaining coins concealed behind your left fingers. Produce the right hand's coin behind your participants' ears, knees . . .

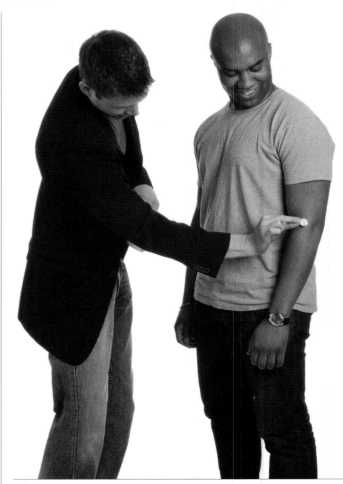

4 . . . elbows, and anywhere else you deem appropriate. Each time you produce a coin, display it in the right fingertips. Pretend to drop it into the mug (as you drop a coin from your *left* fingers), and then move your hands apart again.

⑤ Once you have dropped all of the concealed coins, tip the opening of the mug toward your audience to show all the money you "produced." Pretend to dump the change into your right hand but instead, maneuver the change *back* into your left fingers.

To do this, move both hands together as you invert the mug; note that the left hand does not alter its grip on the mug's side. As the mug is inverted, allow the change to slide back under the extended left fingers.

⑥ Close your right hand and pretend to take the handful of change away and put it in your right pocket, but actually move the right hand away with only the finger-palmed quarter. The change is silenced under the left fingers, and this allows you to reorient the mug so the mouth is upright again.

You are now reset to produce *another* round of coins. The mug appears empty, but the coins are again concealed by the left hand. The right hand still has its trusty quarter in palm position.

Continue as before until the fingers of your left hand conceal only one coin. Produce the coin at your right fingertips but this time really drop it into the mug. Show the audience that your right hand is empty.

⑦ For a grand finale, invite a participant to reach behind your ear and mimic producing a coin. Then ask her to toss the invisible coin into the air, toward the mug. Watch the invisible coin, following its path with your eyes into the air toward the mug, and then on the proper beat, ease your grip on the last coin concealed behind the left fingers, and allow it to fall into the mug . . . "clink."

MASTER CLASS

No verbal presentation is offered here because the effect is everything in "The Miser's Dream." Often accompanied by music, the magician becomes a mime-like figure as he walks between and around his audience, in search of invisible money. Plucking coins from the air is amazing to an audience, and talking a lot (save the occasional sound effect) would only detract from the mystery.

CREDIT: The effect goes back at least as far as Robert-Houdin in 1852, who called it "The Shower of Money." It became known as "The Aerial Treasury" until 1895, when T. Nelson Down dubbed his version, "The Miser's Dream."

SPOTLIGHT ON AL FLOSSO

Al Flosso didn't look like a master magician. He was short, heavy, and spoke with a thick New York accent, but Al Flosso also did the world's most outrageous Miser's Dream.

Flosso honed his coin productions during his performing career at Coney Island. He would invite a child onstage and produce silver dollars from the bewildered child's ears, elbows, and nose. But in Flosso's version, even *the child* produced money from his own pockets and joints, and even midair! Audiences had no idea where the money was coming from, and neither did Flosso's young volunteers.

Unexpected Profits

MATERIALS:
Two quarters, a cloth napkin or handkerchief, and a rubber band.

SETUP: Place a small rubber band in your right pocket. Have a cloth napkin or pocket square handy. This is the only preparation for the vanish.

To make the coin reappear, you have several options. You can simply load the second quarter somewhere unexpected, like under a saltshaker or in the folds of a newspaper. But it's far more fun to take risks and load it in your boss's suit jacket or your assistant's shoe. This trick requires only a light touch or a quiet step.

DIFFICULTY:

THE EFFECT You borrow a man's coin, make it disappear, and then make it reappear *in his pocket!*

THE SECRET You employ two quarters and secretly load one in the participant's jacket pocket. To make the other quarter disappear, you create a secret pocket in a cloth napkin or handkerchief with a rubber band.

THE PERFORMANCE

Ask to borrow a quarter from your participant. While he searches for a coin, casually put your right hand in your pocket and insert all four fingers into the rubber band. Bring your hand back out casually and nobody will notice the rubber band.

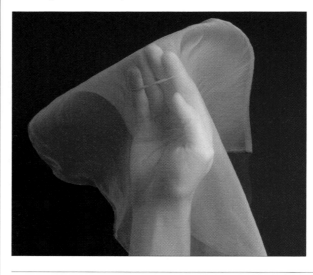

❶ Drape the cloth napkin over your right fingers to cover the rubber band from view.

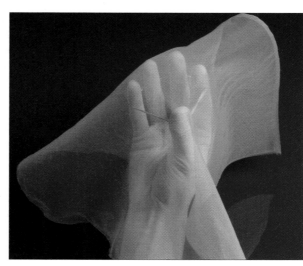

❷ Once the rubber band is covered, insert your right thumb into it and spread all your fingers apart to stretch it slightly (showing a transparent napkin for clarity).

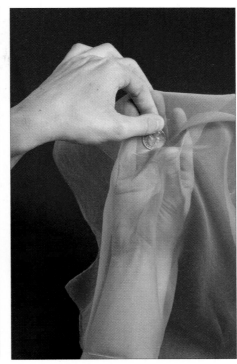

4 Push the quarter into the napkin about an inch so that the coin secretly passes through the opening of the rubber band. Release the rubber band so it encloses the coin.

Then turn your right hand palm down, allowing the ends of the napkin to hang down.

3 Take the participant's quarter in your left hand and openly place it on the draped napkin between the concealed fingers of your right hand.

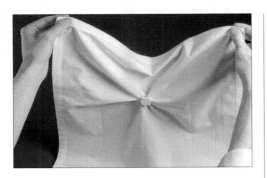

6 Grasp the napkin by its ends with both hands and shake gently. From the front, where your participant is standing, it appears that the coin has vanished. From your angle, it is safely hidden. Pocket the handkerchief after you present it and begin calling attention to the participant's pocket (or shoe, or wherever you hid the duplicate quarter). Allow him to discover "his" quarter's reappearance.

5 The quarter is secretly secured in the makeshift pocket created by the rubber band. You can gently slide your fingers away from the rubber band and it will remain attached to the handkerchief, clinging to the material.

money lost (the coin disappears) and found again (the coin reappears), you have magic with meaning.

MASTER CLASS

Corporate Magician Paul Gertner is the best-known practitioner of this effect. He teaches it to top corporate executives. Gertner uses a presentational theme about "finding profits in unexpected places."

Gertner understands that without a presentation this is a mere amusement. But when the effect is related to

CREDIT: Abbotts has been selling this effect as "Phantosphere" since the 1960s, but rubber bands, invented in the mid-19th century, have been used in conjuring since 1911.

The "Gun Trick," or the "Bullet Catch," whereby a magician somehow survives a gunshot completely unharmed, is without a doubt the deadliest magic effect in history. While there are some acts that have successfully performed a version of the effect (Penn & Teller use a modified Banachek effect; in 1988 "first lady of magic" Dorothy Dietrich became the first female magician to catch a bullet in her mouth), more than a dozen people have been killed during performances of the trick.

One of the most famous fatal performances was on November 8, 1829, when Louis de Linsky was onstage performing for Prince Schwartzberg-Sonders-Hausen.

For his dramatic denouement, Madame de Linsky, his wife, was to withstand a firing squad of six soldiers provided by the royal court at Arnstadt.

Louis de Linsky coached the six cadets in advance. Their guns were real, but each man was instructed to bite both the tab and musket ball during the loading process. This way, the barrels would be packed only with gunpowder—no projectile—and the shots would be harmless.

But a soldier forgot to bite his bullet, so when the squad unloaded their rifles, the unfortunate Madame de Linsky was shot in her abdomen. She died the next day, only twenty-three years old and pregnant.

Another fatality was Chung Ling Soo (William Ellsworth Robinson, 1861–1918), an American magician who performed as a Chinese conjurer. In Soo's version, the loaded bullet was supposed to fall into a secret chamber of the gun. On March 23, 1918, however, gunpowder buildup between the two barrels of his gun ignited and the bullet fired into the performer's chest. Soo, who had for many years onstage pretended not to speak English, exclaimed "My God,

I've been shot." Thus, his first English words in public were also his last.

"Art is long and life is short," wrote Harry Houdini, after the Roman poet Horace, in the September 1906 issue of *Conjurer's Monthly Magazine.* "The stage and its people, in the light of history, make this a verity." In his inimitable style, Houdini recounts the demise of yet another magic fatality—the *Bullet Proof Man:*

For the benefit of those who have not heard of this sensational attraction—which was indeed a great novelty for a brief time—I will explain that the man was a German who claimed to possess a coat that was impervious to bullets. He would don this coat and allow anyone to shoot a bullet of any caliber at him. Alas! One day a marksman shot him below the coat, in the groin, and eventually he died from the wounds inflicted. His last request was that his beloved invention should be buried with him. This, however, was not granted, for it was thought due the world that such an invention should be made known. The coat, on being ripped open, was found stuffed or padded with powdered glass.

Madame Clementine was a popular female conjurer at the beginning of the twentieth century, and during her rendition of the Gun Trick, she opted to forego any bullet switching and use real ammunition. This decision proved fatal, but not for her.

Clementine's performance entailed firing a bullet across the stage in the direction of her targeted assistant. She would purposely and secretly overshoot her target and send the bullet whizzing safely past the assistant, backstage. Simultaneously, Clementine's assistant would produce a bullet from his teeth. Timed properly, the illusion was perfect.

The illusion had worked perfectly when Clementine performed it twice nightly at the Canterbury Music Hall in Westminster, U.K. But when she moved to the Middlesex Music Hall for her next run of performances, she forgot to change the sightings of her weapon. The stage at Canterbury had been a small, intimate venue. The Middlesex stage was more than twice the length and height. Thus, the calculated settings were incorrect, and she accidentally shot her assistant through the forehead.

On June 14, 2007, the Gun Trick claimed its latest victim, Togo's Kofi Brugah. Brugah (stage name Zamba Powers), one of Africa's busiest magicians, was touring Ghana at the time. Having played his show before villages in Asamankese and elsewhere, Brugah found himself in the south at Adukrom, in front of a large, enthusiastic crowd.

Brugah performed traditional conjuring tricks, including a production of money and candy, both immediately distributed to spectators. For his last illusion, he offered to withstand the fire of a gun. Ghana's largest newspaper, *The Daily Graphic,* reported:

> After a tense moment of silence, a gentleman stepped forward from the crowd and Brugah handed him the gun, stood upright and asked the volunteer to press the trigger. Boom! Horror of horrors! There lay Brugah in a pool of blood . . . .

Pandemonium ensued, and the "volunteer" who shot Brugah ran

In 1988, "first lady of magic" Dorothy Dietrich performed the Bullet Catch— a trick that Houdini himself never attempted.

from the scene. The magician's assistant, Kwabla Ali, helped assemble a team to transfer his fallen employer to Adukrom Health Centre. Brugah was dead on arrival.

When the group arrived at the hospital, everyone except Brugah's assistant fled. The landlord of the performing venue and the volunteer who fired the gun are still wanted for questioning. Needless to say, the Gun Trick is not an effect to take lightly.

When the "Chinese Conjurer" Chung Ling Soo was fatally shot in 1918, his greatest illusion was revealed.

Money Laundering

MATERIALS:
Two one-dollar bills and a business card.

SETUP: First you have to make "laundered" money. To do this, fold a dollar bill into fourths, and then wrap it in two tissues (this is your lint source). Place it in the pocket of your dirtiest jeans. Now machine wash and dry everything. The result is a lint-covered, hardened dollar bill (and a clean pair of jeans). If your bill isn't laundered enough, rinse and repeat.

For this presentation, you'll also need a lawyer's business card. I made a gag business card on my computer for an extra laugh; it reads, "Dewey, Cheatem, and Howe Law Firm." Of course, this bit is optional for the effect.

Place the business card in your right pocket. Fold a clean one-dollar bill into eighths and place it in your left pocket.

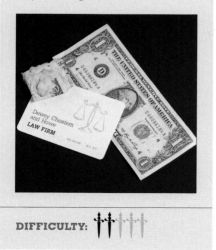

DIFFICULTY: ††††

THE EFFECT You know how money looks when it has been through the washing machine? We've all discovered a crusty, ruined bill in our pocket at least once—and cursed ourselves for forgetting to empty our pockets before doing laundry. **One such ruined bill is displayed, and then magically restored to pristine condition.**

THE SECRET A simple switch accomplishes the feat—yet another application of the false transfer. Here, we use the false transfer as a switch rather than a vanish.

THE PERFORMANCE

1 *"I'm happy to announce that the jeans I'm wearing . . . are clean!"* Take a bow. Nobody is impressed . . . yet. *"I'm not so happy to announce that I forgot to take this out of my pocket."*

As you talk, put your left and right hands into their respective pockets. Bring out the laundered bill with your right hand a split second before removing your left hand. Secretly hide the normal dollar a in left-hand finger palm. If you move your right hand first and look at the laundered bill it holds, the participants' attention will be directed to the strange-looking bill and not to your left hand.

Unfold and display the laundered bill in your right hand. Let the participants examine it if you like. *"I can't talk too loud,"* you whisper, *"because this is laundered money."* Take the bill back, folding it back into eighths. As you do this say, *"I know two ways to solve a money laundering problem. One involves a long walk off a short pier into the Hudson River. The other requires a lawyer."* You then apparently transfer the bill into your left hand. Actually, you'll retain it in your right fingers. To do this, put your right thumb on top of the laundered bill.

2 Next slowly bring your hands together. Turn your right hand palm down as you turn your left hand palm up. With your right thumb, keep the laundered bill pinned against your right fingers.

Close your left fingers around the normal bill and move it up to chest height.

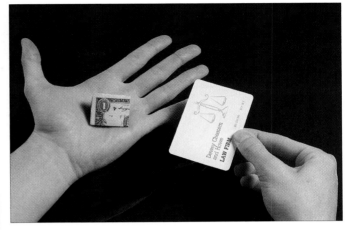

3 Move your right hand into your right pocket. While it's in the pocket, ditch the laundered bill and bring out the business card. Show the card to your participants and allow them to notice the gag printed on it.

Using the business card as a magic wand, wave it over your left fist as you say, *"Now I say the lawyer's magic words: 'three-hundred an hour, payable in advance. . . .'"* Open your left fingers and show that you have magically fixed your money-laundering problem.

MASTER CLASS

"Money Laundering" has all the elements of a good pocket effect. You can perform it anywhere, entirely surrounded by your audience, and without the aid of a table. And it has an amusing presentation that fuses literal and figurative money laundering.

CREDIT: **This method is based on the technique of billet switching that was developed by fraudulent spirit mediums in the late 19th century.**

JADE

Magic from Asia is markedly different from Western magic, and female-magician Jade is world-renowned for her act which uniquely blends East and West. She is based in San Francisco, but draws upon her Chinese roots to perform magic typical of the Asian tradition: manipulation of water, parasol and fan mysteries, and beautiful costume changes, all performed at a graceful, elegant pace. Jade's act also features components of Western comedy, particularly in a number in which she repeatedly escapes from restraints tied by male volunteers.

Jade's show incorporates many elements of performance art and she is quick to suggest the same to other female magicians. "Indulge in other kinds of stage performances: dance, theater, and other variety arts. Then you can capitalize on what the other art forms have to offer. I also recommend taking drama and dance classes to learn how to move onstage."

Table Trouble

MATERIALS:

Any coin and an opaque table

DIFFICULTY: 🗡🗡🗡🗡🗡

THE EFFECT You show a quarter in your right hand. "You've heard gangsters talk about money under the table," you say, "but I don't think this is what they mean." **You visibly and audibly push a coin through the tabletop.**

THE SECRET Our trusty false transfer strikes again! The illusion is enhanced with a sneaky auditory effect.

THE PERFORMANCE

❶ Display a coin in your right hand and pretend to take the coin into your left fingertips while retaining it in your right fingers.

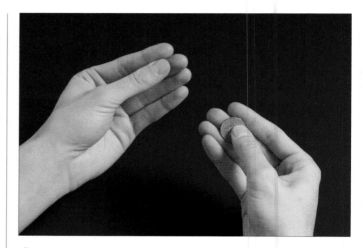

❷ Move your left hand forward on top of the table, apparently holding the coin.

  Just after your left hand moves forward, move your right hand underneath the top of the table, apparently to catch the coin as it passes through. Gently press one edge of the coin against the underside of the table.

❸ Two actions happen simultaneously. Your left fingers press down against the tabletop, as if pushing a coin through. Press with your left middle finger and spread the others so that it is apparent your left hand is now empty.

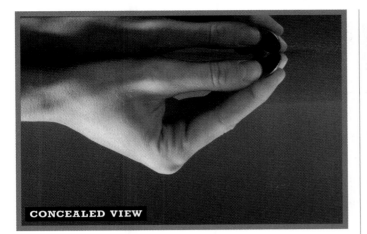

CONCEALED VIEW

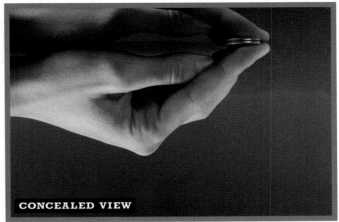

CONCEALED VIEW

4 At the same time, "snap" the right hand's coin against the table's underside, using your right first finger and thumb. Timed correctly, the coin appears to penetrate (vanish from the tabletop) just as everyone hears an audible "snap."

5 Allow the coin to drop back into the palm of your right hand and bring that hand back into view. It will appear as if you caught the coin as it passed through the tabletop.

MASTER CLASS

We've talked about Robert-Houdin's insightful analysis of a magician's role: "A magician is an actor playing the part of a magician." To play that part, we have to believe—on some level—in what we're doing.

You must practice the technique (the false transfer in this case) so that it becomes second nature. You shouldn't even think about the technique when you perform; like eating or driving or changing channels, it should be a habitual action that eventually becomes subconscious.

Legendary close-up magician Derek Dingle had an excellent tip to add conviction to coin magic. "Read the date," he would say, suggesting that you pretend to read the date on the coin in your left hand. Of course, there is no date on the coin in your left hand . . . because there is no coin in your left hand. But this subtle tip convinces participants beyond a shadow of a doubt that you're still holding a coin in your hand.

CREDIT: This effect first appeared in John White's *A Rich Cabinet with a Variety of Inventions* in 1668.

Penny Pressed ON DVD

MATERIALS:
Two identical pennies, one of which has been flattened.

SETUP: Magicians have used train tracks for years to flatten pennies; this is dangerous, however, so I suggest trying other options. Good office-supply shops have paper presses that will flatten a small coin. Or, for a few bucks, a local jeweler can flatten a few pennies for you.

If you plan to give the coins away afterward, flatten a bunch of pennies at the same time. Since you can't anticipate whether your participant's coin will be shiny or dull, make sure you flatten a group of pennies in various stages of oxidation.

Begin with the flattened penny concealed in a finger palm with your right third, fourth, and fifth fingers.

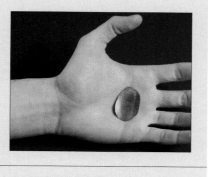

DIFFICULTY: ⚔⚔⚔⚔⚔

THE EFFECT **Demonstrate your superhuman strength by flattening a borrowed a coin.** The permanently altered penny makes a perfect souvenir for your participant.

THE SECRET When you're done with this effect, the participant's penny looks like it has been run over by a train.

THE PERFORMANCE

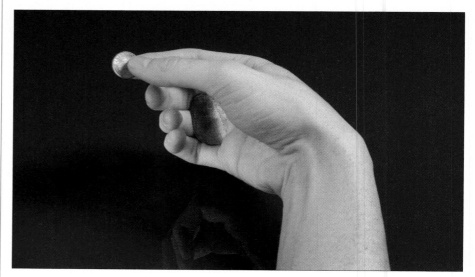

1 Borrow a penny from someone and hold it between your right thumb and first finger. Notice that the flattened penny remains in your right hand, concealed by your other right fingers.

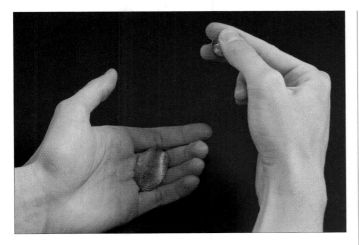

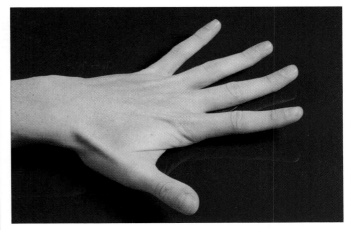

❷ Toss the borrowed penny into your waiting left hand. Close your left fingers around the penny as you catch it. Open the left hand again and retake the penny between your right thumb and first finger. Repeat the toss-and-catch action two more times.

While you toss the penny, say, *"I've been working out lately. Can you tell?"* This will get a laugh. *"I'm serious. Watch this."*

You'll apparently toss the borrowed penny into your left hand again. Actually, you execute a transfer, called a Bobo Switch: Curl in your right wrist just before tossing the penny to your left hand. Instead of tossing the borrowed penny, retain it between the first finger and thumb. At the same time, open your right fingers and allow the flattened penny to fall onto your left hand.

❸ The flattened penny is in constant motion and is thus indistinguishable from the normal penny just displayed. When the flattened penny hits your left hand, quickly close your fingers around it. The switch is done.

In a continuing action, turn your left fist palm down and open your fingers as you slam the penny against the table. Pretend to squash the coin with your palm as you feign physical stress.

Alternately, keep your hand in a fist and act as if you're straining as you *slowly* push the flattened penny from your fist, forcing it between your second and third finger (as if it has gone through a wringer). Casually lower your right hand without flashing the borrowed penny.

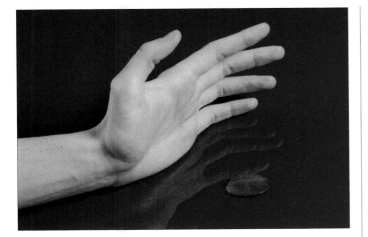

❹ Lift your left hand (or open your fist after you've squeezed the penny out) to reveal your superhuman strength. Give the participant "her" penny back, and conclude, *"I can bench-press an entire roll of quarters, too."*

MASTER CLASS

The Bobo Switch is an unlikely sleight; the audience *sees* the switched object (the flattened penny in this case) but they can't interpret what they're seeing. The flattened penny is blurred in motion, roughly the same color as the original coin, and in view for only a split second.

There are some finesse points to the switch. Follow these guidelines for a perfect illusion.

• You must precondition your audience to the toss-and-catch action. That's why you toss the borrowed penny several times before the switch. This acclimates your participants to the tossing action and puts them at ease. Don't forget to establish this action before performing the secret switch.

continued ☞

- Anticipate the catch with your left hand. That is, close your left fingers *while the flattened penny is still falling.* Don't wait for the coin to land or you risk exposing the climax too soon.

- Your eyes direct the participant's focus. First look at the borrowed penny in your right hand. Look at the participant as you toss the coin so the audience isn't so focused on the move. Then look at your left hand, where the borrowed coin is supposed to be.

The Bobo Switch sounds like a clown kidnapping, but it's not. It's a handy magician's tool with unlimited applications. Here are some examples to get you thinking:

Mint Machine: To change a quarter into a mint, simply conceal a mint in your right fingers as you display a quarter between your right thumb and first finger. Toss the quarter into your left hand a few times, commenting, "My left hand doubles as a candy machine. And a mint candy costs twenty-five cents."

Execute the Bobo Switch and reveal that your quarter has magically changed into a mint. When you pocket the mint's wrapper you can ditch the concealed quarter.

Change for a Dollar: No change machine around? Use magic! Begin with four quarters concealed in your right fingers. Openly fold a dollar bill into eighths and toss it into your left hand. Repeat the tossing action a few times, and then execute the Bobo Switch. The audience hears the dollar bill change as you release the quarters into your left hand. This is particularly effective near parking meters and vending machines.

Rocky: "Some people hide keys under rocks," you say outside your house. You pick up a small pebble. "I hide my keys *as* rocks." So saying, you change the pebble into your house key.

To perform this impromptu stunner, simply keep your house key concealed in your right fingers. Pick up a small stone with your right first finger and thumb and execute the Bobo Switch. It looks as though the rock has changed into the key.

CREDIT: Called the "Bobo Switch," the effect was published by J. B. Bobo in the first edition of *Modern Coin Magic* in 1952.

Trash to Treasure

MATERIALS:

Two one-dollar bills and a table.

SETUP: Defacing currency is technically breaking a federal law, but this is magic on the edge. Tear a dollar bill in half, and then tear one of those halves in half again. You'll need the "half" piece and one of the two "quarter" pieces. You must be seated to perform this effect.

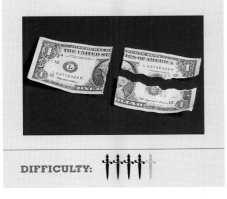

DIFFICULTY: †††††

THE EFFECT You present an unfortunate situation: a dollar bill torn into three pieces. "I found these in a public trash can," you say, "while I was looking for a snack." As you talk, you place the separate pieces between different fingers. "But one man's trash is another man's treasure!" And suddenly, **you magically restore the pieces to make a whole dollar bill.**

THE SECRET A folded dollar bill masquerades as one of the pieces. Through a clever illusion, it's possible to display one bill as three separate pieces.

THE PERFORMANCE

❶ Fold a normal dollar bill in half lengthwise.

❷ Then fold the dollar again, bringing one end of the bill near the other end, about a half-inch short of perfect alignment. Place the two torn pieces (the "half" and the "quarter") on top of this folded bill. At quick glance, it looks as if you hold only the pieces of a ruined bill in your hand.

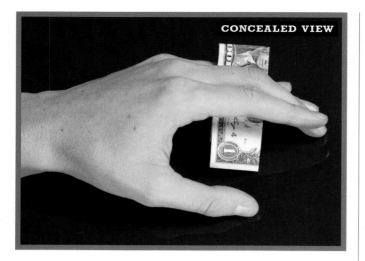

❸ Display the torn pieces of the dollar bill in your left hand (be careful not to flash the underside of the folded bill). As you talk to the audience, rest your left hand on the table's edge nearest you. Your palm should face your body. Drop the torn pieces onto the table, openly retaining the folded bill in your hand (the audience believes this to be another torn piece).

Insert the folded bill between your second and third left fingers so that the folded end protrudes slightly, less than an inch. Notice that the ends of the bill are concealed from view beneath and behind your left hand.

❹ Using your right hand, pick up the smallest torn piece and fold it in half. You can use your left fingers to help fold the torn piece. Next, you will apparently insert the piece between the third and fourth fingers of your left hand. Actually, you are going to switch this piece for an end of the folded bill.

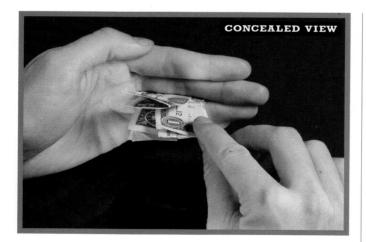

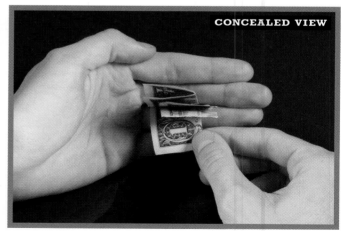

❺ To make the switch, insert the quarter piece into the fold of the complete dollar, between your left second and third fingers.

❻ Immediately pinch the lower, shorter end of the folded bill between your right thumb and fingers.

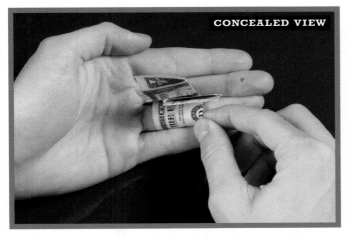

7 Insert this end between your left third and fourth fingers.

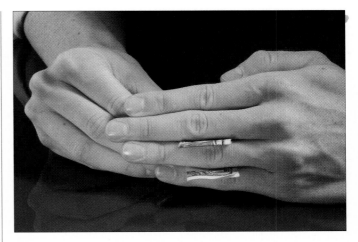

8 It will protrude from the front.

9 With your right hand, pick up the torn half piece remaining on the table. Fold it in half and in half again. Place this piece into the same fold as the previous one, between your left second and third fingers. In a continuing action, bend the longer end of the folded bill so that you can insert it between the your left first and second fingers.

10 From the front, it appears you are displaying three separate torn pieces of a dollar bill.

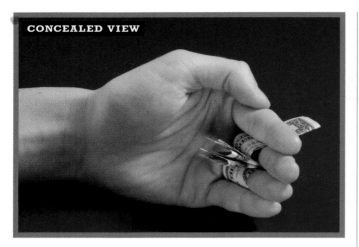

CONCEALED VIEW

11 Actually, the audience is seeing the same bill snaked through your fingers. From your point of view, the concealed pieces protrude from the folds of the complete dollar bill.

CONCEALED VIEW

12 The restoration is automatic and foolproof. Say, *"But one man's trash is another man's treasure!"* With the fingers of your right hand, pull up on the uppermost protruding end of the complete bill. Pull the bill slowly through your left fingers. It appears that each protruding "piece" fuses back together as it slides away.

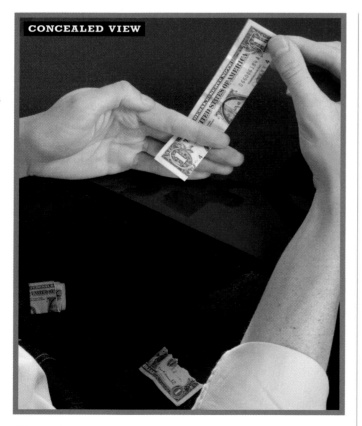

CONCEALED VIEW

13 Simultaneously, the torn pieces fall into your lap, unseen. Offer the dollar bill up for inspection and show your empty left hand.

MASTER CLASS

When we see a dropped ice-cream cone melting on concrete, we all react the same way: "What a waste." The same thing is true with money. The very sight of torn money disturbs people. Restoring torn money affects our audience on an emotional level. You took something worthless and made it valuable again. Your magic matters!

CREDIT: I devised this effect when I was twelve. At that time, my hands were too small to palm the pieces, so I developed a way to restore the bill without any palming.

Old Dog, New Trick: Using a Folding Coin

Coin Through Bottle

THE EFFECT Push a quarter, borrowed from a participant, through the bottom of a bottle.

MATERIALS:
A magician's folding coin (a standard gaff sold at all magic and novelty shops) and any bottle.

SETUP: Secretly place a folded coin in an empty bottle. The bottle doesn't have to be yours. Just bend your folding coin and stick it in the neck of the bottle without anyone seeing you. The coin should remain wedged at the top. If the bottle is relatively opaque, the coin is virtually undetectable. Magic shops sell these gaffs by the hundreds, but the effect they pitch it with where the performer takes a bite out of a coin is, I think, a bit obvious. For sake of completeness, however, I will detail this effect, too (see "Master Class," page 200). But a far more subtle use for the gaff is to push a borrowed coin through a bottle, as follows.

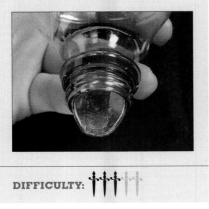

DIFFICULTY: 🗡🗡🗡🗡🗡

THE SECRET

 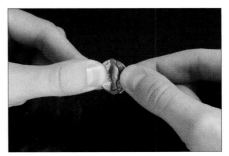

A folding coin, usually a quarter, is actually a coin cut in half or thirds.

The pieces are held together by a small rubber band around the edge of the coin. Glass bottles work best for the following effect.

THE PERFORMANCE

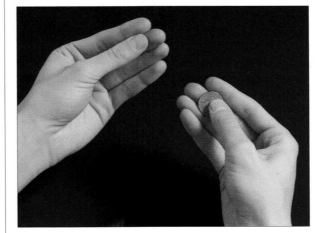

❶ Borrow a quarter, taking it at your right fingertips. Execute a false transfer (page 18), pretending to place it in your left hand, but retaining it on the right fingertips, out of sight. Then form your empty left hand into a fist, as if you hold the coin.

CONCEALED VIEW

2 Pick up the prepared bottle with your right hand, keeping the spectator's coin concealed as you move. You'll apparently push the coin through the bottom of the bottle. To create this illusion, two things happen simultaneously. First, open your left hand as you move it toward the bottle. At the same time, smack the bottom of the bottle against your left palm. This jerking action automatically forces the folded coin to fall from the neck of the bottle to the inside.

This is a wonderful moment because the audience sees and hears the coin pass through the plastic. Your left hand is empty and the participants can peer inside the bottle at the coin. The situation is an impossibility because a quarter is too big to fit inside the bottle, even through its opening.

You can stop here if you like, or venture forward with the coin's removal.

3 To get the coin out of the bottle, simply perform the reverse of the above actions. With the mouth of the bottle toward the floor, give the bottle one firm shake downward to re-lodge the folding coin in the neck. If the coin doesn't wedge itself the first time, shake the bottle until it does. Be careful. Too firm a shake might propel the coin out of the bottle altogether. At the same time, open your right hand and bring the borrowed coin back into view. It appears, at a glance, as if the coin has fallen from the bottle.

After the show, when nobody is looking, you can surreptitiously retrieve the gaffed coin from the bottle's neck.

CREDIT: The "Coin Through a Bottle" routine was marketed by the Hartz Magic Repository in New York in 1873, while the folding coin effect dates back at least one year earlier.

MASTER CLASS

As I outlined in the setup, biting a piece off a coin and "spitting" the piece back on is a popular—and crude— application of this gaff. But if visual is what you're going for, read on.

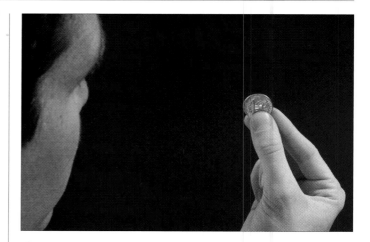

1 Hold the folding coin at your fingertips, in front of your face. Make sure the slit is positioned horizontal, running side to side.

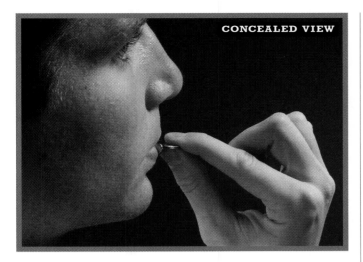

CONCEALED VIEW

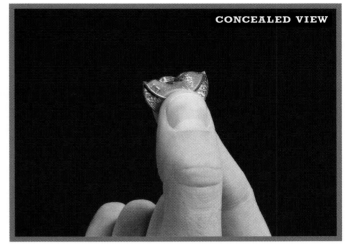

CONCEALED VIEW

❷ Place one flap from the gimmick in your mouth. Once it is partially covered by your lips, fold this piece of the coin backward, toward yourself. Hold it in position with your right thumb.

❸ Now pull the coin away from your mouth as you pretend to eat a piece of the coin. The partial coin displayed at your fingertips is quite convincing, particularly if your gimmick has been cut with curves.

Now spit the supposed "chewed" piece back onto the piece at your fingertips. At the same time, ease your grip on the folded segment, allowing it to flip back into view. With proper timing, it appears you "spit" the coin back into one piece. Your parents will be so proud!

CARING FOR YOUR COIN

Magic vendors rarely tell you about the care and feeding of your gaff. What happens if the rubber band breaks? Here's a quick tutorial.

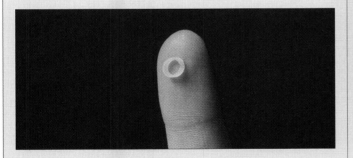

❶ Whether your coin is in two or three parts, it's held together by an orthodontic rubber band, no bigger than a fingertip. Over time, this rubber band oxidizes and becomes brittle; it will eventually break.

❷ To replace it, simply wrap a new rubber band around the edges of the pieces. With gentle, frequent use, a rubber band should last six months.

Bank Roll

Perform this overnight procedure with a stack of dollar-bill-sized papers as well, and place the fake roll in your right pocket. Also place a loose dollar bill and a rubber band in your right pocket.

Your two pockets must have easy access. Jacket pockets, dress pants, loose-fitting jeans are perfect for this effect.

DIFFICULTY: ⚔⚔

THE EFFECT You offer your audience some tips on how to fake a big bank roll. You display a roll of paper and wrap a one-dollar bill around the outside. "From a distance, it looks like I've got a roll full of money. This might impress poker opponents," you say, "but I can tell it isn't impressing you. That's because it doesn't have a rubber band around it!" **You expertly stretch a rubber band around the roll of paper, snap your fingers, and display that it has changed into a roll of bills.**

THE SECRET You have two bank rolls: a fake one and a real one. You'll execute a bold but undetectable switch during the effect.

THE PERFORMANCE

❶ *"Tony Soprano would never be caught with one of these,"* you say. Remove your wallet and show it for a moment. *"Instead, every respectable mobster carries his money in a bank roll."*

Reach into your right pocket and remove the paper roll. Unroll and display the paper. *"And if you don't have a bank roll, you fake it."* Retrieve the loose dollar bill from your right pocket and wrap it around the paper roll.

❷ *"From a distance,"* you explain, *"this would pass for a wad of cash."* Look at your audience. *"Not impressed? That's because it's missing the final touch of class: a rubber band!"*

3 You will now remove the rubber band from your right pocket. But, under the guise of taking out the rubber band, you'll secretly switch the fake bank roll for the real roll of money. Here's how: Transfer the fake roll to your left hand. Look at your audience and place both hands in their respective pockets.

4 With your right hand, retrieve the rubber band. With your left hand, deposit the fake roll in the pocket and take hold of the real one.

5 Bring out your right hand a split second before your left hand emerges from your pocket. The left hand's roll appears unchanged because the bill around the outside of each roll is identical.

Wrap the rubber band around the roll. *"How does it look now? Realistic?"* Your audience will remain unimpressed. *"I think it looks pretty real!"* So saying, remove the rubber band and unravel each bill to reveal an authentic bank roll!

MASTER CLASS

This is the Ham Sandwich Theory in practice. You remember the Ham Sandwich Theory from the Introduction? The idea is that magic is stronger if it fulfills the audience's desire. And changing paper into real money is universally appealing.

CREDIT: This technique is known as the "Rhythm Switch" and was first published in 1967 in *New Jinx* by Max Maven.

Coin Rolling

MATERIALS:
Any coin.

SETUP: None!

DIFFICULTY: ✝✝✝✝✝

THE EFFECT While it isn't magic, no manual on the subject would be complete without the world-famous roll down, exhibited in films by renegade cowboys to keep their trigger fingers nimble. **You roll a quarter down the back of your hand and across your knuckles.**

THE SECRET There is no secret. It just takes a ton of practice.

THE PERFORMANCE

now at the outset that you will drop your coin many, many, many times before you see noticeable results. Welcome to the most difficult entry in *Magic*.

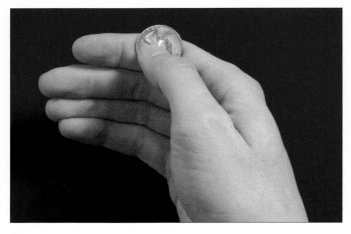

1 Begin with a quarter between the right thumb pad and the right first finger, situated in such a way that your thumb pad rests slightly on top.

2 With your thumb, slide the coin to the side of your first finger.

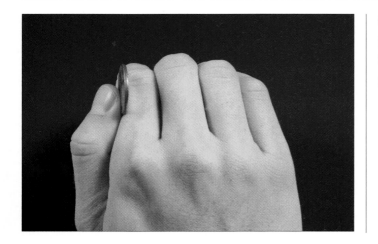

3 Now turn your hand palm down, pinning the coin in place between the side of your right first finger and the thumb pad. The coin should be propped into a vertical position.

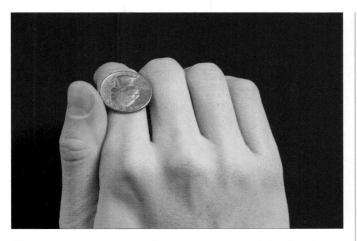

4 With your thumb, nudge the coin *around* the first finger and lever it to a horizontal position, resting across the first finger. Note that the coin is positioned between the first knuckle and the base of the finger.

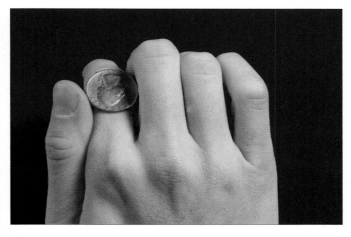

5 Carefully raise your right second, third, and fourth fingers slightly. To make the coin "walk" across your fingers, lower each finger in succession, as if you were playing piano scales.

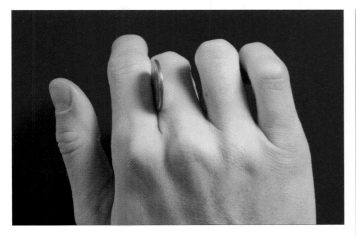

6 Lower your right middle finger first so that it contacts the coin and rotates it back to a vertical position between your first and second fingers.

7 By easing your grip and tilting your hand slightly, allow the coin to fall back to a horizontal position, this time across your middle finger.

8 Continue in this fashion until the coin is pinched between the third and fourth fingers of your right hand. At this point, there is nowhere else for the coin to go. So, curl your little finger inward and rotate your entire hand so the palm faces inward.

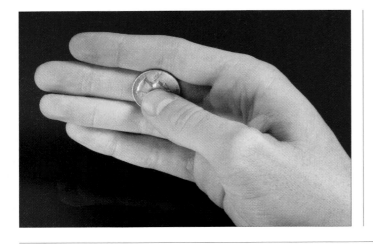

9 Retrieve the coin with your right thumb and slide it back onto the palm side of your hand. From here, you can repeat the roll again and again. It's hypnotic (for you, if not your audience).

MASTER CLASS

Once you've mastered this basic coin roll, try these stunts:

Across Both Hands: Rather than curling your right little finger and cycling the coin back into your hand, practice rolling the coin across both hands. To do this, align your left first (index) finger to your right fourth (little) finger. This creates eight hurdles for your running coin!

Nondominant Rolling: All this stunt requires is practice. Right-handers can master the right-handed roll fairly quickly and vice versa for southpaws. But the true test of your coordination is whether you can learn the sleight with your nondominant hand.

Simultaneous Rolling: When you can roll a coin across both sets of knuckles, try both simultaneously. You'll discover that rolling a coin in each hand isn't terribly difficult *as long as the hands mirror each other.* That is, move both middle fingers at the same time, cycle the coins around at the same time, and so on. As long as both hands do the same thing, you can eventually even do the whole stunt without looking.

Two Coins, One Hand: This stunt takes hundreds of hours to master, but it is possible to roll two coins on the same hand. Begin the roll as described above, but when the first coin has reached the end of its first cycle (pinched between the right third and fourth fingers), place a second coin between your right thumb and first finger (place the second coin with your left hand).

The right thumb retrieves the first coin and cycles it around *as* the fingers roll the second coin down the knuckles.

CREDIT: This flourish was first created by Nate Leipzig in 1902, originally called the "Steeplechase."

Grandpa's Coin Trick

MATERIALS:
Two identical coins. You must also be wearing a wristwatch.

SETUP: Place two coins under the face of your wristwatch. Quarters are ideal.

DIFFICULTY: ⚔

THE EFFECT You offer to demonstrate the ultimate guessing game, but you offer it with an invisible coin instead of a real one: "Which hand is it in," you say, in the time-honored fashion of grandfathers worldwide. A futile game ensues because, after all, guessing which hand an invisible coin is in is pretty silly. **But when you open your hands to "show" the invisible coin, you prove that a real coin has appeared . . . in each hand.**

THE SECRET The two coins are hidden under your watch.

THE PERFORMANCE

❶ *"My grandfather got me interested in magic. He wasn't a magician, but he did one incredible trick. He would take a coin. . . ."* As you talk, pinch your right first finger and thumb together as if you are displaying a coin. *"And then he would put both hands behind his back and then bring both fists forward. He would say, 'Which hand has the coin?'"* So saying, move both hands behind your back, make a fist of each, and then bring them back into view, fists facing down. Allow the participant to indicate either hand.

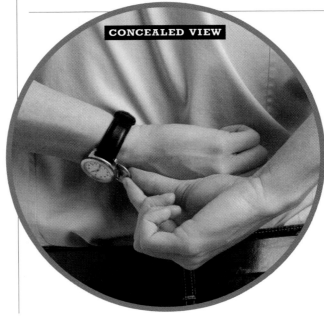

CONCEALED VIEW

❷ Whichever hand she chooses, open the other fist and say, *"No, the coin is here."* Of course, there is no coin, so make sure you deliver this line playfully. Show her that both of your hands are completely empty and put them behind your back again, offering to play once more.

CONCEALED VIEW

❹ *"Sometimes Grandpa would play the game differently. He would show the coin at his fingertips like this, before he closed both fists at the same time."* Suiting actions to words, "display" the right hand's invisible coin between the right thumb and fingers, just as Grandpa would have done.

❸ This time, retrieve both coins from beneath your watch. Finger palm them, pinched between the base of your left second and third fingers and their first joints.

Bring both fists forward again and challenge the participant to guess which hand holds the "invisible" coin. No matter which hand she indicates, open your empty right fist but mime the actions of holding a coin. If she guesses your right fist, say, *"Exactly!"* and pretend to display an invisible coin. If she guesses your left fist, say, *"Wrong again!"* Either way, open only your right fist. Your left fist will be presumed empty, even though it remains clenched.

❺ Extend your left first finger and thumb and move the left hand toward the right. The left first finger and thumb can extend without disturbing the two coins concealed in your left fist. Fake a grabbing action with both hands and form each into a fist. Say, *"Which hand now?"*

Once again, show the right hand empty first. Congratulate your participant if she guessed your left hand. Then, with the fingers of your right hand, reach into your left fist and take hold of *just one* of the two palmed coins. Bring this coin into view. Under the guise of a guessing game, you have turned an invisible coin visible.

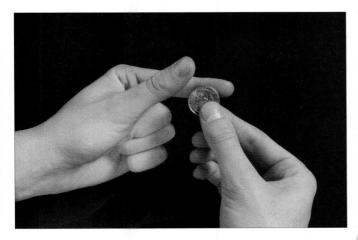

6 Keep your left fist closed after you have removed a coin. Position the visible coin in your right hand, between the thumb and fingers. You'll play your grandfather's guessing game one more time, this time with a real coin.

Move the left hand toward the right, extending the left first finger and thumb as before.

Let the right hand's coin fall onto the right fingers as both hands fake a grab. Immediately form both hands into fists, obscuring where the coin falls as much as possible. "*Last time,*" you say, "*Which hand?*"

7 Whatever she guesses, open both hands at the same time to reveal a coin in each. Say, "*Grandpa cheated. He used two coins. So do I!*"

MASTER CLASS

I've given you a bare-bones presentation here, suitable for impromptu settings. But you can embellish your grandfather's trick if you have a larger captive audience.

The two-coin production is well choreographed within a guessing game, and you'll find that this game is excellent mental distraction from the coins you are concealing.

CONQUER YOUR FEAR OF LARGE AUDIENCES

Stage fright is the number one fear of human beings. Polls reveal that, more than drowning or being struck by lightning, the average person fears being onstage. Yet everybody's job likely has some element of public speaking. For some, it's an annual shareholders' report in front of thousands. For others, it's being in front of a classroom. No matter what the scenario, magic makes it more fun.

This chapter deals with magic you can integrate into your next public appearance. Whether or not you're booked as a magician, these effects will punch up your next presentation.

Imagine reading an expense report from the podium. You cough at one point, and whisper how thirsty you are into the microphone. A moment later, you produce a glass of water. Real magic? No, but it looks that way. Check out "Ovation Position," just ahead, for details.

Or visualize yourself onstage, dressed up for that annoying awards seminar you're obligated to attend. It's your turn to present. Before you begin, you address the audience. "Please excuse the interruption," you say, "but I think I've got a rock in my shoe." So saying, you remove from your shoe a rock bigger than your foot! "Earth Shoes" shows you how.

You'll learn to tear and restore a newspaper, predict a thought-of word, and find hidden money. And each effect in this collection packs small and plays big. They are all visual in nature and simple in plot. Even from afar, they amaze and deceive.

THE WARM-UP

The parlor magic described in this chapter doesn't involve many secret gimmicks or sleights of hand, but it requires your best dramatic skills. For larger audiences who can't clearly see your props or effects, the presentation carries the magic. Here are some tips to keep in mind:

Perform the Magic at Chest Height

A beginner's gut reaction is to perform illusions the way she practices them—in her lap. But when you are before large groups, hold your props at chest height where everyone can see them.

Fill Out Your Space

Although your rehearsal space is likely your basement or living room, remember that your stage is much bigger. Don't confine yourself to the podium or to one corner of the stage. Set your props on tables near the audience, and if possible, use two end tables, one on each side of the stage. Plan to cater each effect, or a part of each effect, to a different audience area. Just make sure you stand still when you're talking or performing an effect. It's jarring to an audience when a performer is walking and talking and doing magic at the same time. Instead, walk from side to side between effects or during applause.

Project

If they can't hear you, they can't appreciate your magic. Speak slowly and audibly but don't shout; project your voice to the back of the room. If the audience is unwieldy, use a lavaliere microphone (you can't very well do magic if one hand is always preoccupied with a handheld mike).

Performing effects at chest height allows for maximum visibility.

Ovation Position ON DVD

MATERIALS:
A straight-edged glass of liquid, filled almost to the top. A couple of ice cubes is a nice touch. And, you must be wearing a jacket or blazer and loose-fitting pants with a back pocket.

SETUP: Just before going onstage, place the glass of water in your right back pocket. As long as you don't trip or get spanked on the way to the stage, the water won't spill. The glass should protrude a little. Your jacket will hide this from the view of the audience.

DIFFICULTY: †††††

THE EFFECT Whatever your public speaking purposes (magic or otherwise), this is a perfect icebreaker. You introduce yourself to your audience and offer to teach everyone *how* to applaud during your act. You proceed to teach the "ovation position." At the end, **you toast the crowd with a glass of water . . . produced from your sleeve!**

THE SECRET The glass of water is concealed . . . in your back pocket!

THE PERFORMANCE

Just after you're introduced, make your way to the stage and greet the audience. *"I have to confess something. I am really thin-skinned. I need lots of affirmation and I never seem to get enough. This must be a weakness, but my feelings are easily hurt. Do you know what? You have actually hurt my feelings. The applause was so modest. I'm used to ovations."* You will get some polite applause here. Hold up your hands to stop the charitable clapping.

"No, I don't want your pity. I've just realized two things. First, you are all stockbrokers, and you're used to giving rewards for high performance, not just for showing up—right?" (If you're performing for engineers or New Yorkers, rather than stockbrokers, you would alter the script accordingly.)

"Another thing I've figured out is that nobody has ever taught you the Ovation Position." Laughter ensues.

❶ *"I'll show you. Hold your hands like this."* Hold your hands about a foot apart, palms facing each other. Then press your hands together with alacrity and enthusiasm. Explain that when everybody does it together, it creates an ovation.

"Everyone assume the position! Please, everyone do it. That's good! Now relax for a second. I want to earn an ovation from you.

"I'll tell you what I'll do. I'll recite the alphabet. . . ." Pause. *". . . backward! And when I get to the last letter, you will burst into applause!"* Pause again.

"I can see this doesn't impress you. You know what I'll do? I'll say the alphabet backward and, at the same time, I'll take off my jacket." Rub your hands against your jacket and sleeves, ostensibly to show off your jacket. Really, you're proving nothing fragile is hidden in your sleeves.

"You're going to be so impressed with this, you'll break into thunderous applause. Just think! You'll be able to go home and tell your friends you saw Joshua Jay stand before you and do two things at the same time. He said the alphabet backward and he took off his coat. Amazing!"

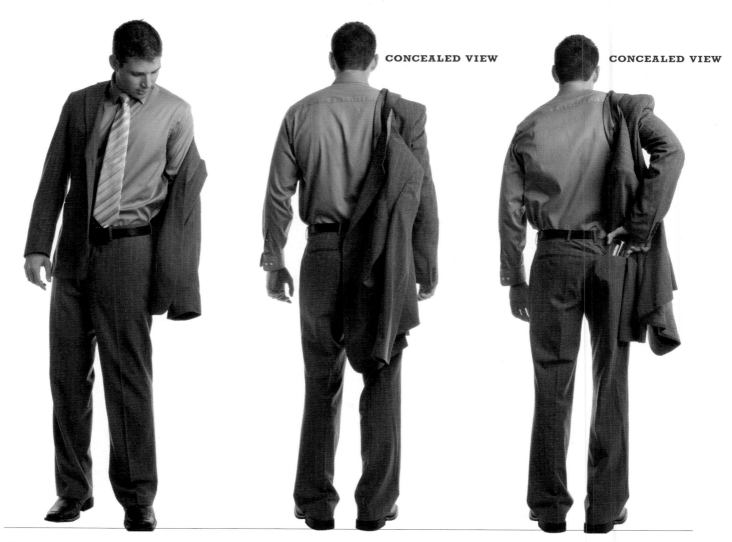

CONCEALED VIEW   CONCEALED VIEW

❷ Now you get serious. *"Assume the position!"* Do this with the audience. *"Everyone, ovation position!"* The whole audience is primed, waiting to applaud wildly. Close your eyes and begin, almost like an incantation: *"Z, Y, X, W, V, U, T, S, R, Q, P . . ."* Pause for a moment, as if thinking.

Slide your left arm from your sleeve without the aid of your right hand. This is awkward at first, but it comes more easily with practice (practice this one alone, lest someone see you sliding your jacket off in front of a mirror over and over and get the wrong idea). Move your left shoulder down and back in a shrugging action, almost flinging the coat off the shoulder.

❸ Once your left hand clears your sleeve, the jacket hangs off your right side. From behind, the jacket continues to cover your right back pocket and the glass concealed within it.

❹ Continue, *". . . O, N, M, L, K, J, I, H, G, F, E, D . . ."* As you talk, you'll secretly steal the glass of water. Move your left hand in front of your body, to your right lapel. Just after you move your left hand, move your right hand to the glass in your back pocket. The right hand's movement is concealed by your hanging jacket. Grasp the glass of water between your right thumb and fingers.

CONCEALED VIEW

5 With your left hand, slide your jacket off your right shoulder. As this happens, begin to pull the glass of water through your right sleeve.

6 In doing so, you'll automatically turn the sleeve inside out. This is good; it conceals the glass of water from view. Continue pulling the glass from the jacket's sleeve.

7 *". . . C, B, A!"* Time your actions so that as you complete the backward alphabet, your right hand emerges from your jacket with an unexpected refresher. Hold up the glass and toast the audience. Take a sip. You deserve it. *"Is that what you call an ovation?"*

MASTER CLASS

We've talked about using concise, simple effects that are easy for the audience to understand. But on a smaller scale, even some movements are more legible than others. Escalate your voice as you recite the alphabet backward, straighten your posture, and hold up the glass of water like you're posing for a picture. Your voice, body, and actions all speak that the piece is finished, and it's time to applaud.

Scripting magic is essential. Because the piece is so simple, every word in this script serves the effect. Here, the audience is coached on how you want them to respond. You prime your participants to applaud, seemingly of their own accord, and reap this benefit throughout the entire program. This sets the tone for fun, unexpected entertainment.

On a technical note, when I first tried this, I was afraid the water would spill from the glass. There's just something about walking onstage with a wet spot on your pants that sends the wrong message.

Reducing the amount of liquid

in the glass is a bad solution, because producing a *full* glass of water is far more impressive than one that is only half full.

Barrie Richardson, who wrote the script above, suggests you use a tennis ball container. You know the ones . . . plastic jars a bit bigger than water bottles. The advantage is that these containers have a lid. Assuming your back pocket is wide enough for such a container, you can simply fill it with water and then snap on the lid. Now you can pace backstage and make your entrance without worry of spilling. Just before beginning the effect, slip your hand behind your back, remove the lid, and tuck it inside your pocket. Problem solved.

For bigger audiences, you may want to use a glass containing colored liquid, like tea or cola. Water isn't as visible from a platform.

Also, for those of you who aren't household names, this effect is an excellent vehicle to get people to remember you. This particular script provides several opportunities to reference your name throughout your performance: "You'll be able to . . . tell your friends you saw [insert your name here] stand before you and do two things at the same time!"

CREDIT: Barrie Richardson, who created "Ovation Position," is a motivational speaker at banquets and functions all over the world. He uses magic as a metaphor for inspiring concepts. As you can tell from his thoughtful, entertaining script, Barrie is also one of magic's most distinguished writers. Note the audience involvement, humor, and simplicity of this piece.

Richardson is the retired dean of The Frost School of Business at Centenary College, and one of the world's most respected magical thinkers. English magician Pat Page taught Richardson this classic street busking stunt, and he honed the presentation throughout years of keynote speaking.

MEMORIZING THE ALPHABET . . . BACKWARD

The hardest part of "Ovation Position" is memorizing the alphabet backward. Barrie Richardson to the rescue again, this time with a story mnemonic that will help you memorize the inverted alphabet in less than thirty minutes (Richardson teaches this mnemonic at the collegiate level). Like most mnemonics, this is just a crutch for learning. With time and practice, the silly images fall away and you're left with complete recall of the backward alphabet.

Just envision the following sequences. Each one has an outrageous and memorable visual image. Memorize each step individually, then build on your image as you add new steps.

1. Z, Y, X, W, V, U
"Zeke, wh**Y** don't you put an **X** on the **W.V.U.** flag." Visualize a crossed-out flag with the initials of West Virginia University (visualize their catastrophic '82 football season).

2. T, S, R, Q, P
Visualize that the flagpole is a **T**ea **S**poon. Robert **Q.** **P**reston's initials are on the spoon.

3. O, N, M, L, K
This one's easy. The teaspoon is balanced **ON** a **M**i**LK** carton.

4. J, I, H, G, F
"**J**ab **I**n **H**is **G**ood **F**inger," is the mnemonic here. Picture a guy's middle finger jammed into the milk carton.

5. E, D, C, B, A
"**ED**'s hand is on the **C. B.** radio **A**ntenna." Just picture the hand (mentioned above) belonging to Ed. Picture Ed's other fingers wrapped around a C. B. radio antenna.

Hand Scam ON DVD

MATERIALS:
Your hands.

SETUP: None.

DIFFICULTY:

THE EFFECT Contort your arm in the most impossible position.

First off you invite your audience to follow along with you. "Hold out both hands," you say, and you wait for everyone in the audience to comply. You further instruct them to interlock their hands as you demonstrate. Then, you rotate your wrist 180 degrees counterclockwise. When the audience members try, their wrists quickly lock up—they're unable to move their arms as you did.

THE SECRET Although it appears you and your audience begin in the same position, your starting position is slightly different, and can accommodate a counterclockwise rotation.

THE PERFORMANCE

❶ Invite everyone in the audience to participate. *"Everyone, please hold out your hands and wriggle your fingers, like this."* Hold out your hands about chest high and wriggle your fingers to demonstrate. *"Turn the backs of your hands toward each other, with your pinkies on top."*

❷ Invite your participants to cross their right arms over left. (Their palms should be facing.) *"Interlock your fingers, like this,"* you continue, demonstrating.

3 *"Now wriggle your left middle finger."* Wriggle yours and then watch as the audience members attempt this.

Now comes the scam: With your right hand, gesture toward someone to your left, commenting, *"No, that's your right middle finger."* When you point with your right hand, leave your left hand extended, in position.

4 You will apparently move your right hand back into position. Actually, the position will be (indistinguishably) different, so that you will be able to do the next maneuver—a counterclockwise rotation—but the people in the audience will not! Move your right hand leftward as your turn your right palm toward your left palm. Interlock your fingers in this position, with the right arm *under* the left. (Study the subtle difference between photos and you'll discover that you can rotate your fists counterclockwise only when the right wrist is positioned under the left.)

"Now don't let go. Whatever you do, don't let go of your hands. Wriggle both thumbs like this, and slowly turn your fists." Wriggle your thumbs and rotate your fists counterclockwise until the thumbs are uppermost. The key to this illusion is to rotate your wrists *slowly*.

Hold the position and watch a sea of knuckles turning white, unable to budge.

MASTER CLASS

A strategy of this book is to involve the audience in some way in every effect you do. And while "Hand Scam" is light fare for a magic show, it's an excellent interlude that involves everyone. It's easy, visual, and funny. And even though you might be twenty rows and two balconies away from your public, it puts the magic in *their hands*.

Torn and Restored Newspaper

THE EFFECT You remove the front page from a newspaper and display it. "A little math quiz," you say. "If I rip the newspaper in half, how many pieces will I have?" You tear the page in two.

"That's right, two pieces. If I tear these pieces in half," you continue, suiting actions to words, "then I have?" The audience responds. "Right! Four pieces. And if I tear those in half?" You get the picture. You display the eight pieces.

"If I tear these eight pieces in half, and half of those in half," you say, "then that leaves . . ." you hesitate, ". . . a lot of pieces! I was never good at math. I'm much better at magic." So saying, **you unfold the bundle of torn pieces to reveal the original newspaper, restored.**

THE SECRET You have two identical pages and switch the torn one for a pre-folded, "restored" piece.

MATERIALS:
Two identical newspaper pages (smaller, tabloid-sized newspaper pages work best) and a table.

DIFFICULTY: †††††

SETUP: You need to find two identical newspapers. The smaller (tabloid) size works best, and you can often find these papers free outside grocery stores or schools. Oftentimes they're weekend updates, real estate listings, or restaurant guides. The content doesn't matter.

❶ Pre-fold the cover page of one newspaper. With this fold, you give the impression that the corners are a bundle of folded pieces. The exact folding isn't critical as long as the end result resembles photo 4. Refold the paper at its "binding" so the top page sits slightly askew, so there are four visible corners along the open edge.

❷ Fold the newspaper in half a second time, folding the bottom edge up to meet the top edge, so the front page is concealed.

continued ☞

SETUP, CONTINUED:

❸ Fold the paper in half a third time.

❹ Fold the paper in half along the diagonal so the corners remain visible at the top of your relatively triangular bundle.

❺ Place this bundle between the second to last and the last pages of the second newspaper, near the edges.

❻ Fold this second newspaper in half. From all angles, the secret, duplicate piece is concealed.

THE PERFORMANCE

CONCEALED VIEW

❶ Pick up the newspaper with both hands. Slide the cover page away from the others, pinning the folded duplicate against the remaining pages with your right fingers. As long as you keep the front of the newspaper toward the audience, they will be unable to see the duplicate hidden behind.

❷ Fold the remaining pages in half, maintaining your grip on the secret duplicate. Hold the cover page in your right hand and the newspaper (and the folded bundle) in your left hand. Slide the newspaper and the hidden piece under your right arm as you turn slightly to the left. As long as you keep your body turned slightly toward the left, the hidden piece will remain out of audience view, hidden behind the newspaper pages under your arm.

❸ Open the cover page and display it between your hands. *"Pop quiz: If I tear this newspaper in half, how many pieces will I have?"*

continued ☞

4 Tear the page in half. Each time you tear, ask the audience how many pieces you have. This rudimentary math exercise provides a good opportunity for humor (you will be surprised at how slowly some audiences calculate the totals; you can exploit this for fun). The questions help cement the idea that the newspaper really is being torn apart.

5 *"If I tear these two pieces in half . . ."* Align both halves and tear them again. *" . . . how many do I have?"* Align these pieces and tear them once more. Continue aligning and tearing (and quizzing your audience) until you have sixteen roughly even pieces.

6 Fold this stack into a triangular shape, approximating the folded duplicate. *"So if I had eight pieces, and then tore them in half, and tore half of those in half. . . ."* The point here is confusion. Up to this point, all your questions have been insultingly easy. The brief moment of confusion is the perfect time for a switch. Transfer the packet of torn pieces to your left hand.

7 Hold the torn packet between your left thumb and fingers, move it to the newspaper under your right arm, and pin it to the outside surface (against the inside of your right arm). This is your first step in apparently moving the newspaper that you have tucked under your arm onto the table beside you. The action should be casual and unstudied.

❽ As you pin the pieces against the newspaper with the fingers of your left hand, make sure you also take hold of the folded duplicate with your left thumb pad.

Pull the newspaper from your arm, holding it parallel to the floor as you lower it. Your left thumb (and the duplicate piece) should be on top. Place the newspaper, with the packet of torn pieces hidden beneath it, on the table as you openly retain the bundle visible to the audience.

❾ That's the switch. It happens *as* you move the newspaper to the table. Since the two packets look similar from a distance, the switch will go unnoticed. As you switch the papers, deliver the punch line to your joke: *"Apparently you weren't math majors either!"* Display the folded page and snap your fingers. Slowly unfold it and point out, *"You can still see the lines where each piece fused back together."* These lines are just folds, but they seem like magical seams from a distance.

MASTER CLASS

The "Torn and Restored Newspaper" is a classic of magic, with good reason: It's visual for five people or for five hundred. It's easy to understand and uses a universally familiar object.

The advantage of this version is that virtually no preparation is required. If you can find two identical newspapers, you can do this effect!

The last line demonstrates a small but important subtlety. When you unfold the page, it is wrinkled from the folds. You point to the folds and say, "You can still see the lines where each piece fused back together." You have turned these folds into part of the magic. This presents the viewer with a vivid mental image of how the magic looked.

CREDIT: There are myriad versions of the "Torn and Restored Newspaper," but I developed this one for *Magic* based on three criteria: It had to be relatively simple, it had to easy to prepare, and it had to look like magic.

GENE ANDERSON

Gene Anderson distinguishes himself from other magicians with an act using only one prop: newspapers! He has performed his newspaper act professionally in twenty-one countries on six continents, and his book *Newspaper Magic* is now in its eleventh printing.

Gene is the undisputed authority on conjuring with newspaper, and he advised *Magic* on the inclusion of this classic. "Newspapers have a grain," Gene says, "and they tear nicely either across the page or in the up-and-down direction. Take advantage of this and make your first three tears with the grain. The fourth tear (to 16 pieces) can be across the grain; by then it won't matter if the tears aren't very straight."

Pick a Word

ON DVD

MATERIALS:
A pen and paper, paperback book, and a coin (quarters work well).

SETUP: Flip through any book, looking only at the first word on each left-hand (even numbered) page. Choose a force word of some substance; avoid words like "of" or "and" or "the." Four letters or more is best.

Place your quarter at your force page near the spine of the book. Notice that when you riffle the pages with your fingers, you automatically stop at the force page because the quarter creates a tiny gap.

If this is a friend's book, load the quarter surreptitiously and then reshelve the book. If you're using one of your own books, you may actually wish to prepare several books, each with a different coin and force word. This way, a participant can choose from several books.

DIFFICULTY: †††††

THE EFFECT "There are approximately three hundred words on each page of a paperback novel," you say as you remove a book from a friend's shelf. "Times hundreds of pages makes tens of thousands of words for you to choose from at random from any page of this book. And without reading the book, I'm going to read your mind." You choose a book from your friend's shelf and she remembers a word from a page of her choosing; **you look into her eyes and guess her chosen word, letter by letter.**

THE SECRET The word is forced from the book.

THE PERFORMANCE

"*There are approximately three hundred words on each page of a paperback novel. This one has four hundred pages. That's roughly one hundred and twenty thousand words, give or take a surprise ending or two. You're going to choose a word at random from any page of this book. And we'll use that word as a target for a telepathy experiment.*"

Here you must give the impression that you have chosen a book at random. If you've secretly prepared a book on someone else's shelf, this fact is self-evident. Don't be too studied when you remove the book. Look away and pull it from the shelf as if you were simply removing a book to illustrate what you're saying.

❶ Hold the book by the spine in your left hand with the cover facing you. With your right fingers, riffle the pages, starting at the end of the book and riffling toward yourself. "*We can use any page you want. Just call 'stop.'*"

2 Riffle slowly until the participant calls stop. As she starts to speak, just riffle to the gap—where your quarter is. This part happens automatically. No matter where she says to stop, riffle to the gap. If she hasn't stopped you until you have already passed the gap, just riffle quickly through all the remaining pages and make a joke of it: *"Sometime between the covers, please."* Then start again until you can properly force the page.

"I'd like you to think of a word from this page," you invite, indicating the left page. *"Can you see the first word?"* Ask her to remember this word. Make sure to look away throughout this whole procedure. Since you already know the word, you don't need to peek.

3 Lower the book and open it a little wider. This causes the coin to dislodge from the spine and fall secretly into your hand. Toss the book to the nearest table and casually stick your hands in your pockets, ditching the quarter.

Borrow a pen and paper and ask the participant to look you in the eyes. The rest is presentation. But don't rush the ending. Instead, make an event out of this. *"So you're thinking of a word—any word—from that book. You chose the page and you chose the word. Just keep thinking of it."*

Suppose the force word is "bedroom." Remove the pen cap and

CONCEALED VIEW

prepare to write. *"I'm not getting the word yet, but I'm getting the impression of some letters. Is there a D? An E? An O? Wait—two Os?"*

Here's a classic mentalism ploy: *"Is there an N? No?"* Act confused. *"Ah! It's an M, but it's a lowercase M, and that looks like an N."* Now write your force word in full, keeping it out of your participant's view.

"For the first time, what was your thought-of word?" Allow your participant to answer. Then turn over your prediction . . . a perfect match.

MASTER CLASS

This effect leaves your audience with the impression that you can actually see *thought-of* words. Of course, you can't. You can't even simulate this. Yet this is exactly how audiences remember "Pick a Word."

The reason has as much to do with the script as the technique. You ask a participant to say "stop" as you riffle the pages. This is hardly the same as asking her to choose her own page. Yet this is how you describe it: "We can use any page you want. Just call 'stop'. . . ."

You ask her to look at the first word on the page—

which is not the same thing as *thinking* of a word. But later you refer to her chosen word as "in her mind," and "her thought-of word." You're sculpting—altering—a memory here to enhance the effect. In so doing, you take a good effect and make it *great*.

CREDIT: This is an example of what magicians call a "Book Test" effect, and the premise dates back to 1607. Girolamo Scotto di Piacenza, however, was recorded performing a book trick for the Emperor of Austria as early as 1572.

Earth Shoes

MATERIALS:
Shoes, a suit jacket or blazer, pants with a deep back pocket, and a smooth, long rock a little smaller than your foot. The rock should taper gently, thinner at one end than the other.

SETUP: Place the rock in your right rear pants pocket.

DIFFICULTY: ✠✠✠✠

THE EFFECT It's an impossible sight gag. Commenting that you think there's a rock in your shoe, you remove your right shoe and withdraw an enormous rock. It falls to the floor with the thud that only a genuine rock makes. The stone is *real*. **You've dumped a rock—as big as your foot—out of your shoe.**

THE PERFORMANCE

At one point during your show, start limping and complain that there's a pebble in your shoe. Turn your body 45 degrees to the right (so your left side is angled toward the audience), but keep your head squared toward the audience.

❶ Lift your right leg and situate the right side of your right foot across your left leg, above the left knee. Bend your torso forward slightly. With your left hand, pull off your right shoe. Hold the shoe from beneath, gripping the heel against your left palm. As you

remove your right shoe, concentrate your attention on it. Meanwhile, you're going to sneak the rock from your back pocket. In this position, your right hand should be completely hidden from audience view so it looks like your hand is naturally balancing your body.

❷ Reach between your jacket and your pants and retrieve the rock.

Pin the rock against the back of your right thigh as you remove the shoe completely. In one action, move your right hand (with the rock) down your thigh as you move your left hand (and the shoe) upward, along your right shin.

❸ As the hands near each other, move the right hand (and the rock) toward the opening of your shoe. As long as both hands move together, quickly, the audience will be unable to see the rock in your hand.

❹ As soon as your hands touch, feed the thinner end of the rock into the shoe's opening. Move your right hand away as you lower your right foot. Now turn your body so you

are squared to the audience. Pause for just a moment, so people can see a rock protruding from your shoe. Then allow the rock to fall from your shoe to the floor (watch your toes).

MASTER CLASS

Scared they'll think you're using a sponge rock? The thud of the rock hitting the stage is proof positive that yours is the real deal.

"Earth Shoes" is the second effect in this chapter that requires placing a large, heavy object in your right rear pants pocket. If you want to perform "Ovation Position" (page 215) and "Earth Shoes" in the same show, simply adapt the handling of one or the other to accommodate a *left* rear pocket.

And just because this effect appears in a chapter devoted to parlor magic doesn't mean it won't fool close-up. The effect was first published as a stunt, to be performed outside, say, next to your car.

CREDIT: "Earth Shoes" creator Looy Simonoff is a retired professor of mathematics at the University of Nevada, Las Vegas. He first published "Earth Shoes" in Paul Harris's *Super Magic* in 1977.

CONCEALED VIEW   ❷

CONCEALED VIEW   ❸

❹

Old Dog, New Trick: Using a Set of Linking Rings

Lord of the Rings

ON DVD

MATERIALS:
A set of Linking Rings, found in any magic shop and included in many magic sets. (If your mom didn't throw yours out when you left for college, they're probably still at the bottom of your closet, next to the X-ray specs.)

SETUP: Many of the best routines use only three or four Linking Rings. This routine uses four: two rings permanently linked, one normal (single) ring, and one key ring. Set the others aside.

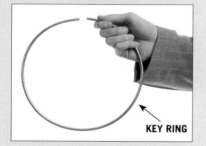

KEY RING

Before performing, stack the rings on your working surface as follows, bottom to top: the two linked rings, the normal ring, and the key ring. You can hold this stack and transfer it from hand to hand; just be careful not to let the rings overlap or disorder.

DIFFICULTY: †††††

THE EFFECT   **You cause solid steel rings to link and unlink at will; this new take on a classic is the real deal.** Everyone has seen a magician butcher a Linking Rings performance; the routines are almost always too long. But seeing this classic performed artistically is a rare treat; when properly handled, the rings baffle. The instructions that come with a set of Linking Rings are usually one page, without illustrations. Nobody can learn the Linking Rings this way—it's like trying to teach an elephant how to surf. What follows is a professional-caliber routine that you can—and will—use.

THE SECRET   The Linking Rings are sold as a set of eight rings. Some of the rings are truly (and permanently linked), and one "key" ring has a small gap. Through a series of displays and sleights, you hide the key ring's secret gap as you pass rings through it, "linking" them like magic.

THE PERFORMANCE

One reason the Linking Rings have garnered such a bad reputation is that few performers have found presentations that engage the audience. My feeling is that steel rings are too abstract to pass off as normal, relatable objects (hoop earrings? Mini hula-hoops? I don't think so). Your best bet is to perform the piece to music.

The Count

Even though three of the four rings you're holding are gaffed, you're going to show them all normal and all *separate* in the following count. This count deceives the eye and the ear, and it couldn't be easier.

❶ Hold the stack of rings in your closed, but palm-up right hand. The key ring's gap is well concealed by your right thumb (it's the ring closest to your right wrist).

2 Insert your left hand, palm up, partway through the center of the stack of rings.

3 Angle your right hand down slightly, and with the aid of the right fingers, allow each ring to fall individually from your right hand into your left.

4 Each ring will make a clinking sound against the others as it falls. This count is counterintuitive—how can linked rings move independently of one another? But as you'll discover, each ring (including the linked ones) appears to fall separately onto your left fingers. Be sure to maintain the order of the rings during this counting.

KEY RING &
NORMAL RING

LINKED
RINGS

The First Link

5 Before visually linking the first two rings, take the key ring and the normal ring back into your right hand. This leaves the two linked rings at the left fingertips. Toss the linked rings into the air a few inches and thrust your left arm through their centers. Store the rings at your elbow for a few moments.

NORMAL RING

KEY RING

6 In a similar action, take the normal ring back into your left hand and toss the key ring to your right elbow. As long as the gap in the key ring rests against your arm and clothing, it will remain unnoticed. Display the normal ring between your hands. Raise this ring to chest height and look through it.

7 With the fingers of both hands curled around it, slide the normal ring through your fingers to show the ring doesn't pull apart. To do this, grip the ring with your left fingers and rotate it, pulling it through your loosely gripped right fingers.

KEY RING

8 Slip the normal ring onto your left forearm and retrieve the key ring from your right elbow. Grasp the key ring with the left fingers, keeping your hand curled around the gap to conceal it. Show the key ring in the same manner as the normal one, but as you apparently slide the ring through your fingers, keep the left fingers anchored over the secret gap.

9 Pass the key ring to your right hand, taking care to conceal the gap with your right fingers during and after the transfer. You have displayed all four rings separately and proved, supposedly, that no gaps exist on any of them.

KEY RING   NORMAL RING

10 Now retrieve the normal ring (from your left forearm) and display it between the fingers of your left hand. To link the two separate rings together, maneuver the key ring's hidden gap to the opening in your right fist, just behind the first finger.

11 Hold the rings at chest height and overlap them slightly so that the normal ring rests between the key ring and your body. From the front, it looks like a Venn diagram.

12 Slide the rings against each other by moving your hands closer together and then farther apart. As you move the rings, turn your wrists first toward . . .

13 . . . then away from each other, as if each hand was holding onto a car steering wheel. During this action, allow the normal ring to slide through the key ring's gap. Immediately after it clears, continue the sliding action as before.

continued ☞

14 From the front, the people in your audience can't tell whether the rings are linked or unlinked (even from up close). Reveal the first link by slowly pulling your hands apart until the rings lock against each other.

15 Release your left hand's grip on the normal ring and allow it to dangle from the right hand's key ring. Drop your left hand and catch the two linked rings, together, as they fall from your elbow. They will fall together; the audience assumes these rings to be separate even though they are secretly linked.

The Second Link

16 The second link is a no-brainer; you will simply reveal the rings that are permanently linked. Here's how to do it with style.

Tap the left hand's two rings against the rings in your right hand.

17 Concentrate for a moment, and then release one of the two rings from your left fingers. One will fall and hang, suspended. Immediately pass out these two rings for examination. Unless Merlin is in the front row, those babies aren't coming apart again.

LINKED RINGS

KEY RING

NORMAL RING

KEY RING   NORMAL RING

18 To unlink the right hand's two rings, you'll execute the linking action, but in reverse. Hold the key ring in your right hand, covering the gap between your right thumb and first finger. Hold the single ring in your left hand. Your hands should mirror each other so you don't call any undue attention to the right hand. This time, grip the rings gently and rock them forward and backward as you inch your two fists toward each other. As before, unthread the single ring from the gap in the key ring the moment your hands touch, and then continue the rocking action as you *slowly* separate them again, effecting an eerie unlinking—as if the rings melt apart.

Linking Again
19 Here's the prettiest sequence in the routine. The key ring is still held in the right hand, the single ring in the left. Flip both rings around your hands so they rest against the back of each forearm.

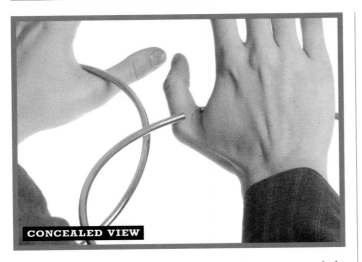

CONCEALED VIEW

20 Maneuver the gap in the key ring so that it is concealed behind your right thumb's webbing.

21 Once you have it in this position, you can open both of your fists, palms outward, for an extremely fair display.

continued ☞

22 Now move your thumbs toward each other and thread the rings together. The bases of your thumbs hide the actual linking from sight.

23 The moment the rings are engaged, form fists again. In a continuing action, flip the rings back over your hands and display the link. For best effect, this sequence is done in rapid succession.

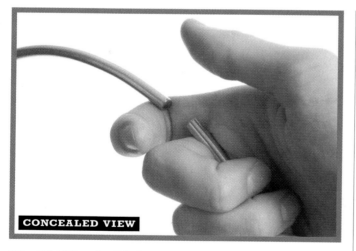

CONCEALED VIEW

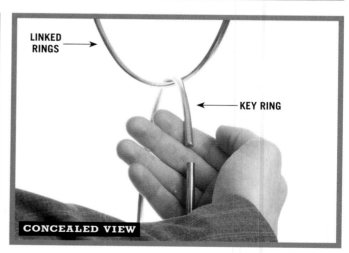

LINKED RINGS →

← KEY RING

CONCEALED VIEW

The Big Finale: Linking All Four

24 Retrieve the two linked rings from the audience and hold them in your left hand. Your right hand holds the key ring, and the normal (single) ring is dangling beneath it.

25 Position the left hand's two rings just beneath the normal ring. Raise your left hand upward, grazing the two linked rings across the rings in your right hand. As the lower, dangling ring in your left hand passes your clenched right fist, gently thread it through the gap in the key ring. You don't have to worry about being silent here. There are supposed to be clinking sounds when the rings are rubbed together. And your left hand's upward motion conceals the smaller motion of threading the two strands together.

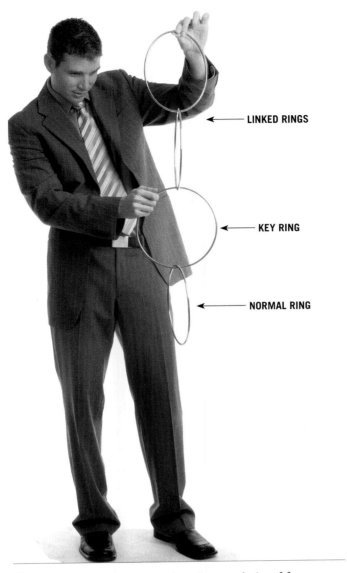

←— LINKED RINGS

←— KEY RING

←— NORMAL RING

26 Continue moving upward to show a chain of four linked rings.

MASTER CLASS

Linking Rings certainly aren't household props or items your audience is familiar with, and this goes against the thrust of *Magic;* but in this case, their use is justified by their simplicity. What is the clearest way to demonstrate solid through solid? Large, visible rings made of strong materials work perfectly.

In this routine, I've done away with lots of links and relinks in favor of the most visual two or three effects to keep this Linking Ring routine short and succinct. The routine has a natural build that culminates with a four-ring finale.

I don't see much inherent entertainment value in the rings themselves (as opposed to effects with money or chosen cards, where participation and intriguing props engage the audience). For this reason, I think performing to music is the way to go.

But there are other ways to make the rings "play." You can use a participant, inviting her to join you onstage to verify each link up close. You can even allow her to link rings together with only a slight alteration to the above routine. Instead of displaying the two permanently linked rings yourself, hand them to your assistant and instruct her to "link" them. To the audience's surprise (and your participant's delight) she has linked the rings.

CREDIT: You have just performed a miracle more than five hundred years old. The Linking Rings are often (and incorrectly) referred to as Chinese Linking Rings, but the effect appears to have 16th-century European origins.

MODERN MASTER

TOM FRANK

Tom Frank is a busker—a magician who performs at festivals and on the streets.

The "Linking Rings" is a staple of the street magician's repertoire because it can be enjoyed close up or from afar. It's also a classic that many audiences *expect* from a magician.

Tom developed a unique, memorable presentation for his routine: As he carries out the choreography of the moves, he recites a version of Edgar Allan Poe's spooky poem, "The Raven." Tom's routine, like the poem, asks the audience if what they're seeing is really happening (the rings link), or if it's all just an illusion (the rings unlink).

"For twenty-five years, I've ended my show with the rings," says Frank. "The [Linking] Rings combine senses of sight, sound, and touch."

Money Mischief

SETUP: Use four envelopes of the same size and color. Mark one on the back with a pencil dot at the upper right corner. This mark will allow you to identify this particular envelope. The mark should be visible enough so that you can distinguish it, but light enough that the audience and your participant won't notice it.

Cut four slips of paper to approximately the size of a dollar bill, and place one in each of the four envelopes.

DIFFICULTY: †††††

THE EFFECT A large sum of borrowed money is sealed in an envelope, and this sealed envelope is mixed among three identical envelopes. You divine which of the four envelopes contains the participant's borrowed bill and **psychically find the participant's hidden money.**

THE SECRET The "money" envelope is marked.

THE PERFORMANCE

"When I was little, I couldn't decide whether to be a pirate or a magician. On one hand, pirates have cooler clothes and get to carry swords. On the other hand, magicians don't have to wear eye patches. So, here I am and here we are, at a magic show. But now I'd like to fulfill one of my pirate fantasies. Let's all get drunk and loot this building!

"Just kidding. Let's find a buried treasure!" Produce the four envelopes. "First we need a buried treasure. Sir?" Invite a man onstage and ask to borrow a large bill. Perhaps his name is David. "The bigger the bill," you say to David, "the funnier the trick." Everyone will find this funny. Everyone except David.

Fold up David's bill and place it inside the marked envelope, next to one of the blank slips of paper. "Your bill goes in one envelope. The other three envelopes have only blank slips of paper, as placeholders." Take out the papers from the three envelopes that do not contain David's bill and display them otherwise empty. You can hold each envelope up to the light, explaining that with the papers in place, it's impossible to tell whether an envelope contains currency or blank paper.

Hand the envelopes to David and ask him to mix them until neither he nor you knows where his money is.

❶ Ask him to hand you the envelopes one by one. Hold each one to your temple in turn, as if concentrating on the contents. Each time, secretly glimpse the back of the envelope and note whether or not it is marked.

"This is not the buried treasure," you say each time you hold an unmarked envelope. When David hands you the marked envelope, concentrate on it and hand it back to him. "I'm not sure about that one yet."

2 Each time you receive an unmarked envelope, declare it is not the treasure and tear it up.

3 Toss the pieces onto the ground and throw in a couple pirate colloquialisms like, *"Argh, matey."*

4 Take back the last, marked envelope and confidently open it. Remove only the blank slip. Act shocked. Glance at the torn pieces on the ground. *"Now it is I who will walk the plank!"* Stare at David, unsure of what to do. *"I really should drop piracy and stick to magic."*

5 Snap your fingers and reach into the envelope again. Remove David's buried treasure and return it to him.

continued ☞

MASTER CLASS

You immediately establish interest with "Money Mischief" because you borrow a sizeable bill from a participant. This helps the audience *care* about what you're doing (and you know your participant will be watching very intently).

The effect also contains a wonderful moment, near the end, filled with comedy and then drama. When you have torn up three envelopes, the audience fills in the rest. "David's bill is in the last one," people think. When you remove a blank slip instead, it's very, very funny. And since David thinks you just tore up fifty bucks, he'll be genuinely concerned. This is even funnier.

But David quickly becomes a sympathetic character. "He didn't *really* ruin David's money, did he?" people ask themselves. You bring the effect to a fulfilling conclusion when you return David's bill, unscathed.

If the Buried Treasure premise is too trite for your tastes, here are some other themes for this effect:

Lie Detector: Invite three people to write true statements on as many scraps of paper. Invite a fourth person to write a lie. The statements are sealed in envelopes and mixed thoroughly. You are able to tell who's lying.

Object Divination: Invite three people to each place a personal object in an envelope. Designate a fourth person as the "target" person, and have her, too, place an object into an envelope. The envelopes are mixed, yet you divine the envelope containing the target person's object.

Card in Envelope: A participant picks a card and places it in an envelope. She then places three other, indifferent cards in as many envelopes and mixes them all together. You determine which envelope contains her card.

CREDIT: This plot was introduced in 1935 as "Just Chance" by Scotland's Tom Sellers.

CHAPTER NINE

TELEPHONE TRICKERY

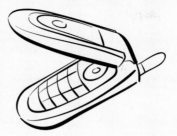

MAGIC WITHOUT BOUNDARIES

You dial up a friend and tell him to grab a pack of cards. You offer to try an effect over the phone. He shuffles, remembers one, and mixes the cards so that you don't know the card—or its location. You instruct him to eliminate cards until only one remains in his hand. You tell him to turn it over. It's his card. Impossible? It would seem that way.

But things aren't always as they seem. Check out "The Australian Shuffle." Within ten minutes, you'll be able to fool a friend with this . . . over the phone.

Another scenario: You ask someone you're with where in the world she would most like to visit. Aruba? Finland? Botswana? She names any place and how long she would stay there. When she finishes telling you about her dream vacation, you ask her to call your "magic" travel agent. The telephone operator answers the phone and, without hesitation, recounts her dream vacation. "Dream Vacation" has a secret so devious—so outside-the-box—that you'll want to spill the beans to your participant as soon as it's over.

Don't do that.

Creating magic effects that work over the phone is understandably difficult. The good news? No sleight of hand, no secret moves, or gimmicks. Instead, we rely on subtle instructions, mathematical principles, and verbal misdirection. More good news: You can perform over-the-phone effects in your underwear.

And while not every effect in this chapter happens over the phone, each one involves a phone. It's time to give your fingers a rest and put your mind to work. It's time for magic without boundaries.

The Australian Shuffle

MATERIALS:
A telephone. Your participant needs a deck of cards.

SETUP: None.

DIFFICULTY:

THE EFFECT **You identify your friend's chosen card . . . over the phone!** You call a friend and ask him to retrieve a deck of cards. He shuffles and cuts the deck into four piles and remembers the top card of any pile. You instruct him on a funky, new way of shuffling, and he mixes his packet further. He eliminates cards at random until he is left with only one card—his!

THE SECRET This is a brilliant mathematical magic effect that works every time.

PERFORMANCE

Call a friend and say, "*Hey, grab a deck of cards from your drawer. I want to teach you a new method of shuffling. It's called the Australian Shuffle, and it has an incredible feature: The shuffle can actually find a selected card. It's really amazing.*" You pause until he's found a deck.

❶ "*Okay, got a deck?*" you confirm. "*Perfect. First shuffle the deck, so everything's fair. Now cut the pack into four approximately equal piles. The piles don't have to be perfect, but you can switch around some cards to even them.*"

❷ "*Now choose any pile.*" Once he's indicated that he's done so, instruct him to pick up that pile and shuffle it again. "*I couldn't possibly know which pile you would choose and which cards would end up in your chosen pile,*" you say. "*And since I couldn't know which cards are in your pile, I certainly can't know the top card, right?*" Let's say he chose the pile second from the right.

❸ Instruct your participant to look at the top card of his selected pile and remember it. Let's say his top card is the Ten of Diamonds. *"Now let me teach you the Australian Shuffle. It's the craziest shuffle I know."*

❹ *"I want you to remember this shuffle so you can show your friends. To make sure you remember the name, spell it with me. As you spell the name, transfer one card for each letter from top to bottom."* He should spell out: *A-U-S-T-R-A-L-I-A-N*, and then *S-H-U-F-F-L-E*. (This subtle action situates the selected card in just the right position.)

❺ *"Now let me show you how to do the Australian Shuffle. Since Australia is the land down under, you're going to deal cards* down *and then* under. *Start by taking the top card, facedown, and dealing it* down, *onto the table.*

"Take the next card and deal it under *the packet in your hand. Take the new top card and deal it down, onto the table. Place the following one under. Continue in this fashion until you're left with only one facedown card. No peeking!"*

While the participant deals, say, *"Think carefully about what you're doing. You shuffled before we started. Then you cut the pack into four piles according to your whim. Then you chose one packet, shuffled it, and looked at a card. Since I have no idea how many cards are in your packet, there's no way I could predict which card you would end up with. Had you cut one card more or less, the outcome would be different."*

❻ *"You have eliminated all the cards except one. Now, what was the name of your card? The Ten of Diamonds? Turn over the card in your hand. Amazing. Even though I'm here and you're there, I found your card. The Australian Shuffle!"*

MASTER CLASS

How does this work? Don't ask. Just be thankful it does. As long as your participant cuts the deck into four *roughly* equal piles, you're fine. If she cuts less than eight or more than sixteen, the effect won't work. But the participant's estimation would have to be really off for this to happen— and the line in the script about adjusting the packets after the cut to "even things up" minimizes the chances of her cutting too shallow or deep.

CREDIT: Alex Elmsley (1929–2006) devised some of the most influential effects of the 20th century. His creative brilliance was equal parts mathematics, sleight of hand, and subtlety. Originally published as "Australian Self Help," this effect is one of Elmsley's hidden gems.

Cell Sorcery

MATERIALS:

A deck of cards and two cell phones (one of them is yours).

SETUP: To perform this effect, first situate the Two of Clubs tenth from the top of your deck.

Then you need to "borrow" your participant's phone—without her knowing. This is easy in bars; people often leave their phones on tables and stools in case they receive a call. Otherwise, just pick a moment when nobody is looking and reach into her purse. Note: To avoid arrest, do this only to friends and family.

Instead of programming your name next to your number, program your force card. I use the Two of Clubs because this card spells with the fewest letters.

Just make sure you do this secretly, without arousing suspicion.

DIFFICULTY: ✝✝✝✝✝

THE EFFECT Your participant's cell phone finds a chosen number.

You offer to perform an experiment with numbers. A participant is invited to deal a secret number of cards and remember the card she dealt to. When you're unable to find her card, you call her cell phone. On the screen, a message appears next to your number: "You selected the Two of Clubs!"

THE SECRET You pre-program a forced card into your participant's phone and execute a classic mathematical force called the *Ten Twenty* force.

THE PERFORMANCE

"*umbers fascinate me,*" you start. "*Even though they're intangible, there is something almost magical about how numbers work together.*"

❶ You offer to demonstrate and instruct your participant to take the deck in her hands as you hand it to her, facedown.

Turn your back so she knows you're not peeking and say, "*Now think of any number between, say, ten and twenty.*" Sound ambivalent, but this is an important number. "*Deal that many cards facedown on the table. Deal silently so I can't hear you.*" Allow the participant to comply. Let's say she deals 17 cards.

❷ Have her pick up the dealt pile and place it back on the deck. "*I'd like you to come up with another number, based on the first number. Add the digits of your thought-of number together and deal that many cards into a new pile.*" Help your participant through this part. If she thought of 17, she adds 1 and 7 together, which yields 8. She then deals eight cards facedown.

Say, "*Through numbers you thought of and generated, you've landed on one card: the top card of the tabled pile. Look at this card and remember it.*" Although what you've said is true, the card on top of the tabled pile is always your force card (the tenth card from the top). This is the Ten Twenty force.

❸ You've just forced the Two of Clubs. Ask your participant to remember this card and think of it over and over again. (You subtly interject this notion of her "thought-of" card—even though she actively selected the card—because thought-of cards are more impressive than picked cards.) Later on, you'll ask her which card she thought of, and she'll identify it as the Two of Clubs.

Ask the participant to shuffle her chosen card back into the full deck.

❹ Retrieve the deck, snap the deck or wriggle your fingers, and turn over the top card. In nearly all circumstances, this will not be her card. Feign disappointment. Shuffle the cards and turn over the new top card. Again, act disappointed when she indicates that you still haven't found her card.

❺ *"Perhaps the secret is in the numbers. If you don't mind my asking, do you have your cell phone with you?"* You know the answer to this, but she doesn't know you know. *"Would you please call out your cell phone number?"*

Take out your cell phone and dial her number. Ask her to concentrate on her thought-of card. When you call her, ask her to look at her phone. To her surprise, her card will be staring her in the face!

MASTER CLASS

As I mentioned in the setup, I use the Two of Clubs for its brevity, but if you want to be clever, type, "Are you thinking of the Two of Clubs?" or "I knew all along you picked the Two of Clubs."

If you want to be *really* clever, use your participant's camera-phone function and take a snapshot of your force card. This way, in addition to a message, your participant sees the image of her card.

In the right situation, this is an extremely strong effect. You must give the impression that you're performing off the cuff—making it up as you go.

CREDIT: **The first telephone trick can be traced back to John Northern Hilliard in 1905. Obviously, his idea didn't involve a cell phone.**

Predicting a Phone Number

MATERIALS:

A deck of cards and two cell phones (one of them is yours).

SETUP: Put your phone on silent and then find a friendly stranger at a party. When she isn't looking, secretly borrow her cell phone and dial your own number. She mustn't see you with her phone. (Note: A party setting—where everyone knows *someone*—is much preferable to a bar scene, where your cell phone borrowing might be misinterpreted!)

Stay connected just long enough for the call to register in your phone's call log. Now you have the number of a stranger you've never met. Replace her phone and walk away. (If the person has her phone set to block this won't work.)

Take out your trusty deck and remove the cards that correspond to her number (without the area code). For example, if her number is 555-9713, you might remove and order the following cards: Five of Clubs, Five of Diamonds, Five of Spades, Nine of Clubs, Seven of Hearts, Ace of Spades, Three of Diamonds. Aces represent 1 and Queens represent 0.

Place this packet on the bottom of your deck so that the last card/number is on the very bottom.

DIFFICULTY:

THE EFFECT   Predict a complete stranger's phone number. You approach a friendly looking stranger and offer to perform an incredible magic effect. "And if it works," you ask, "can I call you?" She agrees.

You ask her to take your deck and cut off half. Starting with the card she cut to, she then deals her packet into seven piles. You instruct her to turn over the top card of each pile. She stares at the numbers, confused. "Say them out loud—just the numbers," you suggest.

She recites the numbers aloud and immediately realizes that she shuffled and dealt the cards into precisely her phone number. "So . . . I can call you?"

THE SECRET   You ascertain the participant's phone number beforehand, and control how she deals the cards.

THE PERFORMANCE

Approach your stranger and introduce yourself. Make nice, and then explain that you're a magician. Offer to demonstrate, and then propose a deal. *"I'll do the coolest card trick you've ever seen. If it works, can I call you sometime?"* Fun people love this stuff. (And if someone isn't up for good magic, she isn't worth calling anyway.)

❶ Hand her your deck and ask her to cut off about half. Place the cut-off cards aside. *"You could have cut deeper or shallower, but you cut at that exact spot. And in so doing, you determined where you'll start dealing."*

last dealt card

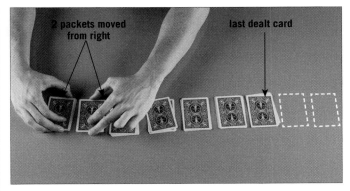

2 packets moved from right   last dealt card

② Instruct her to deal her cards into seven packets. She is to deal like a card game, with all the cards facedown. When she reaches the end of her seven-packet row, she is to start again at the beginning of the row. She should distribute all the cards she holds.

As she deals, reiterate how fair the conditions are. She cut. She dealt. You have never met her before. Watch where she places her last card, and remember this packet.

③ Pay attention to how the last seven cards are dealt—you will likely have to make one small adjustment. The last card she deals is the last digit in her phone number, and you want this number at the end of the row. If the last packet she deals onto is, say, third from the right, you have to *make* this packet last in the row. This involves shifting all the packets to the right, with the ones on the end going back to the beginning of the row. Sliding the packets shouldn't be a secret. Just say, *"And I'll mix the packets around a bit."*

④ Invite your participant to turn over the top card of each packet. She probably won't get it. Yet. It's fun to let this play out slowly. *"Those cards don't mean anything to you?*

What about the numbers on the cards?" Ask her to say the numbers aloud. She'll begin to recognize the sequence as she's saying it. She made her own phone number appear!

MASTER CLASS

Making a complete stranger's phone number appear is a deeply personal effect, and this makes it strong. Finding someone's selected card is fine, but it's only her card because she picked it. But finding her phone number— well, that's *hers*. And that's magic.

CREDIT: Max Maven pioneered the concept of revealing phone numbers with a sequence of cards. The dealing force used here was probably devised by Al Leech and was first published in *Cardmanship* in 1959.

Dream Vacation

MATERIALS:
A cordless telephone (cell or cordless) and a friend who can act.

SETUP: To prepare, just fill in your most animated friend on how to play the game. You explain that you'll dial his number and call him in secret (or in another room). Then you'll approach your participant, phone in hand. It will look like you're just holding your phone. Nobody will suspect that you have a friend on the other end, live. Just tell him to quietly listen to what the participant says.

He should note the *place, activity,* and *length* of her dream vacation. As soon as he has this information, he has to hang up and wait for a call back. When the participant finishes describing her ideal vacation, hand her your phone and ask her to dial your "magic" travel agent's number. Your friend must answer the phone by saying, "Magic Travel Agency: We tell *you* where you want to go!" Then he restates what he just heard.

DIFFICULTY: †††††

THE EFFECT Name any place in the world you want to visit and call the "magic" travel agent, who names your thought-of place. You begin by handing your participant the phone number of your travel agent, and then survey her for her dream vacation. **When your participant calls your travel agent, he perfectly predicts her trip!**

THE SECRET The phone you hold is secretly connected to your "agent's" phone, so he can hear all the specifics your participant desires. When she calls him, he regurgitates what he just heard.

THE PERFORMANCE

Here's one scenario for how your presentation might go.

❶ To begin, you're holding your phone, secretly connected to your friend. You approach your participant and start a conversation, steering the topic toward travel.

"*Do you travel much?*" you say.

"Not as much as I would like," she answers.

"*Well, I've got a travel agent. He's absolutely incredible. I'll write down his number for you.*" Write down your friend's number and hand it to the participant.

2 Now you start gathering the pertinent information: the location, favorite activity, and ideal length of vacation stay. *"So, if you could go anywhere in the world—anywhere at all—where would you go?"*

"Fiji, I suppose. If cost weren't a factor," she answers.

"Wow! I would love to go to Fiji, too. And while you're in Fiji, what would you most like to do?"

"I have a scuba license, so I'd like to do a few diving trips." (You have confirmed two items on your checklist.)

"Oh, wow, the scuba diving is supposed to be incredible in Fiji. Okay, a diving trip. And how long would you stay?"

"Two weeks, if I could," she says.

"Two weeks of diving in Fiji. Awesome. Hey, let's see what the availability is like," you suggest.

"What? Right now? It's like 9:30 at night."

"Don't worry," you say, *"the magic travel agent stays open late. Dial that number I gave you."* You hand her your phone and she calls your friend. (Make sure your friend's phone number isn't programmed in; your cover might be blown when "Jeff S." appears on your screen.) As an alternative, suggest she use her own phone.

3 Your friend answers as a jolly agent. *"Magic Travel Agency: We tell you where you want to go! How are you this evening? Excellent! Before we begin, I'd like to notify you about a special we're having. It's an all-inclusive two-week package to Fiji. And diving is included!"*

MASTER CLASS

This is situational magic at its best. It's perfect for your next house party, assuming at least one of your friends stays at home to take your call.

CREDIT: Joel Givens and I developed "Dream Vacation" to add what we hoped would be the perfect party effect to this chapter. The method is based on a Steve Fearson routine.

JOSEPH DUNNINGER: RADIO MAGICIAN

The Amazing Dunninger (1892–1975) could read your mind . . . over the radio. In the forties, millions of listeners tuned in to Joseph Dunninger's elegant voice: "For those who believe," he used to say, "no explanation is necessary. For those who do not believe, no explanation will suffice."

While Dunninger was in the studio, home listeners participated in his long-distance brand of mind reading, and he was a sensation. So popular, in fact, that he was the inspiration for *The Shadow*, early radio's most popular crime fighter. With the effects in this chapter, you, too, can read minds miles away.

Whatisyourcard.com

THE EFFECT **A website divines a participant's chosen card.**

THE SECRET The Four of Hearts is forced. The website reveals the card in a mysterious manner.

THE PERFORMANCE

The Sid Lorraine force fits perfectly here because you apparently don't see the participant's selected card. Here's a brief review for your convenience as you set up an impressive technological feat.

❶ Hold the deck facedown and bevel the sides so the bottom extends about two inches toward the left. Hold the deck from above with your right hand, supporting the ends with your fingers.

❷ Pinch the bottom card at its left side between your left thumb and fingers, separating from the cards above it. Push this bottom card to the right about an inch so that it's supported by your right hand fingerpads.

Deal the cards from what appears to be the bottom of the deck with your left fingers, taking cards from the leftmost portion of the deck. Slide cards one at a time from the bottom without disturbing the concealed force card (the Four of Hearts).

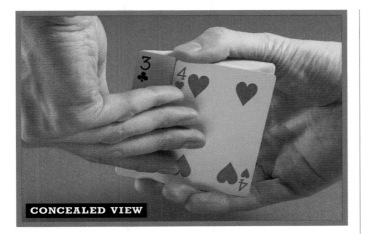

CONCEALED VIEW

❸ Continue to deal and ask a participant to stop you at any time. When she does, you will apparently hand her the next bottom card. Instead, extend the fingerpads of your left hand to the face of the concealed force card (the Four of Hearts). Pull this card from the bottom of the deck and hand it to your participant, facedown.

"*Remember your card,*" you say, "*and don't tell me what it is.*" Go to your nearest computer. "*The Internet has made life so easy,*" you say. "*It's incredible, really, how much you can do online: banking, shopping—even dating. Now there are even websites that find chosen cards.*"

❹ If your participant seems skeptical, forge on: "*I'll show you. Please concentrate on your card. Okay, now log onto the site. It's W-W-W-dot-W-H-A-T-I-S-Y-O-U-R-C-A-R-D-dot-C-O-M. Now just follow the directions.*"

Your participant will be taken through a short video intro in which he is asked to concentrate on his card. Images of cards will flash on the screen and disappear—this is all smoke-and-mirrors stuff.

❺ Eventually an image of a hand will appear and the participant will be asked to place his hand on the image.

❻ When she removes her hand, he discovers a picture of his thought-of card!

MASTER CLASS
The Internet makes most things easier, including magical effects using cards. Here, not much presentation is required. Just force the Four of Hearts and let the website do the rest.

CREDIT: Joel Givens and I collaborated on this concept. I think it started when we were arguing about *2001: A Space Odyssey* (I love the film; he hates it). We wanted to include a "technological" card effect in which the computer itself did the mind reading.

Telephone Osmosis

THE EFFECT "Are you familiar with osmosis?" you ask the person at the other end of your phone conversation. "For our purposes, it's the concept of learning without studying. Let's try an osmosis experiment.

"Think of your favorite basic school subject—but don't say recess or gym—and no extra-curriculars. I know that's what you were thinking!" **You then read your friend's mind, letter by letter . . . over the phone!**

THE SECRET You'll use what magicians call a *progressive anagram*. This is a special chart (opposite page) that helps you divine any school subject, letter by letter.

THE PERFORMANCE

Let's talk about how to use the Progressive Anagram chart. You ask your participant to think of a school subject. Everyone thinks of gym or recess first, and everyone thinks they're the first ones to ever make that lame joke. So, you make it first and tell your participant not to think of either of those fun subjects.

You're playing the odds here. Your participant must think of one of the following subjects: **History, English, Spanish, French, German, Geography, Math, Science, Sociology, Economics.** This is an excellent range, and as long as you indicate that you want a "school subject," most people think of something general, like math or science. Every once in a while, you'll get something obnoxious, like "Special Topics: Film Noir and the Western."

In those cases, be glad you're not in the room with your participant. In these cases, ask him to do it again, with an elementary school subject.

❶ Okay, so your participant thinks of a school subject. It's probably one of the subjects on this list, but you're not yet sure which one. You'll narrow it down with the Progressive Anagram chart (opposite page). You'll guess the word letter by letter. You may get up to two letters wrong, but each wrong letter will help you narrow down your search for the chosen subject. Have your book open to the page throughout the effect. Begin at the "Start Here!" icon.

MASTER CLASS

Reading someone's mind is impressive; reading someone's mind over the phone is inconceivable. But to give the impression that you're actually reading her mind, you have to maintain an air of authority.

The key here is playing down your failures. You aren't guessing the letters, you're "seeing" them. When you get one wrong, don't act disappointed. Instead, act surprised, and then use the suggested dialogue to explain your mistakes.

MODERN MASTER

ANDI GLADWIN

Andi Gladwin is a London-based magician who has published his original effects in many leading magic periodicals, including *MAGIC* magazine.

"All magic," he says, "should have both a human element and a defined power. Here, our human element is school; everyone can relate to elementary subjects because we all slept through them. And the power we're demonstrating here is a kind of mind-reading: osmosis."

PROGRESSIVE ANAGRAM CHART

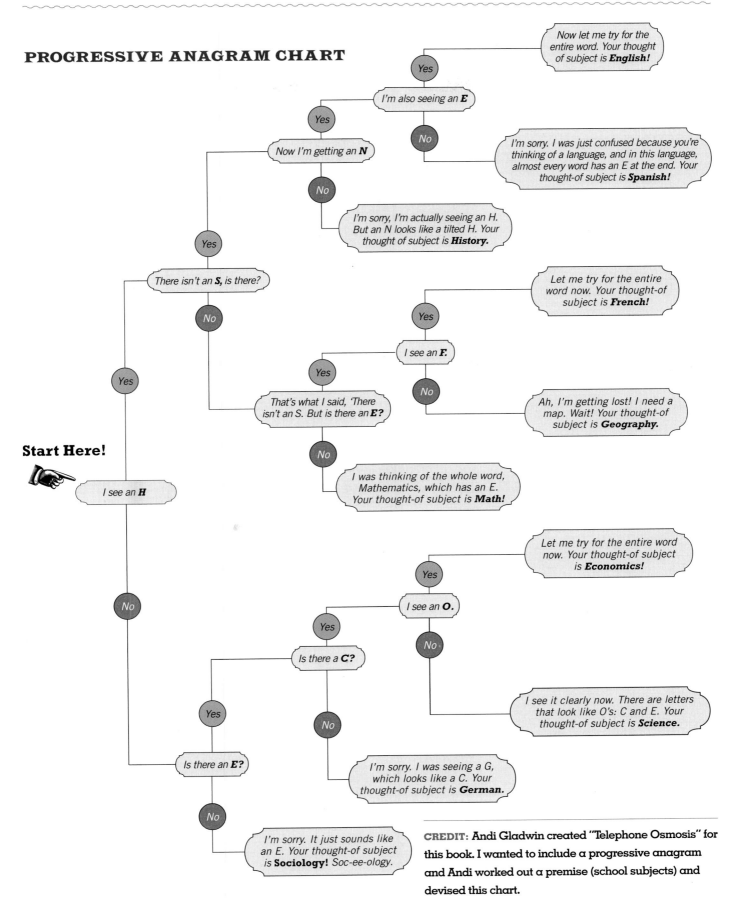

Start Here!

I see an **H**

CREDIT: Andi Gladwin created "Telephone Osmosis" for this book. I wanted to include a progressive anagram and Andi worked out a premise (school subjects) and devised this chart.

Da Vinci Decoded

SETUP: During the performance you'll force the number 1089 over the phone. Your friend won't know you know his "thought-of" number, and you can use this against him.

You will eventually ask him to use his number, 1089, to find a word in his book. You will instruct him to look at the tenth page, the eighth line, and the ninth word. All you need to know in advance is what edition of *The Da Vinci Code* he has. There are two major versions: hardcover and paperback.

If he has the hardcover edition, the word is *blah*.

If he has the paperback edition, the word is *which*.

Remember that, and you're set.

DIFFICULTY: †††††

THE EFFECT You use this enormously successful book—which many people have in their homes—in a mystery of your own. **An amazing demonstration of synchronicity with a participant's thought-of number.**

THE SECRET You force the shapes and page numbers using psychology and a little-known mathematical principle.

THE PERFORMANCE

Call a friend. Ask, *"Have you ever read The Da Vinci Code?"* You'll get a yes or no answer here; hopefully you won't get a biblical sermon. Assuming the answer is "yes," proceed.

❶ *"Perfect! Put the phone down and get it off your shelf. And grab a pen and paper. I'll wait."* When your friend returns, ask, *"Can you use the book's surface to write on, or is it too flimsy?"* This sounds like you're being thoughtful, but you're really asking (without asking) if his book has a hard or soft cover. Now you know which word to use. Let's assume he has the trade paperback.

"What I loved about The Da Vinci Code was how Dan Brown wove little puzzles and wordplay into the story. There were codes and hidden rooms and— let's stay on topic. I'd like to show you something spookier than anything in that book. Do exactly as I say, and this will totally freak you out."

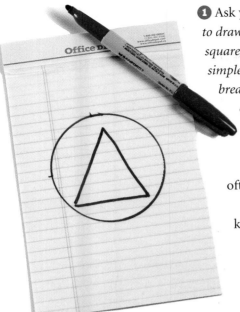

1 Ask your friend to hold his pen at the ready. *"To warm up, I'm going to ask you to draw two geometrical shapes. Make them simple shapes, for example a heart or a square, one inside the other."* As he draws, continue: *"Leonardo da Vinci used simple geometric shapes to illustrate fantastic and complex concepts. And you can break down nearly all of his drawings to these simple shapes."* Ask your friend to concentrate on his drawing.

There are no reliable statistics on this, but more often than not, he will draw a triangle inside a circle. So, you play the odds.

"I'm seeing a triangle inside a circle, yes?" You will be *shocked* how often you're right.

What happens if your participant drew something else? Nothing. Just keep going: *"Oh, then what did you draw?"*

"I drew a star inside a trapezoid," he says. *"Excellent. I asked you to do that because I need to tap into your left brain for this experiment."* If you don't get it right, it isn't part of the effect. Remember, you're in control, and only you know where this is going.

3 *"Now I want you to think of any three-digit number using three different digits, and write it inside your shape."* Allow him to comply. Note: It's very important that none of the digits in his number repeat. *"Now reverse your thought-of number, and write it down below the first number."* For example, 321 becomes 123. *continued* 👉

2 *"Now it's my turn to do the thinking,"* you continue. *"I'm thinking about the future, and about decisions you haven't yet made. I'm seeing an old woman, on a broom . . . a witch! Wait. That's the visual image."* You pause. *"But when I picture the word, I see w-h-i-c-h. Will you write 'which' on the back of your paper?"* Make sure he does this; it's your big ending.

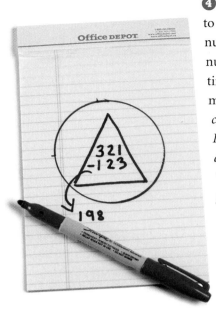

4 Instruct the participant to subtract the larger number from the smaller number, and give him time to complete the math. Say, *"I'm not certain, but I thought I felt a wave of doubt about the subtraction. Would you double-check, please?"* You would be surprised how often people *do* doubt their own math, and how often there is a mistake. This line helps minimize errors.

5 *"Beneath your total number, I want you to write the reverse of this new number, and add them together."*

"Do you have a four-digit number?" If he does, the number is always 1089. If he indicates that his final sum is only three digits, ask him to reverse the number and add it once more. You always end up with 1089.

6 Bring his attention back to the book. *"We'll use your number to find a page and a word. Which number did you pick?"* After he responds with "1089," say, *"Open up The Da Vinci Code to page number 10."* Make sure he turns to the page numbered 10 and not the tenth physical page in the book. *"Count down to the eighth line. Now count over to the ninth word. What is that word?"*

7 His finger will be on "which." Remind him that you prophesied this word (and the proof is written on the reverse side of his paper) before the experiment began. Spooky!

MASTER CLASS

I love magic about topical subjects. *The Da Vinci Code* is a book shrouded in controversy, and this makes it a perfect choice for a prop. And while "Da Vinci Decoded" is most potent over the phone, don't overlook its effectiveness in person. The next time you're at a party at your friend's house, check out his bookshelf. Chances are, he has *The Da Vinci Code*.

What if he doesn't? I've got you covered. Here are some other bestselling titles that folks are likely to have around. The 1089 force is the same, but the book (and the word) change.

Harry Potter and the Prisoner of Azkaban (paperback): **on**

Tuesdays with Morrie (paperback): **frozen**

Men are from Mars, Women are from Venus (paperback): **can't**

CREDIT: The 1089 force is a classic mathematical puzzle. *Magic* creative consultant Joel Givens combined several classic effects in this timely mentalism feat; it appears here for the first time.

CHAPTER TEN

GET YOUR ACT TOGETHER

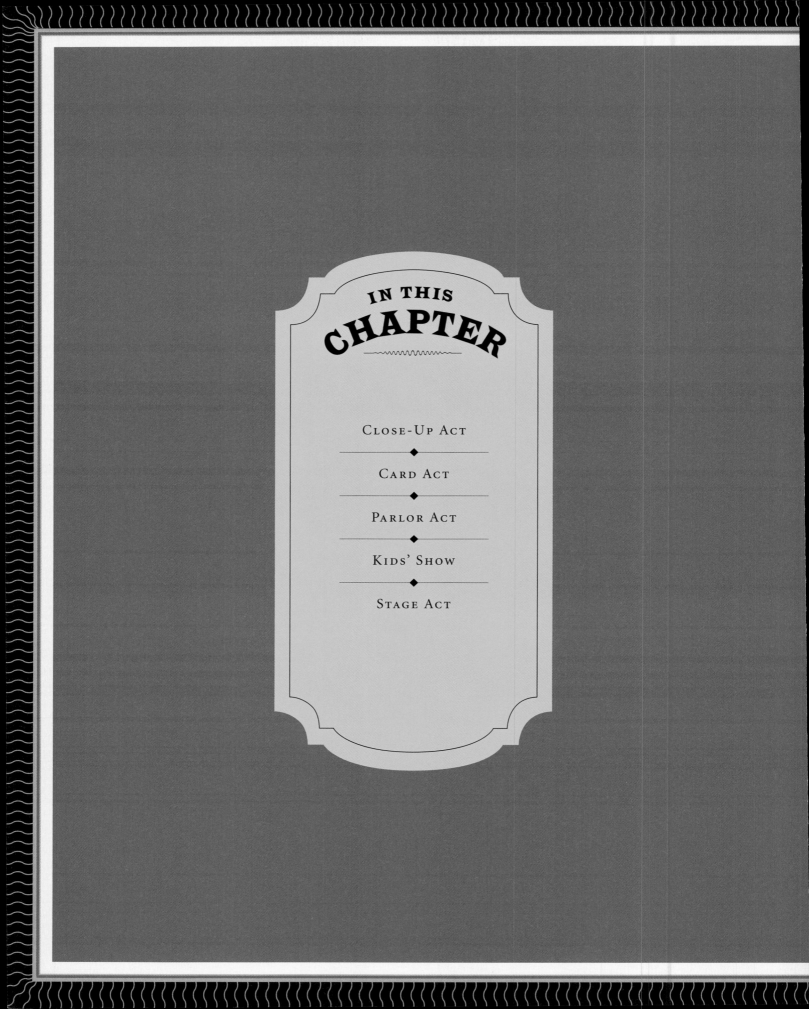

IN THIS
CHAPTER

Close-Up Act

♦

Card Act

♦

Parlor Act

♦

Kids' Show

♦

Stage Act

FIVE COMPLETE SHOWS TO AMAZE ANY AUDIENCE

Magicians are often at a disadvantage in assembling a show because we wear too many hats: performer, writer, choreographer, director, costume designer, and set designer. And never mind that there is a world of difference between *magic* and a *magic act*. Let me explain.

If you pull a coin from someone's ear and then push a bottle cap through a tabletop, you've just completed two effects, *not* an act. But if you produce a coin and then push this same coin through a tabletop, you've got a routine—two effects that *flow*. (See "Grandpa's Coin Trick," page 207 and "Table Trouble," page 190.)

Props aren't the only way to theme a show; you can also choose material by genre. Mentalism, cards, coins, stage magic, dinner table effects: All the major genres are represented in *Magic*. You can search the book by "Effect" and put together a routine based on a premise. For instance, you might try to do an entire show on "mysteries of the mind."

Perhaps you like "Psychic Stocks" and "Telephone Osmosis" (page 158 and page 254). If you predict a participant's thought-of stock symbol and then guess someone's favorite school subject, you have done two separate effects—great effects, but separate ones. Let's turn them into a routine.

The common ground between them is mind reading, so let's link them together this way. "I just predicted someone's thought-of stock," you say between the two effects, "but I'd like to try something more difficult. I want to read someone's memory and find a thought that goes back to, say, grade school. You, sir, think of your favorite school subject . . ." Now there's continuity between these effects. Now you're doing a show.

To help you get started, here are five complete magic shows, each one tailor-made and time-tested for a specific audience. Whether you're performing magic with cards or for kids, for two people or two hundred, you'll find a show that suits your needs.

Close-up Act

A 15-minute magic show . . . before dinner!

CHECKLIST

✔ You must be seated for this performance.

✔ Make sure the table has silverware and a saltshaker.

✔ Prepare a matchbook and straw for "Match-ic Wand." Place it in your right pants pocket.

✔ Keep a false thumbtip in your right pants pocket.

✔ Pre-fold a dollar bill and place it with two torn pieces in your left pants pocket.

✔ "Bank Roll" requires a wad of cash, a wad of paper, and a rubber band. Keep these in your right jacket pocket.

✔ The materials for "The Vanishing Pet" should be stored in your left jacket pocket.

✔ Place two quarters under your watch.

✔ Situate a folding quarter in the mouth of any bottle and store this next to you, out of sight.

You'll need: Matches, plastic water bottle, salt shaker, drinking straw, several dollar bills, photographs, false thumbtip, 2 quarters, knife and fork, blank writing paper.

PERFORMANCE

MATCH-IC WAND
TWO MINUTES, 30 SECONDS
page 22

Open your show by empowering a participant. A booklet of matches appears in her hand.

TRASH TO TREASURE
ONE MINUTE
page 195

"Magic can also be practical," you say. "Just the other day I found this." You display torn pieces of a dollar bill . . . and then restore it!

A PINCH OF SALT
ONE MINUTE
page 52

Roll the dollar bill from the previous effect into a cone and fill it with salt. Then snap your fingers and make the salt disappear!

BANK ROLL
ONE MINUTE
page 202

Notice that you keep using the dollar bill. This recurring prop helps you flow from one effect into the next. Here, the bill is used as the catalyst to change paper into real money.

SUSPENSION OF DISBELIEF
ONE MINUTE
page 57

Now you change gears. "Let's put the sleight of hand aside for a moment and talk about mind power." So saying, you suspend a spoon against your palm.

THE GAME
ONE MINUTE
page 35

This provides the crucial element of audience involvement. Invite several participants to join you onstage for a game. You predict the outcome before the game starts!

THE VANISHING PET
TWO MINUTES
page 128

Everyone loves to share pet pictures. But only you can magically make your pet disappear.

GRANDPA'S COIN TRICK
TWO MINUTES
page 207

"My grandfather got me interested in magic. This is what he showed me." Now you produce two quarters by magic.

TABLE TROUBLE
30 SECONDS
page 190

You're performing seated, and you just did a coin effect. The timing is perfect for this auditory and visual illusion.

COIN THROUGH BOTTLE
ONE MINUTE
page 199

Your closing effect has to be truly amazing, even under close scrutiny. Use what is apparently the same coin from the previous effects and apparently push it inside a glass bottle.

Kids' Show

For 16 minutes, amaze a group of kids!

CHECKLIST

✔ Place a glass of liquid in your left rear pants pocket.

✔ Have two gum balls in your right front pants pocket, along with a false fingertip.

✔ Place two quarters under your watch and a third, flattened quarter in your left front pants pocket.

✔ Situate a large rock (for "Earth Shoes") in your right rear pants pocket.

✔ Store the prepared ribbons for "Cutting a Child in Two" in your right jacket pocket.

Entertaining kids with magic is more about entertaining and less about magic. The material must be visual and interactive. Here is a complete show, full of laughs, suitable for a classroom full of children or a basement full of little cousins.

PERFORMANCE

GUM BALLS FROM THE MOUTH ONE MINUTE *page 123*	Producing an endless number of gum balls from your mouth is a funny, visual way of opening a show. It doesn't require a script, so I suggest putting this piece to music.
SLEEVES AND SNEEZES THREE MINUTES *page 131*	Continue with your musical opening and produce tissues, handkerchiefs, squeakers, confetti, and anything else that will make your audience laugh.
OVATION POSITION ONE MINUTE *page 215*	Forgo the backward alphabet here and use this glass-of-water production for its visual appeal. Toast the audience and continue with your show.
HAND SCAM ONE MINUTE *page 219*	Introduce yourself and offer to involve everyone in your first effect. Instruct everyone to follow along as you guide them through this hand puzzle.
GRANDPA'S COIN TRICK THREE MINUTES *page 207*	Invite a child onstage and perform this guessing game with her, eventually producing two coins. Keep her onstage for . . .
PENNY PRESSED 30 SECONDS *page 192*	Instead of a penny, use a flattened quarter so you can continue with a coin from "Grandpa's Coin Trick." Leave your participant with a unique souvenir: a pressed coin.
EARTH SHOES 30 SECONDS *page 228*	Dismiss your volunteer with a round of applause and then comment that there is a rock in your shoe. Play out this visual gag, allowing the huge stone to fall to the floor.
TELEPHONE OSMOSIS TWO MINUTES, 30 SECONDS *page 254*	Ask an older child to think of his favorite school subject. Predict his thought, letter by letter. If you can't memorize the chart, turn your back and use a cheat sheet.
POKED 30 SECONDS *page 126*	Time for more audience interaction: Invite a kid onstage and, before you begin the next effect, perform "Poked." The effect is funny, but his reaction will be even more hilarious.
CUTTING A CHILD IN TWO ONE MINUTE *page 120*	Wrap the prepared ribbons around your participant. After due build-up, pull the ribbons through his body. Cue applause for your participant, and then bow to conclude your show.

Stage Act

23 minutes in the spotlight!

CHECKLIST

✔ Place a glass of liquid in your left rear pants pocket.

✔ Prepare a dry-erase board for "Mathemagic."

✔ Place a large rock in your right rear pants pocket.

✔ Store four envelopes (one marked) in your right jacket pocket.

✔ Place the Linking Rings in order on a nearby table or chair.

Whether you're presenting an award, receiving one, or emceeing the whole show, magic is the perfect way to punch up an appearance. This show is high on impact and low on sleight of hand. Most importantly, all the effects can be seen from afar—even from the back of a theater.

PERFORMANCE

OVATION POSITION
TWO MINUTES
page 215

Most people start their show with a glass of water on the podium. You produce yours with magic!

MATHEMAGIC
SEVEN MINUTES
page 146

Explain that before you can begin, you must warm up with some calculations.

EARTH SHOES
30 SECONDS
page 228

Magic shows are about peaks and valleys. After an amazing, lengthy demonstration like "Mathemagic," give your participants something quick, visual, and funny. Give them "Earth Shoes."

MONEY MISCHIEF
FIVE MINUTES
page 238

Invite a gentleman onstage and borrow a large sum of money from him. Carry out this hilarious guessing game. For a second, your participant will think you've torn up his money. In the end, the money's okay and you're psychic!

HAND SCAM
ONE MINUTE
page 219

Offer to involve everyone in the crowd for your next piece. Ask the audience to follow along with you.

TELEPHONE OSMOSIS
THREE MINUTES
page 254

Single out an audience member and read his mind . . . from where he's sitting.

LORD OF THE RINGS
FIVE MINUTES
page 230

There's no finer way to close a magic show than with this time-tested classic. Best with music, the routine explained here works perfectly for large groups.

In Closing

A magician is an actor playing the part of a magician.

—Jean-Eugène Robert-Houdin

There is no such thing as real magic, but magicians come impressively close. Even though we can't do real sorcery, this is the impression we give our audiences. Magician Jean-Eugène Robert-Houdin articulated well that a magician must play the part of a magician. But I say there's much more to it than that.

It's not enough to play the part of a magician—that archetypal magician with a wax-tipped moustache and cummerbund two sizes too small. My advice is this: Forget the top hat; you don't want to be *that* guy. Instead, be a magician who is an actor playing the part of *you with magical powers.*

Interesting people make interesting magicians; your interests, passions, and humor should come through in your magical performances. There should be as little "acting" as possible.

Las Vegas performer Michael Close's interests, for instance, are teaching, music, and travel—and all these elements are present in his show. For him, magic is a form of self-expression. It's a performance. He says that "your magic and the way you perform it should be an expression of your life, not a substitute for one."

As you piece together your act, there are three questions your act should answer for your audience:

1. Who is this person?

2. What story is he or she trying to tell me?

3. Why is it worth my time?

Mentalist Max Maven asks himself these questions whenever he sees a magician perform and in their heads, your participants will ask them of you. Discover your performance style by adapting this book's material to your personality and the answers will come naturally.

You have just completed a comprehensive course on the performance of magic. And I have fulfilled my promise to you and the magic organizations to which I belong: I have taught, not exposed. I also hope that you have a deeper respect for magicians than you did before you started reading.

Now I ask that you make two promises to your fellow magi. First, you must promise to keep these secrets. From a recent article in *National Geographic* (called "The Joy of Shoes," but never mind that): "Kept secrets have power. Revealed secrets have none." We stand on the shoulders of giants, and our predecessors published these secrets so you and I could use them to amaze our public. And magic only amazes if the audience is fooled. Your first promise is . . . shhh!

The second promise you must make is that you will respect magic and, specifically, this material. Inevitably, there will be a faction of magicians outraged at the unprecedented quality and detail of the magic explained here in *Magic.* "Too good for the beginner," they'll say. But they will remember that *they* had to start somewhere, too. And they are fortunate their teachers had a philanthropic attitude toward teaching magic. After all, everyone believed as they did, there would be no new magicians.

So impress them. Amaze them. And you will prove them wrong. All you have to do is . . . magic. When you amaze people with magic, you are keeping the art alive.

Congratulations. You're a magician. Now go out there and make magic!

SPOTLIGHT ON JEAN-EUGÈNE ROBERT-HOUDIN

Robert-Houdin is credited as the father of modern magic, and with good reason. His illusions didn't just amaze. They stopped wars.

In 1856, Napoléon III called Robert-Houdin out of retirement. Islamic fundamentalists called the Marabouts were rebelling against French colonialists in Algeria. Believed to have magic powers, the Marabouts had become unruly.

Enter Robert-Houdin. He performed two effects that demonstrated French power. He allowed an Arab to fire a gun at him. Not only did Robert-Houdin survive the shooting, but he displayed the bullet *between his teeth*. The implication was that he could not be killed with bullets.

Next he invited a rebel—the strongest soldier the Marabouts could provide—to try to lift an ordinary-looking chest from the stage floor. Despite the man's best efforts, he was unable to lift the box. But Robert-Houdin bent over and lifted the small chest with only two fingers. Not only could Robert-Houdin stop bullets, he could take away another man's strength.

The illusion was called "The Light and Heavy Chest," and it involved a steel chest and an electromagnet beneath the stage. And, of course, Robert-Houdin switched the real bullet for a wax one. The magic wasn't real, but it *seemed* real, and it stopped the Arab revolt.

Robert-Houdin's combination of science and mechanics (he was a clockmaker by trade) with sleight of hand and presentation made him the most influential magician of his time. A young Hungarian immigrant named

Ehrich Weiss was so moved by Robert-Houdin that he took on a stage name in tribute: Harry Houdini.

Robert-Houdin is my favorite magician, and in 2006 I went on a pilgrimage to his hometown in Blois,

France. A monument dedicated in his honor reads:

There is a "before" and "after" Robert-Houdin.

Resources

~~~~~~~~~~~~~

FIVE WAYS TO STAY INVOLVED

You read the book. You learned the effects. Then you did magic. What now? Here are five ways to stay involved.

1. Go to a magic meeting.

There are two large organizations for magicians in the United States and Canada, the International Brotherhood of Magicians (IBM) and the Society of American Magicians (SAM). There are affiliated groups all over the world. And it's likely there's one in or near your hometown. Each one offers a magazine with membership.

Visit www.magician.org for information on the IBM, the International Brotherhood of Magicians.

Visit www.magicsam.org for information on the SAM, the Society of American Magicians.

2. Read.

All of magic's secrets are buried in books. Here are some of my favorites:

GENERAL MAGIC

The Tarbell Course in Magic by Harlan Tarbell. Eight volumes of effects, moves, ideas, and illusions.

The Books of Wonder by Tommy Wonder and Stephen Minch. I spoke of Tommy Wonder in the Introduction, but in 1995 he wrote the two finest modern works on magic. These books are for serious students only.

CARD MAGIC

Card College by Roberto Giobbi. This is a five-volume series on card sleights and is the most comprehensive tutorial on the subject. It's a progressive course, so start with the first volume.

Expert Card Technique by Jean Hugard and Fred Braue. This densely written 1940 manual has some very sneaky card effects.

COIN MAGIC

The New Modern Coin Magic by J. B. Bobo. You learned his switch in Chapter Six. He wrote the coin magician's bible, and if you like money magic, this should be your next purchase.

Expert Coin Technique by Richard Kaufman. David Roth is the greatest living coin magician, and in this book he tips over a hundred professional-caliber coin routines.

MAGIC THEORY

Magic and Showmanship by Henning Nelms. This 1969 classic is a thorough examination into the performance of magic. It's mostly theory, but this book contains the real secrets of magic.

Strong Magic by Darwin Ortiz. Darwin Ortiz is one of magic's leading thinkers, and here he offers a modern, critical approach to the art of magic. Only for serious students or those who wish to become serious students.

3. Subscribe to a magazine.

The industry's leading magic periodical is *MAGIC*. For cutting-edge effects and articles, check out www.magicmagazine.com.

Genii Magazine is the oldest American magic periodical. It contains many fine tricks and introduces readers to magicians on the scene (www.geniimagazine.com).

4. Visit a magic shop.

Sadly, the Internet is quickly making brick-and-mortar magic shops disappear—a very bad trick. Support your local shops, and these fine establishments:

Elmwood Magic (Buffalo, NY): www.elmwoodmagic.com
Fantasma (New York, NY): www.fantasmamagic.com
Tannen's (New York, NY): www.tannens.com
H & R Magic Books (Humble, TX):
   www.magicbookshop.com
Denny and Lee's (Las Vegas, NV and Baltimore, MD):
   www.dennymagic.com

5. Volunteer.

Before you accept your first paying gig, get some stage time under your belt. Hospitals, nursing homes, and orphanages are full of people who need magic in their lives. Make a difference with your magic and offer your services to local facilities.

And so our little game is done;

The cards are played,

   the prize is won.

My Four of Spades

   belongs to thee...

In turn thy soul belongs to me.

Extended Credits

—∿∿∿∿∿—

It comes as no surprise that we magicians are a secretive bunch. But magic is also an honorable brotherhood, and although the public never sees creative design, magicians honor their inspirations meticulously. Many effects used in *Magic* are original or substantial variations on existing themes. All existing effects were used with permission, and any omissions are entirely accidental.

Introduction

Rabbit from the Hat
See Engstrom, A.B. *The Humorous Magician Unmasked*, 1836.

Dawes, Edwin. *The Magic Circular*, January 1987, p.60.

CHAPTER ONE
Magic School

Tommy Wonder

Magic Words
"Getting the Mis out of Misdirection" was originally an essay by Tommy Wonder. See Minch, Stephen and Tommy Wonder. *The Books of Wonder*, 1996, Hermetic Press, pp. 9-34.

Spectators Don't Exist. British magician John Allen released an instructional video of the same name, and its main thesis was a rethinking of the words "spectator" and "participant."

CHAPTER TWO
Impromptu Magic

Match-ic Wand First published in *Magic*, December, 2003, pp. 99-100.

Trick Shot This effect first appeared in video form in Jay Sankey's *Sankey Very Much*, 1996. It is used here with Sankey's permission.

Michael Close

Michael Close's excellent essay on Assumptions appears on pp. 3-6 of *Workers Five*, 1991, and is excerpted with Close's permission. Michael Close's entire *Workers* series has had a profound influence on how I think about magic.

Martin Gardner

Blister Vanish Martin Gardner's quotation comes from his book, *The Whys of a Philosophical Scrivener*, 1983, St. Martin's Press, p. 340.

Four Elements For a published reference, see Daniels, Martin. "Rising Damp," *Cunning Stunts*, 1995, pp. 42-43. I published a more theatrical version. See Jay, Joshua. *Session: The Magic of Joshua Givens*, 2007, pp. 105-107.

CHAPTER THREE
Dinner Deceptions

Change Machine "Change Machine" was inspired by a Ross Bertram change called "My Favorite Drink." See Bertram, Ross. *The Magic and Methods of Ross Bertram*, 1978, p. 115.

Banachek

Silverware Sorcery As one of the world's leading mentalists, Banachek convinced scientists at Washington University in the 1980s that he could *actually* bend silverware.

CHAPTER FOUR
The Ten Greatest Card Tricks of All Time

Invisible Deck The concept of "smooth" cards goes back to the slick card, a special card used by cheaters as early as 1530. "Rough" cards were probably introduced by Johann Hofzinser in the nineteenth century.

Simon Aronson

Do As I Do Simon Aronson's quote is excerpted from his fabulous book for advanced magicians, *Shuffle-bored*, 1980.

Dai Vernon

Mixed-Up Kings When Dai Vernon performed his version of this effect, he would spin a tale about an inebriated participant who shuffled the magician's cards faceup into facedown, giving the effect context.

Tenkai Ishida

Mixed-Up Kings Japanese magician Tenkai Ishida invented the secret turnover move used in this effect.

Jim Steinmeyer

Five Cards by Touch Jim Steinmeyer created this card effect and first published it in the "The Real Magic Souvenir Program."

Max Maven

Wagers of Sin Although Max Maven is known to his public as a master mentalist, he is known to magicians as one of the leading scholars in the field. With this effect, he combines a subtle force with a chilling presentation.

CHAPTER FIVE
Kid Conjuring

Cutting a Child in Two Jim Steinmeyer, legendary inventor, originally published it in "The Real Magic Souvenir Program".

Gregory Wilson

Poked Gregory Wilson is a world-class pickpocket, but in this effect, you don't pick anything. But you must think like a pickpocket; approach calmly and reach slowly. Gregory Wilson's performance with a false thumbtip inspired me to include this effect in the book.

The Vanishing Pet The idea of trimming the card to facilitate switching it is attributed to Dai Vernon, who created the concept as an easy alternative to the second deal, a classic cheating sleight.

CHAPTER SIX
Working Miracles

Daniel Garcia

Telekineticlip Daniel Garcia, a young professional magician from Texas, invented this effect years ago when he was in grade school.

Disappearing Ink See Lorayne, Harry. *Tarbell Course in Magic: Volume Seven.*

Alain Nu

Post Bent Alain Nu, the creator of Post Bent, was featured in his own television series on The Learning Channel.

Coffee Conjuring First published in *Minotaur*, volume 8, no. 6, pp. 6-7. It was expanded in a trade publication called *Session* I wrote about the magic of Joel Givens. See "Cup o' Joel." Jay, Joshua. *Session,* 2007, pp.17-22.

Karate Clip See David Roth's "Karate Coin." Kaufman, Richard. *COINMAGIC*, 1981, pp. 24-28. The inventor of the plot is unknown, but the earliest printed account appears to be a terse description in Will Goldston's *The Young Conjuror;* Part 2, 1921, p. 75.

Curtis Hickman

Virtual Magic First developed as "Hickman's Amazing Card Engine," this effect fuses Curtis Hickman's two passions: magic and computer graphics.

CHAPTER SEVEN
Money Magic

Paul Gertner

Unexpected Profits Paul Gertner is a top corporate magician and speaker and one of the finest exponents of money magic. He used several money effects like this one to win first place at FISM, the largest magic competition in the world.

Bankroll Max Maven first published the Rhyme Switch technique in *New Jinx,* 1967.

CHAPTER EIGHT
Parlor Prestidigitaton

Barry Richardson

Ovation Position Barrie Richardson cites Pat Page and Eric Mason as influences for his presentation. The script is excerpted, with permission, from Barrie's first hardbound collection. See Richardson, Barrie. *Theater of the Mind,* 1999, pp. 5-9.

I asked Barrie if he had suggestions on how to memorize the alphabet backward, and he obliged with the original mnemonic described in the sidebar, which he published for teaching purposes in 1986.

The Linking Rings The routine in this book is an amalgam of classic moves and sequences. I'd like to recognize Whit Haydn, the first magician I saw perform a routine with four rings, and magician who helped popularize the notion of putting the linking rings in a participant's hands.

Tom Frank's routine and poem are a reworking of Jack Miller's Linking Ring routine. Miller crafted a variation on "The Raven" that fit perfectly with his routine.

CHAPTER NINE
Telephone Trickery

Cell Sorcery John Northern Hilliard published "Twentieth Century Telepathy" in *The Sphynx,* February 1905. Houdini biographer Bill Kallush recently found evidence that Houdini performed effects over the phone ten years previous to this date.

Predicting a Phone Number See Wagers of Sin, Chapter Four.

Telephone Osmosis Expert sleight-of-hand artist Andi Gladwin has devised more than

Andi Gladwin

a hundred original effects including this one. The principle behind the progressive anagram dates back to Stanley Collins. See "The Nonpareil Book Mystery," published in 1920. Max Maven was the first to explore offering the participant complete freedom in his thought-of choice.

In Closing

I excerpted Michael Close from his *Workers,* Volume 3.

Cathy Newman wrote "The Joy of Shoes" in the September, 2006 *National Geographic.*

Additional Resources:

The Illustrated History of Magic by Milbourne Christopher, 1976.

The Art of Magic by Frank Coffey, Jamy Ian Swiss, and Carl Waldman, 1998.

Thanks also to Bill Kallush and the Conjuring Arts Research Center, where I conducted much of the historical research for *Magic.*

Index

Acknowledgments

Writing a book and performing a magic show are similar experiences. Both are perceived as singular efforts, yet both require a loyal cast and crew. Hidden just behind this curtain, my family, friends, and colleagues are packed to the wings. It's curtain call.

My thanks to David Pogue for the appearing agent trick. Also thanks to literary magician James Levine and his assistant, Lindsay Edgecombe, for their tireless efforts in bringing this book to market, and making a reputedly difficult process painless. Thanks to Suzie Bolotin and Peter Workman, who have been so supportive. They both love magic, which made meetings interesting. Thanks also to Anne Kerman, Janet Parker, Kate Lin, Aaron Clendening, and Barbara Peragine who are responsible for making this book look so magical. Much appreciation also goes to Felipe Abreu and his team, Tina Laterano, David Arky, Rafael Fuchs, Matthew Benjamin, and Tom Boyce. And to my editor Megan Nicolay: Your commitment to every detail concerning this project (which involved learning nearly every effect in this book) amazes me; you would make a fine magician.

Thanks to the following contributors and readers: Gene Anderson, Banachek, Denis Behr, Rod Doiron, Gabe Fajuri, Trisha Ferruccio, Daniel Garcia, Paul Gertner, Andi Gladwin, Curtis Hickman, John Lovick, Raj Madhok, Barrie Richardson, Jay Sankey, Looy Simonoff, and Jim Steinmeyer and to magic consultant Joel Givens. Max Maven, the most knowledgeable magician on the planet, who was kind enough to consult on *Magic*—thanks for your passionate commitment to keeping alive the rich contributions of the magicians who continue to inspire generations. Thanks to Simon Aronson and Gregory Wilson for your magic and your friendship.

Thanks to Michelle Herman, Cameron Filipour, and Christopher Coake: All three are my teachers, all three are my friends. A big thanks to my entire family, and particularly to Uncle David for his sage advice. And thanks to Sarah, who was helpful and patient at every stage of this process.

And finally, my parents. Thanks to Mom, who's here, and Dad, who isn't. I love you.

About the Author

Joshua Jay is an internationally recognized performer, author, and lecturer. He has performed at corporate and private engagements in more than fifty countries, and performs regularly at Hollywood's prestigious Magic Castle. In 1998, Joshua won the coveted first prize at the World Magic Seminar in Las Vegas.

Joshua has authored four trade books for magicians and is the trick editor for *MAGIC,* the largest independent magazine for magicians. He currently resides in New York City.